FUTURE SOUTHS:
DIALOGUES ON ART, PLACE, AND HISTORY

Verónica Tello, Dylan A. T. Miner, Zoe Butt, Edgar Alejandro Hernández,
Rolando López, Carla Macchiavello, Walter D. Mignolo,
Rachel O'Reilly, and Ruth Simbao

AF380903

Published in 2023 by Discipline in collaboration with Third Text Publications, an affiliate of *Third Text* journal.

Melbourne/Naarm and London

Essays by Verónica Tello, Dylan A. T. Miner, Zoe Butt, Edgar Alejandro Hernández, Rolando López, Carla Macchiavello, Walter D. Mignolo, Rachel O'Reilly and Ruth Simbao, and dialogues with the aforementioned and Jennifer Biddle, Katherine Carl, Fernando do Campo, Chandra Frank, Srdjan Jovanović Weiss, Angela Mitropoulos, James Nguyen, Salote Tawale, and Jean-Sylvain Tshilumba Mukendi.

Contents

> What is missing from existing studies of the souths is evidence and thinking on the possibility that there never was a divide within the souths and their way of crafting future(s). This may be the new condition that can be explored and lived by academic, art, and architecture practices. We can discuss, and be open to, conversations that offer up positive aspects of the souths that are overlooked by overestimated powers. Just by turning the map upside down we can see new possibilities.
>
> —Srdjan Jovanović Weiss, excerpt from unpublished *Future Souths* dialogue, January 2018

It takes time to turn the map upside down, and as such this book took longer than anticipated to finish. I want to firstly thank all the contributors for their patience and willingness to participate in an extended editing process. The dialogues that form the core of this book began in 2017 but were reflected upon and polished until 2022. Working with multiple authors on a single text has its challenges. But whatever the administrative pain that collective writing may have caused, I wouldn't have done this book any other way. *Future Souths* was conceived as an experiment in border-crossing art history, intending to dispel both the loneliness of conventional scholarship and geographic singularity. The book, I think, achieves this aim—but were it not for the labour of many hands the *Future Souths* project may have remained on my hard drive for eternity.

For getting the book into print, I want to thank Richard Dyer, editor of Third Text Publications (and editor in chief of the affiliated *Third Text* journal), and Nick Croggon and Helen Hughes, editors of Discipline. Richard was the first person I approached who was willing to take on the book, even as others said that a collectively written text was too difficult to market. And then when Nick and Helen came on board as co-publishers, they offered the necessary editorial support I needed to get the job done just as I was running out of steam (as one does at the end of a book project). I thank them for cracking the whip and maintaining the high benchmark that Discipline and *Third Text* are renowned for.

The book benefited from the keen eye of several amazing thinkers, all of whom generously gave their time and brain power to extend or refine the capacities of this project: Diana Baker Smith, Bianca Hester, Yu-Chieh Li, Lucille Paterson, Tomás Peters Nuñez, and the anonymous peer reviewers. Without their comments some of the nuances of the arguments made in the book would surely be lost.

The project benefited from financial support, without which a book such as this would not be possible. The UNSW School of Art & Design supported this project through a few different grants at different stages of the project: firstly, to develop the *Future Souths* website, which hosted the first iterations of the essays and dialogues of this book, and then to support the book's production. I want to especially thank the current Directors of Research of the School of Art & Design, Bianca Hester and Ollie Bown, for consistently understanding and supporting experimental research in the arts. Create NSW, the arts body of the New South Wales Government, also offered much needed and timely support via its Quick Response Grant just as the costs for the project—including hikes in printing costs in 2022—were spiralling.

Several people, and non-people, have produced or maintained the infrastructure and/or interrelations that are central to *Future Souths* and the communication of its ideas. Ella Sutherland, artist and designer extraordinaire, designed the website for *Future Souths,* working alongside artist and programmer Benjamin Forster. We linked Freenode (1995–2021)—an open-source, and now defunct, Internet Relay Chat program—to the website to host the transnational dialogues for the book. Freenode had been around since the early days of the World Wide Web and we thank its developers for its no frills, low-bandwidth-friendly, and accessible invention. To address one of the technical problems we faced, programmer Sandeepsinh Jadeja designed a Log Bot for the *Future Souths* Freenode account, allowing us to archive the transcriptions.

I had two research assistants during the project who were indispensable. Meredith Birrell is an amazing project manager and, working with Time and Date AS, an open source online international meeting planner (www.timeanddate.com), she orchestrated the dialogues with over twenty collaborators across multiple time zones, and assisted in developing and copyediting the content for the website. June Miskell came on board to help with the manuscript, liaising with contributors and soliciting image rights, working with great efficiency. Jennifer Sijnja, the rigorous and talented copyeditor of the book, has ensured that a rather unwieldy project is lucid. I am grateful to have worked with Zenobia Ahmed and Alexandra Margetic on the design of this book. They have attended to the conceptual underpinnings of the book to produce a strong synergy between the content and its material container.

This book is, in some ways, an attempt to connect to my Chilean heritage and my family there. I grew up in Santiago with my uncle Alejandro Moreno as well as my late grandmother, Adriana Maldonado, both of whom feature in chapter 1. I dedicate this book to them, as well as to the women who have been their fierce allies: my mother, Patricia Moreno, and Alicia Opazo Ruiz.

I want to dedicate this book to another person, Srdjan Jovanović Weiss, who passed away on the 3rd of March, 2022. I first met Srdjan in the spring of 2015 in New York, and I was instantly charmed by his vivaciousness and intelligence. I was thrilled when he agreed to be part of *Future Souths*, and his distinct capacities to turn geopolitical thinking upside down is indelibly felt in this book.

—Verónica Tello, Sydney/Gadigal land, December 2022

FORMER WEST/FUTURE SOUTHS
Verónica Tello

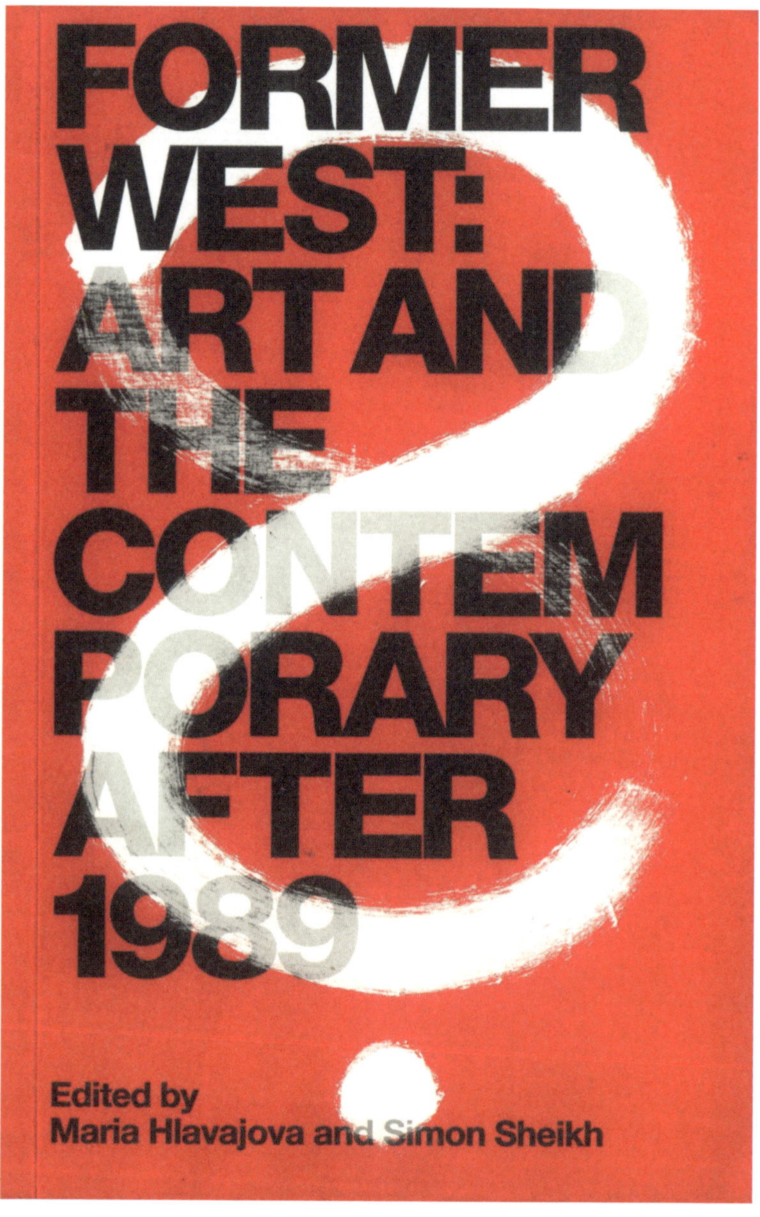

Front cover of *Former West: Art and the Contemporary after 1989*,
edited by Maria Hlavajova and Simon Sheikh, Cambridge, Mass: MIT Press, 2017.

I first began thinking about *Future Souths* in Sydney/
Gadigal land, where I live, after I returned from a trip to the
Netherlands in 2016. I'd visited BAK, basis voor actuele kunst,
the internationally renowned art space and home to *Former
West* (2009–2016), a research project I'd long harboured
an art crush on.[1] *Former West* takes as its historical and
conceptual starting point the 1989 fall of the Berlin Wall,
an event which in the Western imagination has come to
symbolise the final triumph of Western liberalism and the
end of the Cold War. Symbolically, the fall of the Berlin Wall
marked the end of "the East" (the bloc of socialist states
from Central and Eastern Europe, East Asia, Southeast
Asia, Africa, and Latin America), relegating their alternative
to Western liberalism irrevocably to the past. *Former West*
takes this logic of erasure and stands it on its head. It asks:
What if it was not the East but the West that was former?
What would it mean for the East to flourish, for its various
economic and social possibilities to be reactivated? *Former
West*, in short, uses the West's own logic against it. Still, the
question lingers: To what end?

I'd been logging on to www.formerwest.org since
the project's very early days from my desk in Melbourne/
Naarm and then, after I moved in 2011, in Sydney/Gadigal
land. I was keen to learn from its online research seminars
and lectures on topics such as "Where the West Ends?,"
"Migrations, Citizenship, and the Limits of Territoriality,"
or "Multiculture in Europe: Melancholia or Conviviality?"
These topics all resonated with my then PhD research
on contemporary art and the so-called migration crisis.[2]
Yet, while my thinking on the nexus of migration and
art was shaped by local watersheds, such as Tampa[3] and

1 "Former West," basis voor actuele kunst,
accessed June 20, 2018, https://formerwest.
org/Front.

2 Verónica Tello, "The Aesthetics of Counter-
Memory: Contemporary Art and Australian
Refugee Histories after Tampa" (PhD diss.,
University of Melbourne, 2013).

3 Tampa, or the "Tampa affair," refers to the
Australian government's refusal to allow
refugees, rescued by a Norwegian cargo ship
by the name of *Tampa*, to enter Australia
and disembark on the nation's offshore
territory of Christmas Island during late
August 2001. Instead, amongst other
hostile acts, the government excised the
Island from Australia's migration zone and
developed the "Pacific Solution," placing
refugees arriving by boat, including those
on the *Tampa*, in offshore detention centres
in Nauru and eventually Manus Island.

SIEV-X[4]—or my own experiences of migration from Chile after the 1973 coup led by Augusto Pinochet—for *Former West*, global migration patterns, and globalisation more broadly, were always read via a singular, increasingly monolithic, historical moment: 1989. While at BAK, as I engaged with its exhibitions and public programs in a distracted daze, I came to realise the extent to which *Former West*, with its key terms "1989," "East," and "Berlin," is a critical Western studies project, enacted by Europeans, diverse as they may be, in relation to histories and politics that are largely contained within the borders of Europe. In other words, for all its rhetoric of formering the West, *Former West* remained deeply Eurocentric.

Former West likely became a Eurocentric project because the discourses which shaped it were also Eurocentric. The invisible foundation of *Former West* is Francis Fukuyama's "end of history" polemic, developed in 1989 for the US publication, the *National Interest*.[5] In his essay "The End of History?," Fukuyama argued that the fall of the Berlin Wall represented not only the end of the battle between communist and capitalist states, but between fundamentally different ways of organising society. From ancient Greece to ancient Egypt, to the Roman Empire to our present, Fukuyama argued, the history of civilisation has been a battle over how to best organise society, a battle over which political and social systems and ideologies would prevail. After centuries of different models of civilisations, Western liberal democracy

For a more detailed history of Tampa see: Verónica Tello, "Prologue: Refugee Flows and Networked Events," in *Counter-Memorial Aesthetics: Refugee Histories and Contemporary Art*, (London and New York: Bloomsbury, 2013), xvii–xix.

4   SIEV-X refers to an event which saw over 400 refugees drown in the Indian Ocean on route to Australia. After their ramshackle ferry sank, survivors reported to the news media that they had seen an Australian navy vessel pass them without offering help. The SIEV-X event occurred on October 19 in 2001, just weeks after Tampa and amidst the Australian government's development

of draconian "border protection" policies soon after the attacks on the Twin Towers in New York on September 11, 2011. For a more detailed history of SIEV-X see: Verónica Tello, "History Painting, Fiction, and Paranoia: Dierk Schmidt's *SIEV-X—On a Case of Intensified Refugee Politics*," in *Counter-Memorial Aesthetics: Refugee Histories and Contemporary Art*, (London and New York: Bloomsbury, 2013), 125–154.

5   Francis Fukuyama, "The End of History?," *National Interest* 16 (Summer, 1989): 15–25.

had finally emerged as *the* winner—there would not, from now on, be another, better alternative. As communist states collapsed circa 1989, perhaps not all would become liberal societies, Fukuyama conceded, yet neither could they any longer pretend that they offered a better model of civilisation. "At the end of history," he noted, "it is not necessary that all societies become successful liberal societies, merely that they end their ideological pretensions of representing different and higher forms of society."[6]

By now, Fukuyama's polemic has been thoroughly critiqued.[7] And in a way *Former West* joins in on this critique by refusing, and inverting, his teleology. Yet, *Former West*'s critique does not offer an alternative to the logic of Western hegemony. Because it opts for a strategy of inversion, it keeps intact the binary geographic logic of East/West, a legacy of the Cold War, and its implicit power dynamic (hegemony). Further, by adopting Fukuyama's dialectical, oppositional mode of historical thought, it also adopts the West's technique of rendering the "other" primitive, in the past, dead, still, formered. Even if this strategy is applied to the West, such a move replicates the logics and violence of the West. Moreover, insofar as *Former West* empowers the non-West, it does so only on the basis of a fictional past: the West is, after all, not former (a daily read of your local newspaper or scan of most university syllabi will reveal this). Thus, the move to "former" the West effectively erases both the *actual* past and present non-Western ways of life.

Another polemic emerged at the moment of *Former West*'s conception which I want to bring to the fore: Dipesh Chakrabarty's concept of "provincialising Europe" (first

6   Fukuyama, "The End of History?," 21–22.

7   Fuller, Timothy, David Satter, David Stove, and Frederick L. Will. "More Responses to Fukuyama," *The National Interest* 17 (1989): 93–100. http://www.jstor.org/stable/42896764; Jack Lawrence, *The Revenge of History: Why the Past Endures, a Critique of Francis Fukuyama* (Luzkow Lewiston, New York: Edwin Mellen Press, 2003); John Mueller, "Did History End? Assessing the Fukuyama Thesis," *Political Science Quarterly* 129, no. 1 (2014); Benjamin Noys, "Ends in Sight: Marx/Fukuyama/Hobsbawm/Anderson," *Historical Materialism: Research in Critical Marxist Theory* 17, no. 4 (2009).

published in 2007).[8] Here, Chakrabarty argued that Europe is not just a territory but an idea that underpins academic epistemologies, including those that entrench themselves in galleries and museums, and thus governs the position from which we read the world. Yet, if we are to provincialise Europe, we must read this geographical region as just one of multiple regions in the world and undo its privileged location. It is but one, albeit dominant, case study in how to shape and see the world.

Rarely, and only in limited form, did *Former West* engage with epistemologies outside of Europe, or from Europe's colonies across Africa, Asia, Latin America, and the Pacific.[9] And when it did engage, it predominantly limited itself to including essays in the publication to mark the end of the project. *Former West: Art and the Contemporary after 1989* (2017), edited by Maria Hlavajova and Simon Sheik, who conceived *Former West*, may have belatedly registered that something other than the East could offer an alternative to the West: in the book, you'll find writings by prominent theorists of decolonial and postcolonial studies such as Chakrabarty, Walter D. Mignolo, Bonaventura de Sousas Santos, and Achille Mbembe. These writings on decolonising and the global south are tacked on, sitting awkwardly beside the project's focus on 1989. (1989 is not a significant date for many parts of the global south, as is discussed in chapter 8).

In many ways, *Former West* is a product of, and thus perhaps was going to inevitably reflect, the limits of 1990s art and globalisation discourse. Such a discourse, as editors Hlavajova and Sheikh acknowledged in their introduction to the *Former West* anthology, was deeply optimistic, and took the fall of the Berlin Wall as an impetus for tearing down national barriers in contemporary art. The danger of such optimism, they note, was made apparent during

8   Dipesh Chakrabarty, *Provincialising Europe: Postcolonial Thought and Historical Difference–New Edition* (New Jersey: Princeton University Press, 2007).

9   To my mind, this engagement mostly occurred in its very late iterations, mainly in Maria Hlavajova and Simon Sheikh, eds., *Former West: Art and the Contemporary after 1989* (Cambridge, Massachusetts: MIT Press, 2017). See for example essays by Boaventura de Sousa Santos, Walter D. Mignolo, Achille Mbembe, and Campus on Camps amongst many others.

the 1992 Venice Biennale. In the lead-up to the Biennale, its artistic director, Achille Bonito Oliva, called a meeting of the commissioners of the national pavilions.[10] He wanted to take the opportunity presented by recent geopolitical developments and asked the commissioners of national pavilions in the Giardini to work with artists who were not citizens of the national pavilions they managed. As Hlavajova and Sheikh articulate, such a move—which gestured toward the transnational, global art to come— was welcomed by Western nations, such as Austria (which commissioned Andrea Fraser, a US citizen), but less so by Eastern European nations. The East didn't want to give up the (already limited) space allocated to it at this crucial historical moment, when it could finally reappear on its own terms. It pushed back on the terms upon which Bonito Oliva suggested the de-nationalisation or globalisation of art could emerge, bringing to the fore the ways in which discourses of art and globalisation (as discussed in chapter 7) are often set by Western curators and institutions at the expense of the non-West.[11]

The idea of "Future Souths" was an attempt to avoid this pitfall. I wanted to see if the essence of *Former West*'s proposal—to contest the hegemony of the West and animate minor histories "formered" by the West—could be done differently. Why just "former" the West? Why not also speculate on the potentialities of the south? And rather than 1989—a Eurocentric marker of history—what temporalities guide thinking on the histories and futures of the south?

10 Maria Hlavajova and Simon Sheikh, "Formering the West" in Maria Hlavajova and Simon Sheikh, eds, *Former West: Art and the Contemporary after 1989* (Cambridge, Massachusetts: MIT Press, 2017).

11 Amelia Jones, "Ethnic Envy and Other Aggressions in the Contemporary 'Global' Art Complex," *Journal of Contemporary African Art* 48 (May 2021); Ruth Simbao, "What 'Global Art' and Current (Re)turns Fail to See: A Modest Counter-narrative of 'Not-another-biennial'," *Image & Text: A Journal for Design* 25, no. 1 (2015).

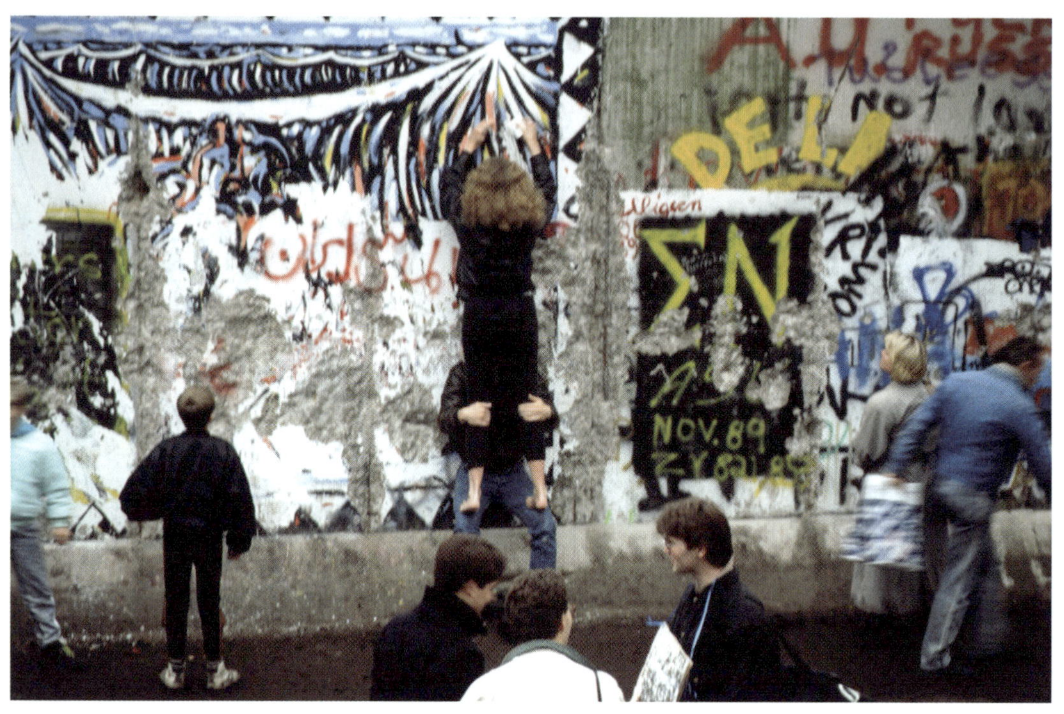

Berlin 1989, Fall of the Berlin Wall.
Photograph by Raphaël Thiémard from Belgique. Creative Commons.

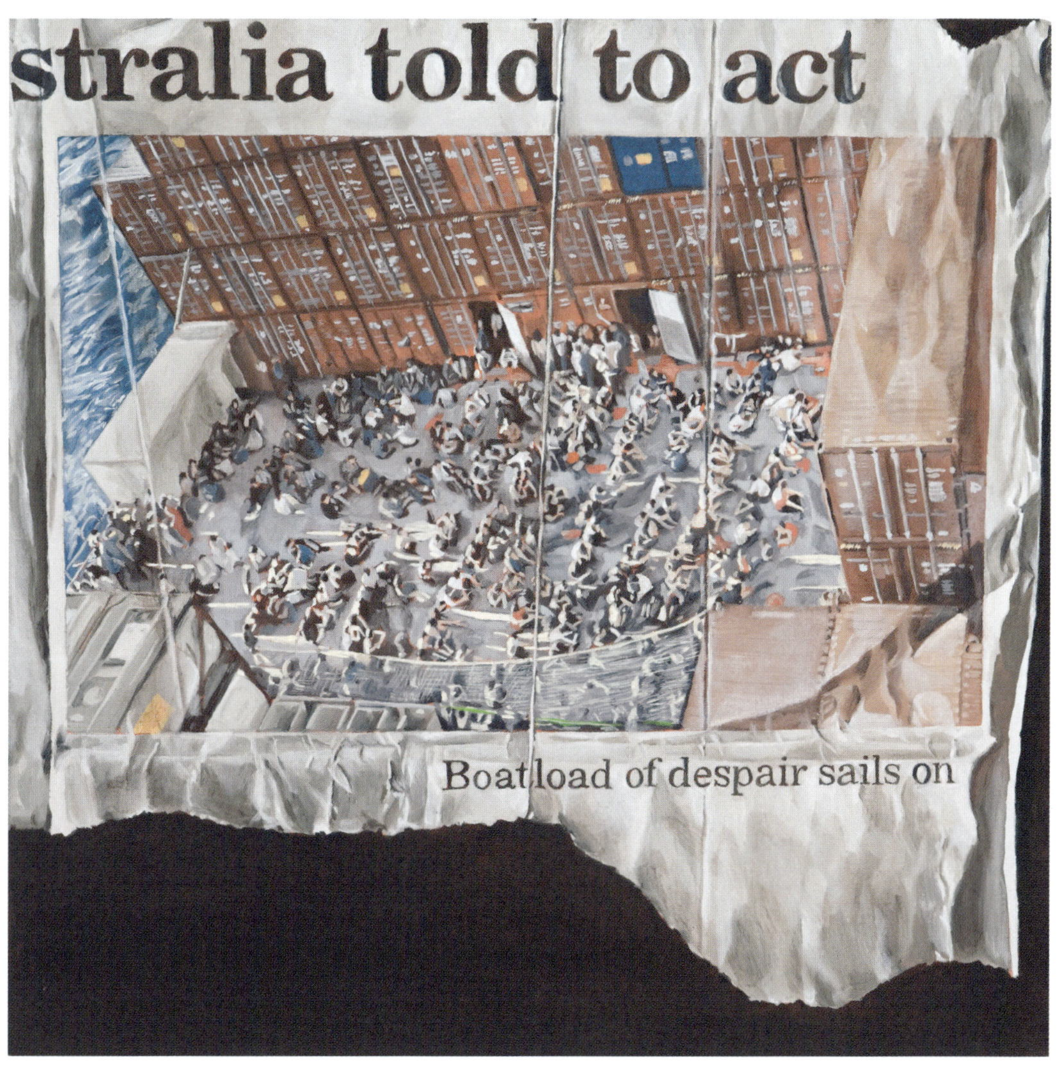

Refugees on board the *Tampa* on 27 August 2001. Wallenius Wilhelmsen/AAP.
Image reproduced in: Lyndell Brown and Charles Green, *Boatload of Despair*, 2006,
oil on linen, 31 x 31 cm. Image courtesy the artists.

Future Souths offers an alternative to the logic of hegemony. It does this, as I detail below, by:

1   Fucking with geography: Shifting from an East/West discourse (where the West always wins) to a southern one, which is premised on resistance to globalisation and its erasures; and demonstrating the non-binary nature of the global south (below I pluralise "souths," a move evident in the book's title, because there is no single or stable south);

2   Fucking with time: The book focuses not on fictional pasts (the former East or West), but rather actual southern presents and futures, as well as entirely different modes of temporality (e.g., *anikoobijigan*, weak histories).

Fucking with Geography

When I began researching the conceptual underpinnings for *Future Souths* it became clear that the concept of the "global south" has brought to the fore multiple and often incompatible definitions.[12] The global south has its historical roots in the Cold War, and is a Western concept championed by former German Chancellor Willy Brandt (1969–1974) to classify countries otherwise labelled as "Third World," "underdeveloped," or "developing," mostly located in the southern hemisphere (across Latin America,

---

12   See, for example, Jean Comaroff and John Comaroff, *Theory from the South: Or, How Euro-America Is Evolving Toward Africa* (New York: Routledge, 2012); David Francis, Imraan Valodia, and Edward Webster, *Inequality Studies from the Global South* (London: Routledge, 2020); Amy Piedalue and Susmita Rishi, "Unsettling the South through Postcolonial Feminist Theory," *Feminist Studies* 43, no. 3 (2017): 548–570; Walter Mignolo, "The Global South and World Dis/Order," *Journal of Anthropological Research* 67, no. 2 (2011): 165–188; Justin Dargin, ed., *The Rise of the Global South: Philosophical, Geopolitical, and Economic Trends of the 21st Century* (Singapore: World Scientific Publishing, 2013); Nour Dados and Raewyn Connell, "The Global South," *Contexts* 11, no. 1 (2012): 12–13; Raewyn Connell, *Southern Theory: Social Science and the Global Dynamics of Knowledge* (London: Polity Press, 2007); Alfred J. Lopez, "The (Post) Global South," *The Global South* 1, no. 1 (Winter, 2007): 1–11; David Slater, *Geopolitics and the Post-Colonial: Rethinking North–South Relations* (Hoboken, New Jersey: Wiley Publishing, 2008); Kerry Bystrom and Joseph R. Slaughter, eds., *The Global South Atlantic* (New York: Fordham University Press, 2017).

the Pacific, Africa, and parts of Asia). The Third World was differentiated from the Second World—countries aligned with the Eastern socialist bloc (USSR, East Germany, etc.)—as well as the wealthy "developed" countries of the First World, or what is now termed the global north (north-western Europe, Canada, the US, and southern-hemisphere nations Australia and New Zealand).[13] The south emerged as a concept, via Brandt, to mobilise "neutral," non-aligned countries and construct south–south cooperation in order to, for lack of better language, combat poverty (alongside Brandt's attempts to shift south–north relations during the Cold War and catalyse the north to invest in developmental aid in the south).

Whatever the origins of the concept of the south, the term was quickly appropriated by neutral/non-aligned territories to counter the hegemony of the north.[14] As the influential Bandung Conference held in Indonesia in 1955 reminds us, the south is a political concept advanced by countries historically categorised as "underdeveloped" or "developing," which sought to collaborate and leverage their resources, epistemologies, and infrastructures to former their status as "backward" or "Third World" (an idea which is further explored in chapter 3, "Networks").[15]

As history shows, the Bandung Conference and subsequent south–south cooperation efforts didn't yield the desired economic changes (global economic inequality persists and continues to privilege nations historically classed as First World). Yet Bandung did give rise to various and sustained transnational exchanges cultivated by the south, including the significant cultural project of the Havana Biennial inaugurated in 1984.[16] Along with the intensification of globalisation post-Bandung, the south is, by now, not able to be classified into strict countries or

---

13   For example, see Dados and Connell, "The Global South."

14   See, for example, Deniz Altinbas, "South–South Cooperation: A Counter-Hegemonic Movement?," in Dargin, ed., *The Rise of the Global South*, 29–65.

15   See Altinbas, "South–South Cooperation."

16   See Altinbas; Rachel Weiss, *Making Art Global (Part I): The Third Havana Biennial 1989* (London: Afterall, 2011); Anthony Gardner and Charles Green, "Biennials of the South on the Edges of the Global," *Third Text* 27 no. 4 (2013): 442–455.

regions. It is better read as porous and de-territorialised. After all, globalisation and colonialism structure lives across borders; their force is not contained by geography, and therefore neither is counter-hegemonic resistance.

Such a conception of the global south—as dispersed— has evaded some of the most influential discourses of contemporary art on the south, especially where I live in Australia.[17] Australia is often folded in to an overly expansive understanding of the south, one that encompasses all countries or colonies in the southern hemisphere.[18] Such discourse, while offering an accommodating notion of the south that goes beyond the geopolitical formations of the Cold War or developmentalism, still renders the south as a set of neatly partitioned territories, located in specific sites. An expansive mapping of the south is not the same as thinking of the south as fluid. Australia contains norths and souths.

The south is everywhere, just as the north is; the terms are not defined by specific national borders. Indeed, as Walter D. Mignolo contends in chapter 2, "The global north is in the global south through investments, military bases, corporations, media, and NGOs." Likewise, through acts of migration, resistance, memory, and the trafficking of archives, the south is unbound, living in the north. To quote Mignolo again, "The point isn't to assert boundaries or borders, but to reveal the ways in which both the south and the north pass through all of us, no matter what our origin point." The south and north are not singular but plural.

By pluralising the souths (and norths)—as noun, adjective, verb, and concept—we can, to borrow a phrase from a friend, "fuck with geography." A friend, who chooses to remain anonymous, said this to me during one of our

17   Nikos Papastergiadis, "The End of the Global South and the Cultures of the South," *Thesis Eleven* 142, no. 1 (2017); Kevin Murray, ed. "The South South Way," *Artlink Australia* 27, no. 2 (June 2007); Anthony Gardner, ed., *Mapping South: Journeys in South–South Cultural Relations* (Melbourne: The South Project Inc, 2013); Anthony Gardner and

Charles Green, *Biennials, Triennials, and documenta: The Exhibitions that Created Contemporary Art* (New York: Wiley-Blackwell, 2016).

18   Gardner and Green, *Biennials, Triennials, and Documenta*; Gardner, *Mapping South*.

discussions of *Future Souths,* and while I didn't probe her to expand at the time, I inferred that she meant to fuck with geography is to take pleasure in fucking with existing colonial mappings of the souths—the various ways in which it is partitioned, or positioned as the other of the norths, somewhere out there. To fuck with geography is to also sense that the souths, and the effects of colonialism and geopolitics, are corporeal. They are better articulated through lived and embodied experience than pointing to a map.

This embodied position seems especially important to emphasise given that I write in/from Australia. Here, the souths have largely been theorised from a northern/Anglo fairly disembodied standpoint.[19] They have thrived, in part, because the rational tones of academia maintain the fiction of neutral or objective positions—the voice from nowhere.[20] However well intentioned, such Anglocised discourses in Australia shape conceptions of the "south" because of an inherently privileged position, and one which has failed to bring to bear the authors' location. Solidarity (with the south) is not the same as overidentification. In Australia, because Anglo discourse on the souths dominates discourse and the means of production, overidentification with the souths feels like possessiveness. As Quandamooka theorist and historian Aileen Moreton-Robinson notes, "Whiteness is the invisible measure of who can hold possession."[21] In Australia, while the category of whiteness has more recently shifted, for example, to include Italian and Greek migrants of European descent, Anglo-Australians always have been the whitest.

19   Connell, *Southern Theory*; Papastergiadis, "The End of the Global South"; Murray, "The South–South Way"; Gardner, *Mapping South*; Gardner and Green, *Biennials, Triennials, and Documenta.*

20   As Haraway argues, "I am arguing for the view from a body, always a complex, contradictory, structuring, and structured body, versus the view from above, from nowhere, from simplicity. Only the god trick is forbidden." Donna Haraway, "Situated Knowledges: The Science Question in Feminism and the Privilege of Partial Perspective," *Feminist Studies* 14, no. 3 (1988), 581.

21   Aileen Moreton-Robinson, "I Still Call Australia Home: Indigenous Belonging and Place in a White Postcolonizing Society," in *Uprootings/Regroundings: Questions of Home and Migration*, ed. Sara Ahmed et al. (London: Routledge, 2003), 23.

As someone living in the antipodean global north (Australia), and who has roots in the former Third World, migrating from Santiago de Chile to Melbourne/Naarm in 1987 (before the terms "global south" and "global north" were widely in use), I am invested in histories of the global souths and the potentiality of southern thinking. But for me southern thinking is not shaped by an Anglo postcolonial consciousness (which aims to acknowledge the Eurocentricity of art history's position Australia in relation to its neighbouring, non-Western regions). That's a valid theoretical project, and one which has been important for undoing the settler-colonial foundations of art history in Australia, and elsewhere. But if discourse is a space shaped by social processes and social change, then calls to de-Westernise language, scholarship, and art institutions from the bottom up has opened a space for something else. Maria Lugones, Gloria Anzaldúa, Cherrie Moraga, Macarena Gómez-Barris, Nelly Richard, Jennifer A. González, and Juan Dávila, but also figures I'm much more intimate with such as my grandmother, Adriana Maldonado, whom I write about in chapter 1, "Futures," have long been shaping a different conception of the souths.[22] For them, the souths are a space shaped by cultural inheritances—of what is acquired or that which has been imposed.[23] They sieve through history, memory, and archives to examine the lies—and that which doesn't resonate or fit—and bring to the fore otherwise repressed ways of being (circumventing

22   Maria Lugones, "The Coloniality of Gender," *Worlds & Knowledges Otherwise* 2, no. 2 (Spring, 2008): 1–17; Cherríe Moraga and Gloria Anzaldúa, *This Bridge Called my Back, Writings by Radical Women of Color*, 4th ed. (New York: SUNY Press, 2015); Cherríe Moraga, *Native Country of the Heart: A Memoir* (New York: Farrar, Straus, and Giroux, 2019); Macarena Gómez-Barris, *Where Memory Dwells: Culture and State Violence in Chile* (California: University of California Press, 2008); Nelly Richard, *Masculino/Femenino: Practicas de la Diferencia y Cultura Democratica* (Santiago, Chile: Fondo de Desarrollo de la cultura y las Artes, 1993); Nelly Richard, *Masculine/Feminine: Practices of Difference(s)* (Durham, North Carolina: Duke University Press, 2004); Jennifer A. González et al., eds. *Chicano and Chicana Art: A Critical Anthology* (Durham, North Carolina: Duke University Press, 2019); Rex Butler, ed., *What is Appropriation? An Anthology of Writings on Australian Art in the 1980s & 1990s*, 2nd ed. (Brisbane: IMA Publishing, 2004).

23   Gloria Anzaldúa, *Borderlands/La Frontera: The New Mestiza* [1987] (San Francisco: Aunt Lute, 2012).

the normativity of machismo, heterosexuality, Eurocentrism, etc.). The souths are a space for making oneself appear on one's own terms. They are a space for radical self-portraiture. But it's also, as cultural and literary theorist Alfred J. López said in the inaugural issue of the *Global South* journal (2007), a concept for resisting the erasure of difference under the umbrella of inclusion or assimilation (as happens in processes of colonialism and globalisation).[24] It resists by insisting on shifting the conditions upon which one can appear, speak, and think—rather than settling for inclusion/assimilation. Language, memory, history, and experience intervene in what is possible. It is through an embodied approach to reading and speaking about the souths that we can fuck with what and where the souths are.

Fucking with Time

Another major aspect of *Future Souths* is its fucking with time. Unlike *Former West, Future Souths* does not have an equivalent to 1989, a watershed on which it is founded, and which signals a universally resonant moment in time when everything changed for all. Numerous dates are named in this book—by the numerous contributors—as impacting historical experiences of the global souths: 1492, the arrival of Columbus in the Americas, or 1500 for the arrival of the Portuguese in Brazil, or the arrival of Cook in Australia in 1770 (or in the Pacific more broadly in 1768–1771) (see chapter 8, "Contemporaneities"), or the 1973 coup led by General Augusto Pinochet in Chile. As Métis artist Dylan A. T. Miner reminds us in chapter 8, while such varied yet interconnected events have left indelible marks across the souths, for First Nations peoples, there is only "time immemorial. There is no beginning, nor end." For Miner, by privileging dates adhered to colonial histories (1492, 1500, 1770, 1973, etc.), we risk foregrounding northern teleology, that is, thinking of history as a linear evolution

24   Alfred J. Lopez, "The (Post) Global South," *The Global South* 1, no. 1 (Winter 2007).

(marked by tension of civilisations, loss, etc.). Even if we single out particular dates in the name of identifying and critically analysing the colonial project, such an exercise still subscribes to linear temporalities. To escape or be parallel to or beyond teleology, Miner privileges First Nations ontologies. As he details in chapter 8, the Anishinaabeg (Ojibwe, Odawa, Potawatomi) word *anikoobijigan* simultaneously names one's ancestors and descendants, invoking a complex and highly subjective, rather than universal, way of reading time—that is, as a constellation of pasts and presents contingent on subjective genealogies carried, felt, and interpreted by those who hold heritage which sits outside of History.

Thinking of time as the simultaneous summoning of the past and the present, embodied and contingent on kinship, is also extended in the first chapter of this book: "Futures (or Weak Histories)." Here, Salote Tawale, James Nguyen, Chandra Frank, and I draw on our family archives to give shape to otherwise minor histories of the global souths, spanning Chile, Vietnam, the Netherlands, South Africa, and Fiji. As Miner notes, chapter 1's focus on weak histories—the faint histories of the disabled, elderly, queer, dispossessed in our families—is closely aligned with *anikoobijigan,* to the extent that it is only through highly personal encounters with archives that any of us is able to displace monumental signifiers of History (e.g., 1989) and thus locate ourselves in any meaningful, and accountable, way within the shaping of history/kinship.

Even if Miner's thinking, and Tawale's, Nguyen's, Frank's, and mine, emerge out of different contexts, what materialises is the generative power of comparative anti-colonialisms, temporalities, and historiographies of the souths. Whether through the concept of *anikoobijigan* or weak histories, *Future Souths* refuses—says "nah" to— a modality of time and history that is based on watershed moments of universal significance.[25]

25   I use the term "nah" after Marquis Bey, *Them Goon Rules: Fugitive Essays on Radical Black Feminism* (Tucson, Arizona: University of Arizona Press, 2019).

An aim of *Future Souths* has been to engage and critique stubborn stereotypes of what I think of as the "temporalities of the souths." As an effect of developmentalist discourse, the souths have long been cast as being "backward" (or its synonyms, such as "underdeveloped," "Third World," etc.).[26] Yet however persistent such a characterisation from the global norths might be, in more recent times the souths have paradoxically been positioned as sites of futurity. It is increasingly common, for example, to come across such statements as, "it is regions in the south that tend *first to feel* the concrete effects of world-historical processes as they play themselves out, thus to *prefigure the future* of the former metropole";[27] and that it's important to "learn from the South."[28] At its most critical, such discourse has the capacity to place the false belatedness of the souths under pressure.[29] For example, in chapter 6, "Species(isms)," Carla Macchiavello leads a discussion on how Tierra del Fuego—a territory long characterised by the norths as being at "the end of the world" and standing still in time—has fertilised curatorial methods for establishing ethical human/nonhuman relations in the midst of a climate catastrophe. Yet, as Rolando López and Edgar Alejandro Hernández particularly remind us in chapter 4, "Contracts (and Colonial Law) I," discourses on the futurity of the souths also potentially hold a cynical undertone: the souths are designated as places of futurity because they most clearly embody the symptoms of global crisis that affect us all (economic austerity, climate change, welfare cuts, and epidemics).[30]

---

26 Comaroff and Comaroff, *Theory from the South.*

27 Jean Comaroff and John L. Comaroff, "Theory from the South: Or, How Euro-America is Evolving Toward Africa," *Anthropological Forum* 2, no. 2 (2012): 121. Italics added by author.

28 See for example documenta 14's project "Learning from the South," analysed in Elpida Rikou and Eleana Yalouri, "Learning from documenta: A Research Project between Art and Anthropology," *On Curating* 33 (2017): 132–138, www.on-curating.org/issue-33-reader/learning-from-documenta-a-research-project-between-art-and-anthropology.html#.YeoIBS8RpTY.

29 I am thinking, for example, of Zoe Butt's project "Conscious Realities" (2013–2016), Sàn Art, accessed September 24, 2021, https://san-art.org/programs/conscious-realities/.

30 This, to my mind, is ultimately the narrative in both documenta 14 and Comaroff and Comaroff, *Theory from the South.*

Chile, to offer another example of the souths' futurity as crisis, is often thought of as a socioeconomic laboratory for what would become global neoliberalism. It was the first nation to systemically (and eventually constitutionally) implement economic policies during the 1970s and 1980s which, supported by US economists, prioritised individual liberty, unregulated markets, and free trade while also diminishing the role of the government in provision of services (education, health, pensions).[31] The abject poverty and profound economic inequity that ensued—leading to the privatisation and therefore limited accessibility of land, water, and basic public goods—are not unique to Chile, but the extent to which this place has been thought of as a crystal ball for other nations to predict, and catalyse, the future of free markets *is* unique. As the example of "Chile as a laboratory for neoliberalism" shows, the souths are less sites of futurity than a colonialist fantasy of finitude. Chile, as a south, reveals the crisis that is to come for all in the form of a discrete case study (the same can be said of, for example, the sinking Pacific island of Tuvalu as a case study of climate crisis).

Rather than resist the existing framing of the souths—as a future of crisis, or as signifier of backwardness in teleological thinking, or as parochial or derivative, etc.—*Future Souths* maps the conditions upon which such framings emerge, mapping the histories of such thinking across anthropology, continental philosophy, and economic theory. In doing so, this book asks: What are the epistemological foundations of the souths? What is to be made of recent conceptualisations of "futurity" about/within the souths? Is the (false) belatedness of the souths now under erasure? What are some of the critical imaginings of the souths and their futures today?

31   David Harvey, "Neoliberalism as Creative Destruction," *The Annals of the American Academy of Political and Social Science* 610 (March 2007).

Collective Vocabularies of Contemporary Art
in/out of the Souths

The questions I pose above are intentionally blue-sky because part of the aim of this book is to theorise the souths (anew). But like any effective theory, the theories of the souths developed in *Future Souths* are deeply grounded in specifics—lived experience, location, bodies, and practice. The book brings together eighteen contributors living across the norths and souths—Australia, Chile, North America, Central and Latin America, Fiji, Vietnam, South Africa, and Eastern Europe. Most of us are part of what my colleague Ramaswami Harindranath calls "the mobile global souths": exiles, refugees, migrants, and First Nations peoples who, while connected to histories and genealogies from the souths, now predominantly live in the norths.[32] (That is the reality of the dispossession or the push-and-pull effect of migration.) Some of us live in a state of in-betweenness—neither here nor there—mediated by memories and archives of the souths in the norths. Others are southern subjects who have always lived in the souths or who have returned to live there as adults. A few of us are northern subjects, deeply Anglo, who seek to work in solidarity with southern futures. Many of us are mixed race and all of us want to bring to bear a complex position which does away with binaries of south/north. Collectively, the *Future Souths* authors generate vital juxtapositions, and at times incommensurabilities, of thought, experience, and praxis. *Future Souths* is an attempt to enact affective, relational, and comparative approaches for articulating the souths through collaborative dialogue.

Through dialogues *Future Souths* engages terms central to contemporary art and humanities discourse—"Futures," "Souths," "Networks," "Contracts," "Colonial Law," "Contemporaneity," "Human/Non-human Species," "Global Art"—co-developing a vocabulary for understanding the politics of place, history, and art in/out of the global

32   Ramaswami Harindranath, in conversation
      with the author, ca. 2016.

souths. I chose these terms because they were easy enough to grasp—they are both ubiquitous to contemporary art and humanities discourse, and yet almost always exclusively defined with a northern bias. The ubiquity of these terms meant they provided much-needed common ground, and a clear conceptual scaffold, for dialogue to ensue amongst a group of thinkers who were mainly strangers to each other. While common ground was important to get them started, the dialogues ultimately bring to the fore the disparate subject positions of the book's contributors—from art, art history, curatorship, museology, poetry, literature, design, linguistics, anthropology, and decolonial theory—generating dissonance, uncertainty, and openness.[33] That is the effect of a dialogical approach: unfinished, even ambiguous, readings of concepts. And this is the point—fixity or a singular authorial voice, authority, is undone. The book's dialogical method creates a space of competing perspectives where acts of enunciation as much as acts of listening are key—the gaps between the interlocutors, and their subjective experience and knowledge is, if not understood, then at least noted. It's through the unknown—the gap—that the dialogues of *Future Souths* open possibilities for new vocabularies in/ out of the souths. It doesn't seek to offer a comprehensive or authoritative take on key concepts of contemporary art and critical theory. Even as this book engages with, and tries to define, terms such as futures, souths, contemporaneity, networks, and global art, for example, it is ultimately an anti-dictionary. It undoes the stability of definitions, and thus undoes the competitive neoliberal approach to scholarship where the aim is to have the last, or best, word on a topic.

The *Future Souths* dialogues unfolded on the internet, more precisely via Freenode, an open-source internet relay chat (IRC) platform usually used for collaborations by software developers. I chose Freenode because its open-source structure made it possible to install a bot to record the dialogues for posterity and publication, but also because

33   Frances Barrett, "Meatus: A Curatorial Passage" (PhD diss., Monash University, 2021).

its aesthetics—white background, black text, no emojis or ads—held the promise of 1990s-era chat rooms, where talking with strangers across the world could lead to new paths of flight.

After working out compatible time zones for interlocutors spread across multiple continents, the dialogues took place for one hour each in July 2017 and January 2018, with certain contributors (according to their specialisation) invited to certain dialogues. We typed our ideas out via our keyboards at various speeds; most of us dialogued in English, though contributors also spoke in Anishinaabeg (Ojibwe, Odawa, Potawatomi—a Métis language, spoken by Miner), Warlpiri (an Aboriginal language, spoken in self-professed terms as a student by Jennifer Biddle, a settler-colonialist), and Spanish (spoken by Rolando López, situated in Chichimeca land/Aguascalientes, Mexico), and I used my knowledge of Spanglish and Google Translate to help translate López's words, live, at his request with the assistance of Carla Macchiavello (when she was present).

This book includes the original Anishinaabeg and Warlpiri language texts within the dialogues, alongside English, the lingua franca of the contemporary art world, which despite representing Western hegemony, also allowed the contributors to dialogue at all. As the book will remind you repeatedly, the norths are everywhere—in how we speak, think, and interrelate—but so are the souths. It's the latter that still need more attention and we hope the book—despite its limitations, i.e., a limited number of contributors and thus positions, predominantly crafted in English language—contributes to formering the West, especially the binaries of the norths/souths.

As much as this book aims to articulate what in chapter 7 Ruth Simbao calls "strategic southerness," it would be naïve to think it can do this in a vacuum which erases hundreds of years of colonisation. Rather, entanglement and discord between the norths and the resistant souths is the *Future Souths* way.

Futures

1

FUTURES: OR, WEAK HISTORIES
Verónica Tello

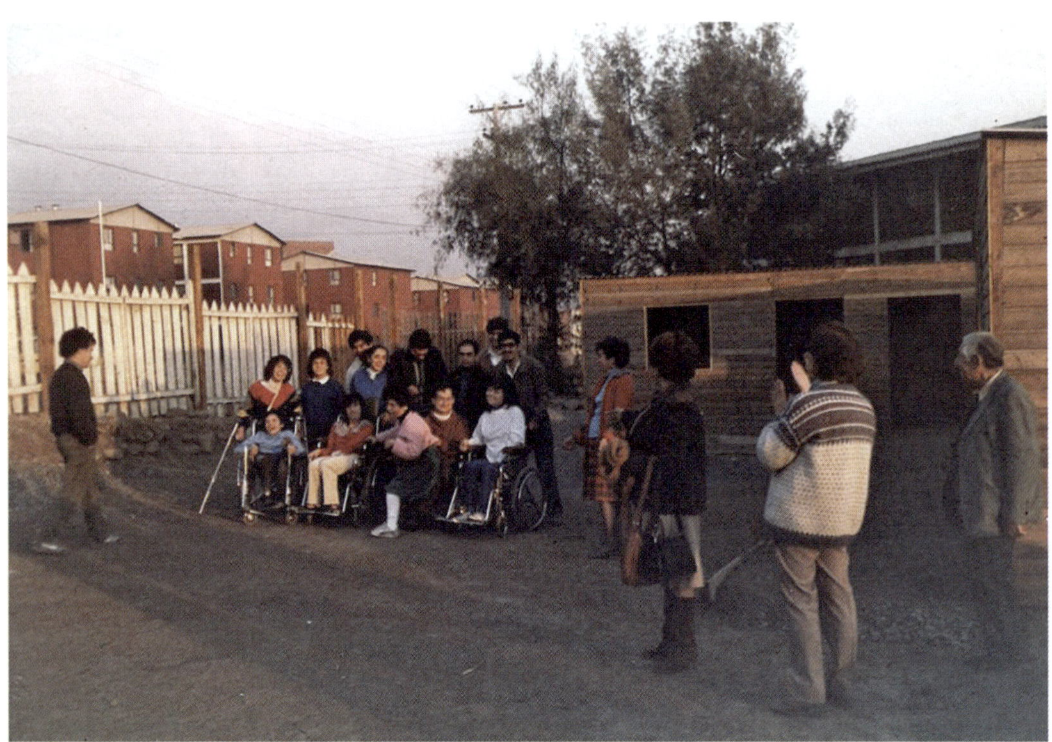

The opening of the Asociación para Espásticos Chilenos (ASPEC), Santiago, 1982:
the first *taller* for adults with cerebral palsy, founded by Adriana Maldonado.
Image courtesy Verónica Tello.

Sometimes the archive is too weak to hold even the most important memories, or traces thereof. Sometimes our experiences don't span far and wide enough to encompass the memories we wish we had.

I'm sitting at my desk in Sydney/Gadigal land, searching Google.cl for traces of a history that might be too weak to connect with. In 1982, my maternal *abuelita*, Adriana Maldonado (1923–2005), initiated the Asociación para Espásticos Chilenos (ASPEC). ASPEC, a *taller,* is best described as something between a workshop, school, and community centre for young adults and adults with severe cerebral palsy. Its mission is simple: to refuse both the relegation of people with cerebral palsy, like my *tio* (uncle) and Adriana's son, Alejandro Moreno Maldonano (1952–), to a lifetime of isolated domesticity and the false prognosis of a short life.[1] Adriana conceived ASPEC as a vital if ad hoc infrastructure—its parts originally comprised a ramshackle building, a small van with a ramp, a group of parent/ mother volunteers, and an enthusiastic physiotherapist graduate—that held open an alternative future for people like my uncle. ASPEC was an act of solidarity with those subjected to what is now termed "necro-politics"—the "letting die" of bodies via the state's withdrawal of support and the privatisation of both health and community infrastructure during the dictatorship of General Augusto Pinochet in Chile (1973–1990).[2]

In 1981, eight years after Pinochet's *coup d'état* and one year before the founding of ASPEC, the Chilean health system was subjected to neoliberal reforms. The military dictatorship inaugurated the Instituciones de Salud

---

1   ASPEC was founded in 1975 as the state no longer offered support to my uncle and others with cerebral palsy, including the many friends he'd made in rehabilitation centres, once they turned 18 and became adults. ASPEC was formally registered in 1982, as the organisation's website details (I lost all connection to ASPEC after my grandma passed away): ASPEC, accessed June 18, 2021, www.aspec.cl.

2   For an analysis of the impacts of the state's withdrawal of public access to medical systems, see Dikaios Sakellariou and Elena S. Rotarou, "The Effects of Neoliberal Policies on Access to Healthcare for People with Disabilities," *International Journal for Equity in Health* 16 (2017), https://doi.org/10.1186/ s12939-017-0699-3.

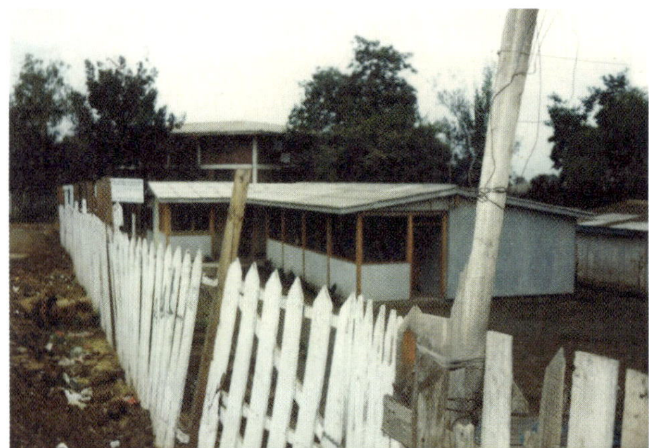

ASPEC, Santiago 1982, the first *taller* for adults with cerebral palsy,
founded by Adriana Maldonado. Image courtesy Verónica Tello.

Previsional (ISAPRES, Institutes of Social Security) to allow people to opt out of the government-managed health insurance system Fondo Nacional de Salud (FONASA, National Health Fund). The change was part of a broader move by the Pinochet regime to institute neoliberalism across the country via constitutional reform. Whereas before all workers contributed seven percent of their salary to FONASA, after 1980 the wealthiest members of Chile's population were able to withdraw their contributions and opt for private health insurance.[3] This led to an uneven distribution of health care based on wealth, as opposed to solidarity between old and young, rich and poor, healthy and not. Health care workers began to predominantly service ISAPRES because of higher salaries, and the capacity of the public health system became greatly diminished (long wait times, poor infrastructure, limited services).[4]

Adriana further explained the context for the founding of ASPEC one day while we watched the popular Chilean television variety show *Sábado Gigante* (*Giant Saturday*, 1962–), hosted by the famous Chilean personality Don Francisco (1940–). For decades, Don Francisco used his media power to support children with developmental disabilities and cerebral palsy, raising over US$286 million and founding numerous rehabilitation centres via his annual telethon, *Teletón* (1978–). Adriana criticised the show's host due to his fixation on youth rather than adults with cerebral palsy, thus mirroring the dictatorship's policy of letting die in adulthood or the fiction of a short life.[5] ASPEC remains the only centre that offers support for adults with developmental disabilities and cerebral palsy in Santiago.

3   Jean-Pierre Unger et al., "Chile's Neoliberal Health Reform: An Assessment and a≈Critique," *PLoS Medicine* 5, no. 4 (2008).

4   Mario Parada Lezcano, "End of the Road for Chile's Neoliberal Healthcare System?," Peoples Dispatch, accessed January 7, 2022, https://peoplesdispatch.org/2022/01/07/end-of-the-road-for-chiles-neoliberal-healthcare-system/.

5   Lack of access to health support for adults with disability in Chile during and after the dictatorship is analysed in Elena S. Rotarou and Dikaios Sakellariou, "Inequalities in Access to Health Care for People with Disabilities in Chile: The Limits of Universal Health Coverage," *Critical Public Health* 27, no. 5 (2017), https://doi.org/10.1080/09581596.2016.1275524.

When I searched the internet to try and find something documenting Adriana's role in founding ASPEC, all I managed to locate was a series of photos deep in ASPEC's Facebook page in an album entitled "*ASPEC historia*" (ASPEC is run by a new group of volunteer parents since Adriana, and the other original parent volunteers, have passed away). Most of the photos are of the ramshackle building that first housed ASPEC, which my mum and uncle tell me was built using donated or found materials. In one photo, I see Adriana, my uncle, and his friends outside the building's muddy grounds. My uncle, wearing a white skivvy and red jumper, is seated in his wheelchair, second from the right; his then girlfriend, Monica, is trying to sit on his lap. Adriana stands on the far right of the image, her back turned to the camera; her hands, mid-clap, show her joy; she is wearing beige pants and a white and brown woollen cardigan she probably knitted herself (I recognise the knitting pattern as one of hers). This pixelated image, and others like it on the ASPEC Facebook page, render present my grandma's role in ASPEC's history, and the history of the centre more broadly. And while it's not much, I'm going to latch onto these digital artefacts.

While public records of my *abuelita* are thin, the internet holds an excess of information on another woman: Lucia Hiriart de Pinochet (1922–2021), the *Primera Dama de Chile* (First Lady of Chile) and Pinochet's right-wing wife. I think of Hiriart de Pinochet as my *abuelita*'s dialectal other. Between 1973 and 1991 Hiriart de Pinochet headed CEMA, the Centro de Madres (Mothers' Centre). CEMA was originally an initiative of Graciela Letelier Velasco, the wife of Chilean President Carlos Ibáñez del Campo, and was conceived as social infrastructure to offer a space and solidarity for women farmworkers, peasants, and mothers during the 1950s. Like ASPEC, it filled a gap for the underclass in Chile.

After the coup of 1973, Hiriart de Pinochet took over CEMA's administration with the support of volunteer military wives, converting the organisation into a bourgeois "women's centre," where women would come and perform "womanly" duties such as quilting and cooking.

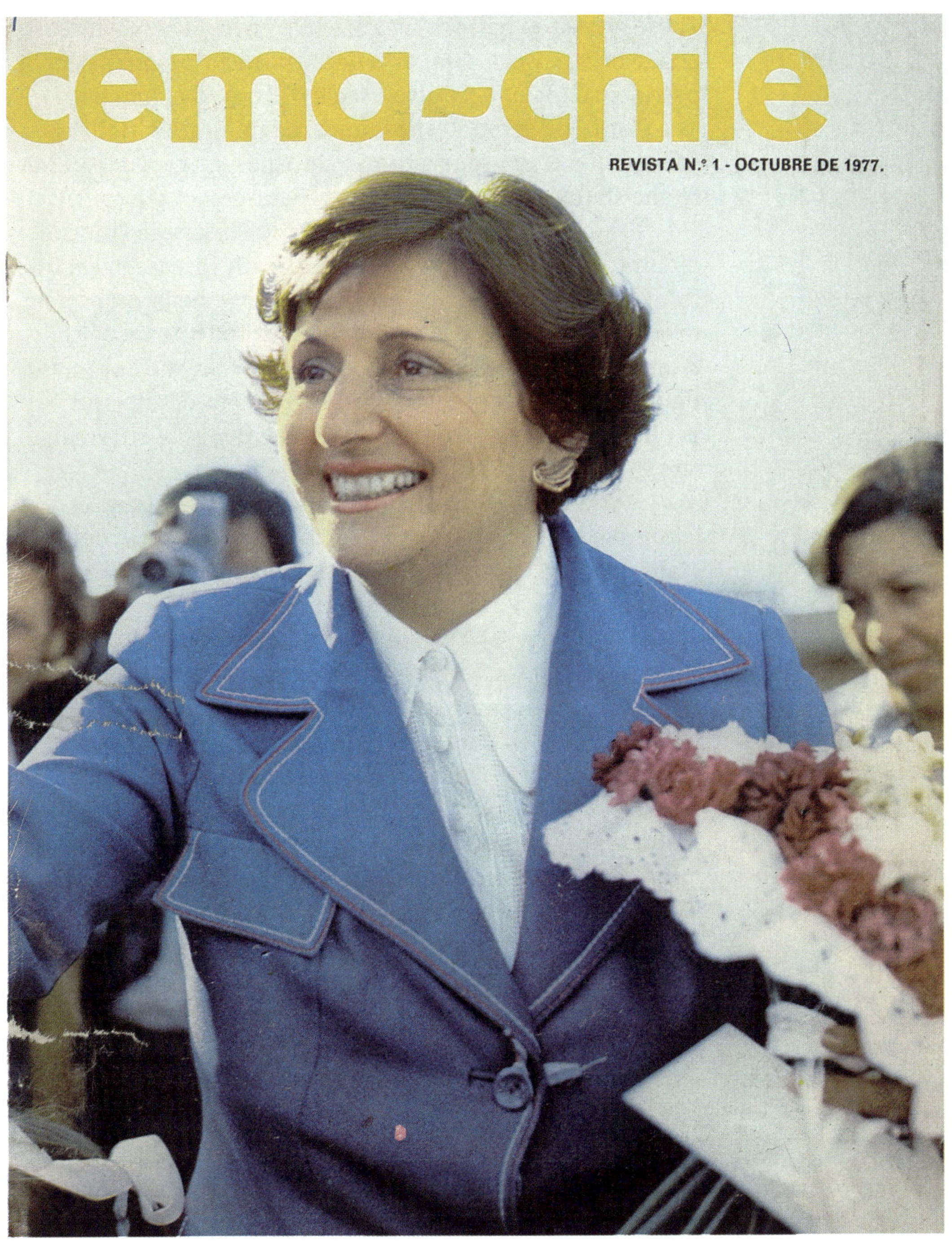

Cover of *Cema Chile* (no. 1, October 1977): Lucía Hiriart de Pinochet, president of the Centro de Madres (Mothers' Centre, CEMA). Image courtesy Biblioteca Nacional de Chile.

These gendered performances, while giving a benevolent image of care work sympathetic to the dictatorship's deeply patriarchal logic, were also used by Hiriart de Pinochet as a front. For decades, she laundered millions of dollars, selling off public property and Mapuche land ceded to CEMA by the state during the dictatorship for personal profit.[6]

The lifestories of my *abuelita* and Hiriart de Pinochet did not, as far as I am aware, ever directly intersect. Yet by thinking their weak and strong stories together, I am hoping to establish a new set of coordinates for the history of Chile after 1973, ones which make legible not only the dominant figures, institutions, and narratives of dictatorship and neoliberalism, but also the less visible modes of surviving and thriving that subtended them.

When I was procrastinating writing this essay, I stumbled across an online lecture by the Polish writer Ewa Majewska on "weak resistance."[7] The "weak"—housewives, the elderly, sex workers, queers, the disabled, and others on the periphery—resist in often "unremarkable" ways, Majewska tells us. "Unheroic," "everyday," and "slow" are the aesthetic categories of the weak, incongruous with the usual characterisation of resistance in patriarchal cultures: "strong," "heroic," "forceful" (the well-known works of Chilean protest mural movements, the Brigada Ramona Parra or Agrupación de Plásticos Jóvenes, come to mind as an example of "strong" resistance). As Majewski states, "The weapons of the weak are ordinary, and demand persistence rather than strength."[8] A sit-in,

6   "The laundered funds were used to support Pinochet while he was under house arrest in the United Kingdom as he awaited the outcome of extradition charges for human rights abuses during the dictatorship. He was released without charges due to his declining health and a 'memory deficit' for which he could not provide accurate testimonies in court." Jonathan Franklin, "Pinochet's Widow under Investigation on Suspicion of Swindling Millions," *The Guardian*, August 19, 2016, www.theguardian.com/world/2016/aug/19/pinochet-widow-lucia-hiriart-cema-chile.

7   Ewa Majewska, "Everyday Struggles and the Politics of Failure" (paper presented at Weak Resistance, Institute for Cultural Inquiry, Berlin, May 27, 2015), www.ici-berlin.org/events/weak-resistance/. Also see Ewa Majewska, "Peripheries, Housewives, and Artists in Revolt: Notes from the 'Former East'," in *Former West*, ed. Maria Hlavajova and Simon Sheikh, 601–604.

8   Ewa Majewska, "Weak Resistance," *Krisis Journal for Contemporary Philosophy*, 2 (2018): 16.

a letter, the work of administration. While the weak may be everywhere, their quiet and unheroic gestures are not monumentalised. The weak, instead, are always in question: "their gender—a trouble, and their origins—unholy."[9] Failure—never meeting neoliberal, racialised, classist, ableist expectations or milestones—is a given.

As I look at the photo of my *tio* and *abuelita*, and their friends at ASPEC, I begin to wonder if forms of weak resistance such as theirs must always be fated to wither, in the shadows. Yet the traces of weak resistance occasionally rear their head to remind us that they're still here, even if testimony, evidence, and memory are often hard to come by.[10] Weak resistance produces weak history. Historians who seek to find a place for weak history are left with little certainty or specifics, yet with much to speculate on.[11]

9   Majewska, "Weak Resistance," 16.
10   Heather Love, *Feeling Backward: Loss and the Politics of Queer History* (Cambridge, Massachusetts: Harvard University Press, 2007).
11   I am drawing on both Heather Love's and Hal Foster's readings of archive and fiction: Love, *Feeling Backward*; Hal Foster, "An Archival Impulse," *October* 110 (Autumn 2004): 3–22.

Dialogue
Verónica Tello, Chandra Frank, James Nguyen, and Salote Tawale,
with Comments by Carla Macchiavello and Dylan A.T. Miner

VERÓNICA TELLO (VT) For this dialogue I want to think about
the connection between "weak histories" and "futures."
In other words, I'm interested in histories which
emerge out of the work of the "weak"—a grandma,
for example—and hobble their way into the present
and future.

Salote and James, you both work with what
I think of as weak family histories spanning Fiji,
Vietnam, and Australia. Chandra, in your curatorial
work and research you are concerned with the weak
archives of queer, black, and migratory feminisms.
To what extent does the concept of weak histories
resonate with you? How do archives feed into your
concept of futures? How do you engage archives to
remember the experience and resistance of the weak?

CHANDRA FRANK (CF) I think of weak archives and
histories in relationship to my research into
the feminist and queer Black, Migrant, and
Refugee (BMR) movement in the Netherlands.
I spent a considerable amount of time speaking
to women active in the movement and combing
through archival materials such as personal
archives, newsletters, magazines, radio shows,
flyers, and pamphlets to get a better sense of the
BMR movement.[12] Most of these materials are part
of the IAV (International Archives for the Women's
Movement) Collection at Atria in Amsterdam,
which is a white feminist archive. The idea of weak
histories resonates with me because during several

12	For a history of the BMR movement and
	archives see Chandra Frank, "Sister Outsider
	and Audre Lorde in the Netherlands:
	On Transnational Queer Feminisms
	and Archival Methodological Practices,"
	Feminist Review 121 (2019).

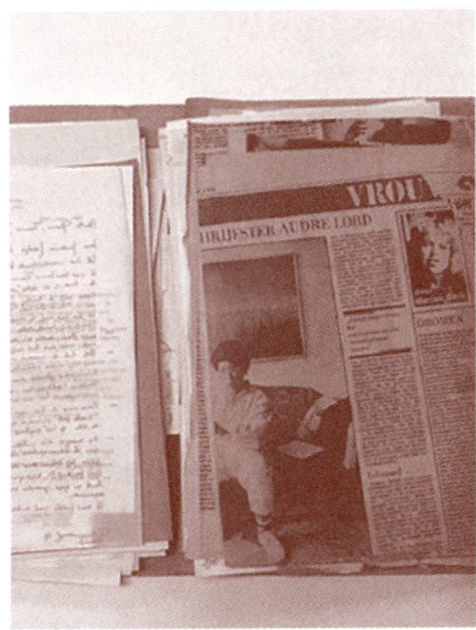

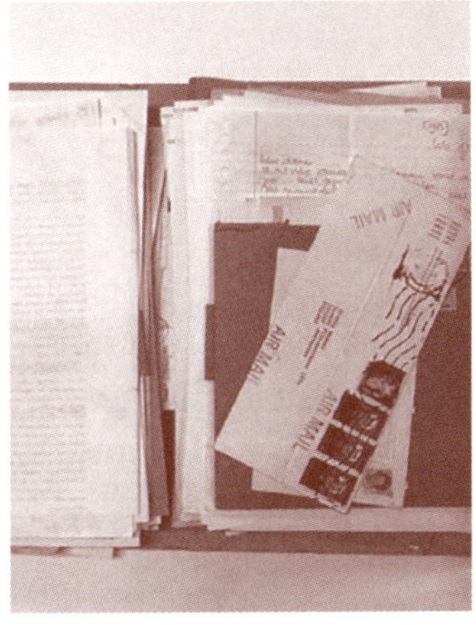

Sister Outsider materials at Atria.
Image courtesy Chandra Frank.

moments in my research I was faced with the racial taxonomies of white institutional archives. I think here of the politics of coding and labelling, but also the ways in which marginalised histories often reside outside of official preservation processes. I became interested in the different modes of relationality that exist between archival materials and researchers. In this process we can also reflect on where weak histories take us, why they might be perceived as weak, and how our engagement with materials might offer us new orientations.

Care also plays a big part in this larger conversation. How might we take care of these histories? Does the use of words like "weak" or "marginalised" offer us another frame or entry point? Care for these histories needs to be future-oriented. However, it's important to ask what we mean by caring for Black and brown feminist and queer histories, and what this care looks like.

I don't think of institutional archives as an end goal for social movement work. That is to say, I don't think simply preserving feminist and queer materials for future generations is enough. And I've had plenty of conversations with feminist and queer elders of colour who aren't necessarily interested in becoming part of a white feminist archive. We should therefore question our investment in archives, and how we might envision archival sites and spaces outside of traditional archival structures.

I am still working through these ideas, but I'm interested in other approaches to futurity and archival spaces. Futurity is evidently no longer about just the act of documentation, and the archive is not necessarily a future promised site. This is especially true for histories and materials that are fragmented and scattered.

VT   Can you elaborate a bit more on this idea of fragmented or scattered archives?

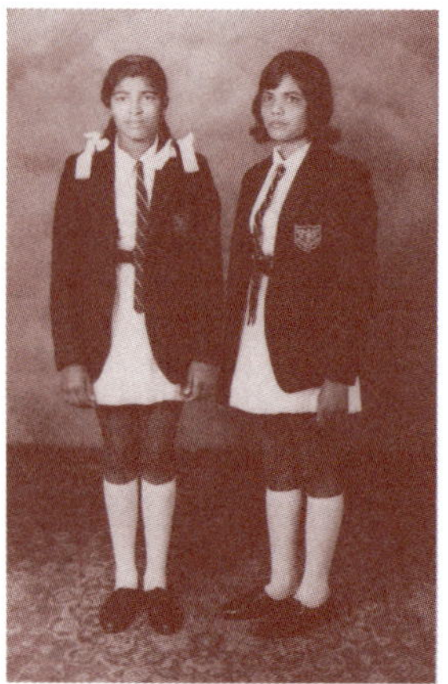

Mary and school friend
at Tongaat Indian
High School in 1970s.
In *Proclamation 73*,
curated by Chandra
Frank and Zara Julius.
Photograph courtesy
Mary Moonsamy.

CF   I've approached my archival research by
acknowledging that we cannot "know" the archive.
BMR materials, for example, do not exist in one
collection; they are scattered across a much larger
collection and are therefore more vulnerable.
In general, though, it's important to not posit
institutional or traditional archives as being
complete, either. In using archival materials, I'm
not concerned with presenting neat linear feminist
and queer histories. Rather, I think it's more useful
to work with the cartographic qualities of archival
fragments.

VT   …and in the process of fragmentation, some histories
are left stronger or weaker, some histories are absorbed
into hegemonic narratives and others aren't?

CF   Yes. I see this in relationship to how the Dutch tell
stories about themselves. These stories are often
rooted in a misconstrued sense of self. Gloria
Wekker offers a very poignant analysis of what
she calls "white innocence" in the Netherlands:
the passionate denial of race on the one hand
and the aggressive colonial violence and racism
on the other.[13] Of course, this poses an important
question as to how we tell other stories without
them solely existing in opposition to hegemonic
narratives. That's why I'm keen to further explore
what we mean by alternative histories, for
instance, and what becomes legible as alternative
or marginalised histories.

VT   Chandra, you often work as a curator. What is your
curatorial method to mobilise a futurity for those
archives?

13   Gloria Wekker, *White Innocence: Paradoxes
of Colonialism and Race* (Durham, North
Carolina: Duke University Press, 2016).

CF   As a curator, I'm interested in the different ways that archives enter the exhibition space. Artists use archives in so many different forms and ways. It's been very inspiring to see artists work with family archives, colonial or state archives, or creating new archives. Visual practices are really powerful in terms of thinking through displaced histories, but they also offer us imaginative entry points. Invented characters or the use of speculative fiction can be a great way to engage with the intersections between archives and art. Collage techniques have really inspired me, too, in terms of contemplating how we might rethink the meaning of archival images.[14]

I wouldn't say I have one specific curatorial method. I think my approach is always dependent on the geographic context and the artists I collaborate with. But I do think it's important to be mindful of how we engage with the colonial grammars of the exhibition space. Exhibitions that address colonial histories often also tend to reproduce the very violence they are trying to interrogate, and the labour to address these issues often falls on the shoulders of Black and brown curators, artists, and cultural workers.[15]

In 2018, I worked with Zara Julius in Durban, South Africa, to produce an exhibition, *Proclamation 73*, based on family photos of people racialised as Indian and coloured. We spent a considerable amount of time thinking about how to arrange these family photos, and how to bring attention to the violent, and often anti-black, categorisations of race within the South African context, in addition to unpacking how local families made sense of race. The futurity of such

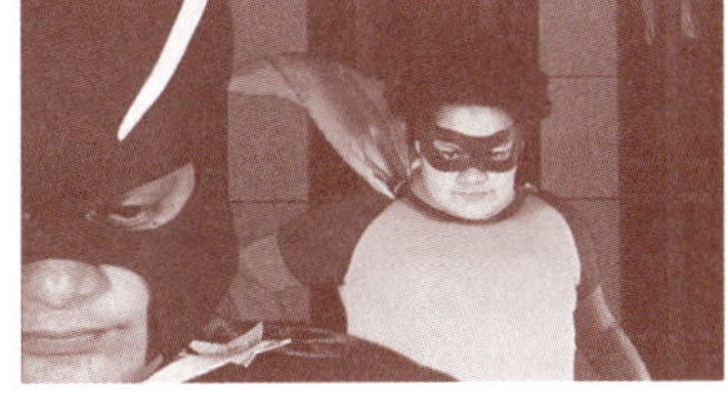

Salote Tawale, *Super*, 2003, single-channel video, colour, sound, 2:45 minutes. Image courtesy the artist.

14   Chandra Frank, "Fugitive Desires" (paper presented at 198 Contemporary Arts & Learning, London, March 3–4, 2017), www.chandrafrank.com/new-events/2017/2/26/opening-fugitive-desires-at-198.

15   For example, see Alberta Whittle, "Biting the Hand That Feeds You: A Strategy of Wayward Curating," *Critical Arts* 33, no. 6 (2019).

personal family archives resides in acknowledging and grappling with those very complexities.

VT   Let's bring Salote and James into the dialogue, starting with Salote.

SALOTE TAWALE (ST) In my early work, I started thinking about making work for future audiences because at the time I felt no connection to the works of artists around me.

VT   What was the context for making this work, Salote?

ST   It was difficult to find works by queer people of colour in Melbourne/Naarm, where I grew up and studied (I'm now based in Sydney/Gadigal land).[16] Back then I didn't know where to look. My approach to this situation was to begin placing myself into my own work. I began by placing myself into pop cultural contexts in my photo and video works. I knew then that I was making my own archive, remaking histories.

For example, with the work *Super* (2003) I positioned myself in the pop-cultural imagery of the original television series *Batman* (1966–1968) by reperforming the archetypes, or perhaps more fittingly the stereotypes, utilised within the show: the villain, the victim, the hero. I played characters that were, and are, usually reserved for Anglo identities, except the villain is often a person of colour. Through works such as *Super*, I wanted to initiate a dialogue on the visibility and presence of people of colour in Australia and other Anglo-dominant cultures from a personal, embodied position; I was analysing white pop culture from both the inside and outside.

16   For a recent reflection on the politics of colour in Salote Tawale's work, see Salote Tawale et al., *I Don't See Colour* (Perth: Perth Institute of Contemporary Arts, 2021).

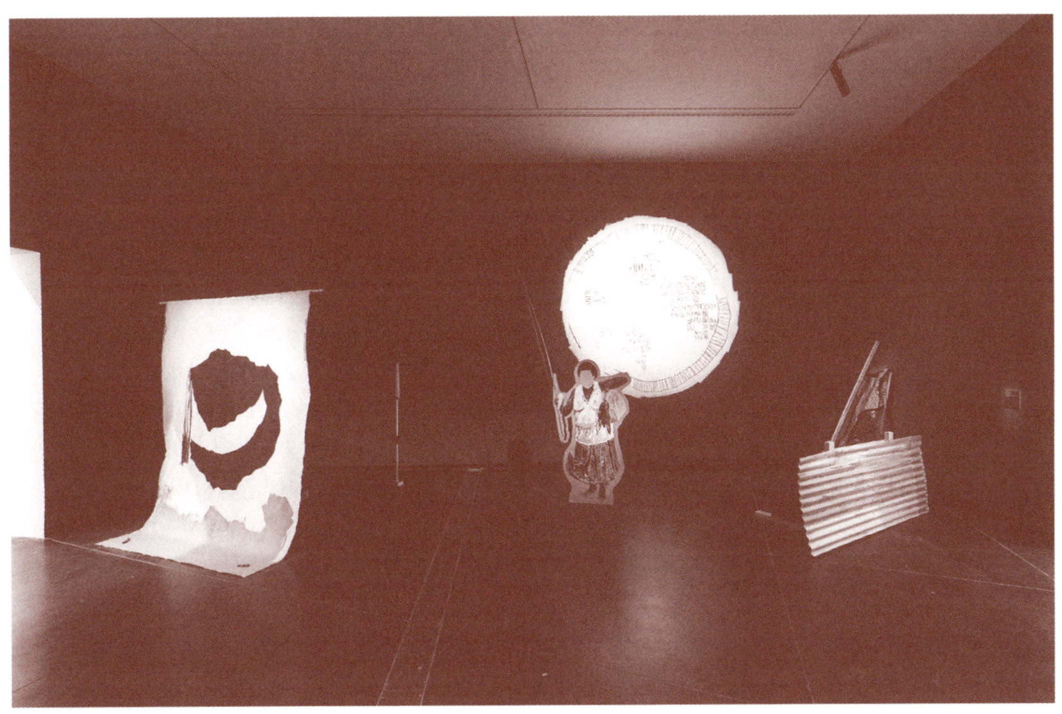

Salote Tawale, *Burebasaga Maramas*, 2017–18. Installation view.
Photograph by Andrew Curtis. Image courtesy the artist.

In my more recent work I've been focusing on family archives. This turn in my practice emerged after I visited the Museum of Archaeology and Anthropology at the University of Cambridge, which holds an archive of ethnographic photos of Fiji and a collection of Fijian cultural objects and artefacts. In this museum there is a lot of detail and information on the makers and collectors of ethnographic imagery and/or the colonial owner of objects; the coloniser's relationship to the materials is recorded with accuracy and depth. Meanwhile, there is a void of knowledge around the subjects of the photographs and archives and the creators of the objects in the collection. When I visited Cambridge, I realised that the museum's "official records" were pseudo-scientific and unable to reveal the intimate stories and knowledges these objects contained/transmitted.[17]

From this visit I began the creation of a video installation to speak of these missing stories, *Burebasaga Maramas* (2017–2018), which reimaged the reflections of Fijian people on the water seen in ethnographic imagery. At the same time, I began a video project with my family, recounting family stories through a series of interviews in my village. My aunts, uncles, and cousins prepared the information and then recounted it to the family. Through the process of gathering these family stories and talking to Fijian people, friends, colleagues, and family, creating *Burebasaga Maramas* was like developing a collage or piecing together a puzzle, which gathers different perspectives to produce

17   Charlotte Joy, *Heritage Justice* (Cambridge: Cambridge University Press, 2020); Khadija von Zinnenburg Carroll, *The Contested Crown: Repatriation Politics between Europe and Mexico* (Chicago: University of Chicago Press, 2022).

a shared history. Each of these different perspectives are connected by my body, my histories, and my current place of being.

Added to this, my work is now being archived in museum collections, and I feel the need to share as much information during the archival process for a future audience who can't just email me and ask a question. So, that means that when a museum collects my work, I try and offer as much detail to the registration team as possible.

VT Let's think a bit more about relations between archives and futurity in your work, especially in relation to this notion of a future audience.

ST I guess there was a lot of hope in my early works that the world would change, and I would have an audience.

VT Has that future audience arrived?

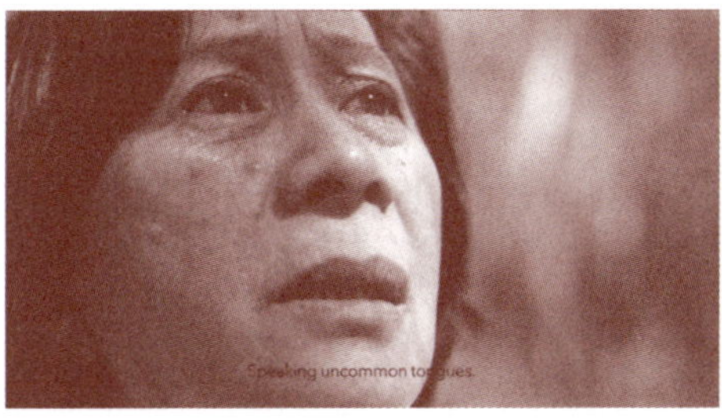

Detail: James Nguyen with Nguyễn Ngọc Cư, Nguyễn Thị Kim Dung, and Joey Nguyễn, *Portion 53*, 2019. Multi-channel digital video, colour, sound. 9:21 minutes, 13:33 minutes, 9:53 minutes. Museum of Contemporary Art, purchased with funds provided by the MCA Foundation, 2020. Image courtesy the artist.

ST Yes, more so than before. In my early work, the risk for me was that I was the only artist of colour, at least directly around me, who was using their own body in their works. Added to this, the audience didn't always understand my gestures and use of materials, or why and how I was directly positioning myself as a person living in the diaspora on unceded territories in opposition to settler-colonial narratives of Australian-ness. Today, this is much more legible.

VT James, I am interested to hear your thoughts.

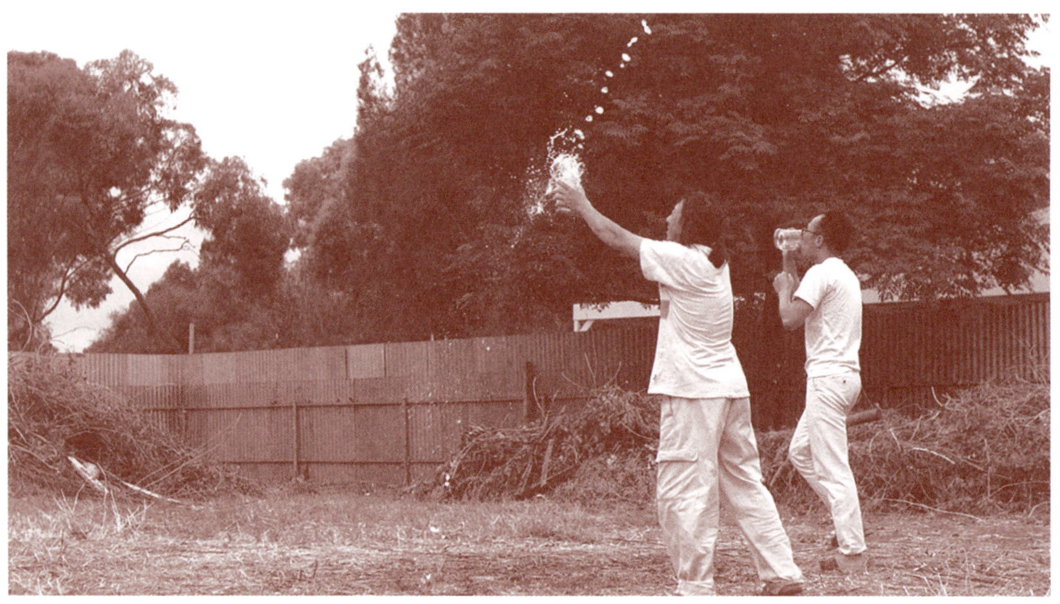

James Nguyen with Cong Ai Nguyen and Nguyễn Thị, *On The Border of Things*, Part 2, 2018. Commissioned by ACE OPEN, a Today Tonight exposé of PFOS (Poly-fluoroalkyl substances) contaminating ground water in areas surrounding Adelaide reveals the ongoing marginalisation of migrant labourers. Image courtesy the artist.

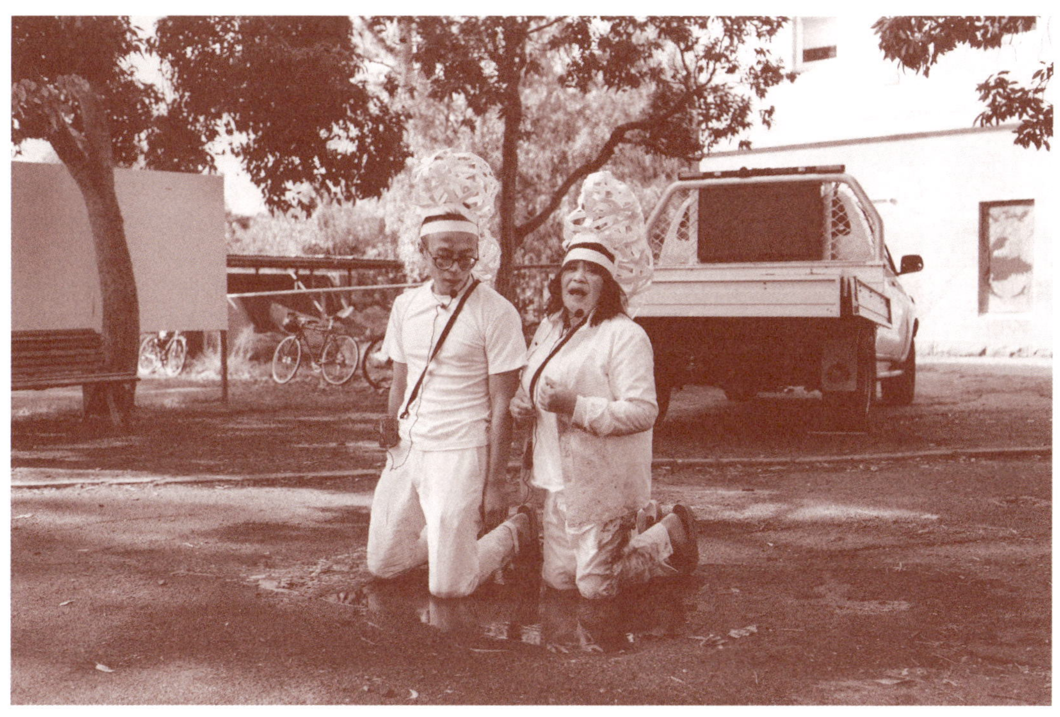

James Nguyen with Nguyễn Thị Kim Nhung, Nguyen Công Aí, and Hayley Forward, *On The Border of Things*, Part 3, 2018. A roving performance on the back of a ute, combining farmwork with connecting to the NBN (National Broadband Network). Made for NEXT WAVE FESTIVAL. Photograph by Anne Moffat. Image courtesy the artist.

JAMES NGUYEN (JN) Okay, I have two things to put forward:

1   Official and conventional archives are often assumed as whole (and I agree with Chandra and Salote on the role of thinking of archives, and history, via fragmentation).
2   To produce an archive is intrinsically to think about a future.

On the first point: I think people generally feel that archives are the most significant source materials for research. Whilst archives are made and produced for the purpose of collecting data, it's clear that these archives are inherently non-comprehensive, often flawed, and limited by design and capacity.[18] With uncollected or uncollatable gaps and holes, these archives are routinely used as evidence or data for policy or thought production. When they are retrospectively used, the gaps and holes become easier to ignore, and what is collected, kept, and organised by these archives becomes the primary source for history-writing. They become representative of a whole or assume a primacy that was never intended. Functionally, these archives are ultimately assumed to be complete, and are only challenged when anomalies or alternate materials appear to remind us of their incompleteness.[19]

VT So you mean, generally, people assume archives are complete, and that institutions possess complete archives.

18   On the entropy of archives, see Sven Spieker, *The Big Archive: Art from Bureaucracy* (Cambridge, Massachusetts: MIT Press, 2008).

19   This reading of the archive is aligned with Saidiya Hartman, *Wayward Lives, Beautiful Experiments: Intimate Histories of Social Upheaval* (London: Serpents Tail, 2019); and Tina Campt, *Image Matters: Archive, Photography, and the African Diaspora in Europe* Durham, North Carolina: Duke University Press, 2012).

JN   Yes. Consider for example, the Operation Legacy program (ca. 1950s–1970s) of British colonists, which saw them deliberately destroying and sending sensitive material back to the United Kingdom (the so-called "migrated archives") so as to prevent them being used for legal and administrative purposes in the process of independence.[20] The materials that weren't destroyed became one of the ways in which institutions in the colonies could build their historic narratives. Whatever was destroyed by Operation Legacy is forever relegated to the realm of the speculative. That's why I say that colonial archives are as incomplete as any other. They are actually more so, because they claim authoritative completeness in spite of the obvious erasures that shape them.

VT   So displacing and erasing knowledge to construct a fiction of authority or completeness?

JN   Yes, that's my set-up…fiction is just as important as "official archives" with their claims to totalising knowledge, since such archives are themselves fictions.

VT   For sure. James, I am curious how the relations between fiction and the archive emerge in your work and how, if at all, they help you connect to futures? Or weak histories?

JN   I get excited by speculation and gossip. I'm always listening for stories about people and places in my local area that fall outside of conventional

20   Foreign and Commonwealth Office and predecessors: Records of Former Colonial Administrations: Migrated Archives, 1835–2012, FCO 141, The National Archives, https://discovery.nationalarchives.gov.uk/details/r/C12269323.

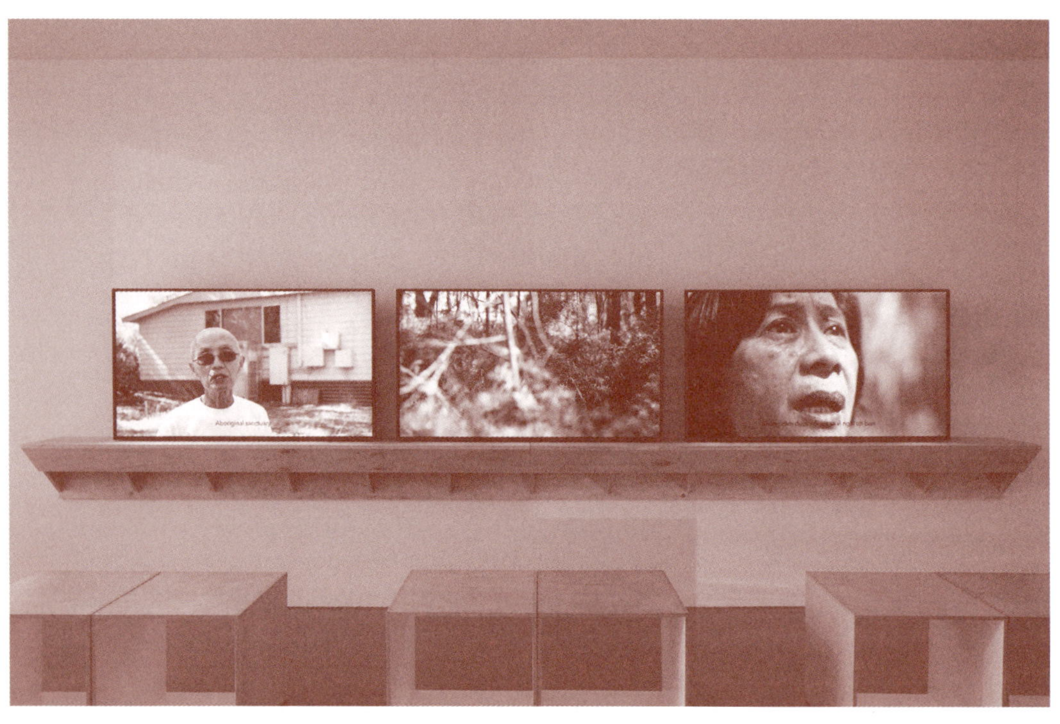

Detail: James Nguyen with Nguyễn Ngọc Cư, Nguyễn Thị Kim Dung, and Joey Nguyễn, *Portion 53*, 2019.
Multi-channel digital video, colour, sound. 9:21 minutes, 13:33 minutes, 9:53 minutes.
Museum of Contemporary Art, purchased with funds provided by the MCA Foundation, 2020.
Image courtesy the artist.

archives or narratives. For example, I've been learning about how Australia produced and tested Agent Orange in Sydney and Queensland for the war in Vietnam, how my dad's first "home" in Australia—an immigration and refugee processing site—was once an Aboriginal sanctuary (on D'hrawal/Tharawal Country), and how my aunty, Bác Hương, worked in a leprosy camp in Nha Trang. These are weak histories: They aren't conventionally substantiated, and only manifest themselves in the present via hearsay and contested local memories. I guess these weak histories don't have the conventional institutional, journalistic, and documentary materials of major histories.

I often think about how I might process or participate in the weak resistance of maintaining these increasingly weak histories and memories. Although weak histories often disappear unnoticed, dying with the people who hold them, weak histories offer respite, resistance, and resilience because of their elusive ability to avoid loud, spectacular, and blustering self-importance.

The concept and politics of weak histories also prompt me to remember how my parents learnt to speak English. Their struggle with the English language taught me the effect of weak power; of knowing when to keep their mouths shut, knowing how to withhold speech, to have the patience to wait for the right word, to not have the last word. For native English speakers, these silences might appear weak, but they are profoundly disruptive and frustrating. These silences refuse participation, they are not easily recorded, and so might not be even noticed or archived.

ST   Do you see the works you make with your family as archiving, James?

JN   Yes, I think so. I started filming my family because my parents were too time-poor to make family videos. I kept seeing these white filmmakers "delving" into their family archives—videos, photo albums, slides—and I felt excluded. I had no family archive apart from oral stories. I make works such as *Portion 53* (2019) to allow my future self to "delve" and naval gaze.

In this sense, I feel very connected to the idea of weak histories, Verónica. My archive—like yours—works to both preserve and resist memories within a colonial context that is underpinned by exclusionary logics (sexual, gendered, racial, ableist).[21]

VT   We are about halfway through, and so we might ask if any of the other *Future Souths* contributors, quietly waiting for their dialogues to begin, has a question or comment?

CARLA MACCHIAVELLO (CM)   I'll comment. As an art historian, I know that in Chilean art discourse, a narrative—an art history even—has been propagated that emphasises "strong" myths of conceptualist resistance to the military dictatorship (1973–1990).[22] This narrative—espoused by figures from the *escena de avanzada*, in particular Nelly Richard—has obliterated other narratives and other possibilities for thinking about possible futures. It has even effaced other archives that exist, which offer counter-histories. This narrative is so strong that it still affects what is possible to include in the archive of contemporary art history.

This narrative—the one espoused by the *escena de avanzada*—probably once saw itself as

21   For an account of James Nguyen's work with his family, see James Nguyen, "Translating Diaspora in the Settler-Colony," *Antithesis* 31 (2021).

22   Nelly Richard, "Margins and Institutions: Art in Chile after 1973," trans. Juan Dávila and Paul Foss *Art & Text* 21 (1986).

weak, historically positioning itself on the margin of both the dictatorship and the art world. Perhaps that was once true. But the margin has, by now, created its own margins.

I am increasingly interested in current artists and artistic projects on the margins of this canonical art history of resistance after 1973. These marginal projects often begin from very personal situations.[23]

VT   From a personal perspective, I'll add that I've been working with the archive of the Chilean-Australian artist Juan Dávila, who has been marginalised by the strong narratives of the *escena de avanzada*. While he is very well known in Australia, in Chile his position in art discourse is still very weak.[24]

CM   Yes, it's been very difficult to access archives and write histories of artists involved in the resistance (after 1973) who were not part of the *escena de avanzada*—and it still is difficult to articulate these histories, since the canon has obscured so much.[25]

VT   Yet the canon and the archives are always incomplete and thus sites of futurity. Incompleteness catalyses futurity?

23   For instance, for personal reasons, the artist Francisca Benítez started learning sign language, subsequently developing a series of artworks that engaged deaf communities in Chile, and through invitations from art institutions in other places, such as Havana. Each time she does the project, she learns the specificities of the local (national) sign system and develops pedagogical and performative projects (involving sign language poetry, for instance). Benítez makes present groups that are on the borders, emphasising communicating through the body, and creating an archive of corporeal signs as the works move from place to place.

24   Verónica Tello and Sebastián Valenzuela-Valdivia, "A Partial History of South–South Art Criticism: Juan Dávila's Collaborations with *Art & Text* and Chilean Art Workers during the Pinochet Dictatorship, 1981–1990," *Third Text* 35, no. 6 (2021), https://doi.org/10.1080/09528822.2021.2019954.

25   Carla Macchiavello, "Vanguardia de exportación: La originalidad de la 'Escena de Avanzada' y otros mitos chilenos" in *Ensayos sobre artes visuales: Prácticas y discursos de los años '70 y '80 en Chile* (Santiage: LOM Ediciones–Centro de Documentación de Artes Visuales, 2011).

CF   I am drawn to the incompleteness and the messiness of archives. Messiness has become an orientation for me, too, specifically, in working with my own family archives and stories. I've gone through the personal family archives of my late father and grappled with questions of what futurity might mean in relationship to diasporic presence.[26] Incomplete letters, scribbles, photos with friends, a Capricorn necklace, lingering notes about mental health issues and addiction. For me, this was a place where I could dwell without thinking about futurity or resolve, or linear time.

JN   Can I ask if an archive is also strategy for deferment? For things we can't resolve in the now and for which we rely on futurity—forged through processes of reflection, care, collaboration, and dialogue—to make sense of these incomplete archives, if not now, then at some point?

VT   Yes. I feel that in this sense futurity is intimately linked with loss and speculation. For me there's a connection between the desire to cling on to fragments from almost erased histories and having the will and agency to construct a history, however incomplete it might be. You're right James, the archive is open and contingent enough to offer the space for ambivalence and unresolved concepts of what may come. This is the politics and potential of the archive that I think we are all trying to engage with.

DYLAN A.T. MINER (DM) During this conversation, I've been thinking about the Anishinaabeg (Ojibwe, Odawa, Potawatomi) word *anikoobijigan,* which simultaneously

26   On subjective engagements with the archive, including family archive, see Nydia A. Swaby and Chandra Frank, "Archival Experiments, Notes and (Dis)orientations," *Feminist Review* 124 (2020).

names one's ancestors and descendants. In particular, the word speaks the names of one's great-grandparents and great-grandchildren at the same time. Epistemologically, I find that Indigenous notions of time— particularly here on Mikinak-minis (Turtle Island)—break down the linearity of (Western) concepts of futurity.

ST   What a great word, Dylan; such a beautiful concept, that in an instant brings together many bodies, moments in time and space together in the singular. Futurity in my practice is a way to speak about how the past passes through and marks my spirit and body, a temporality I am constantly negotiating in the contemporary (with kin).

Souths

SOUTHS: HEMISPHERIC PARTITIONS AND BORDER DWELLING
Walter D. Mignolo

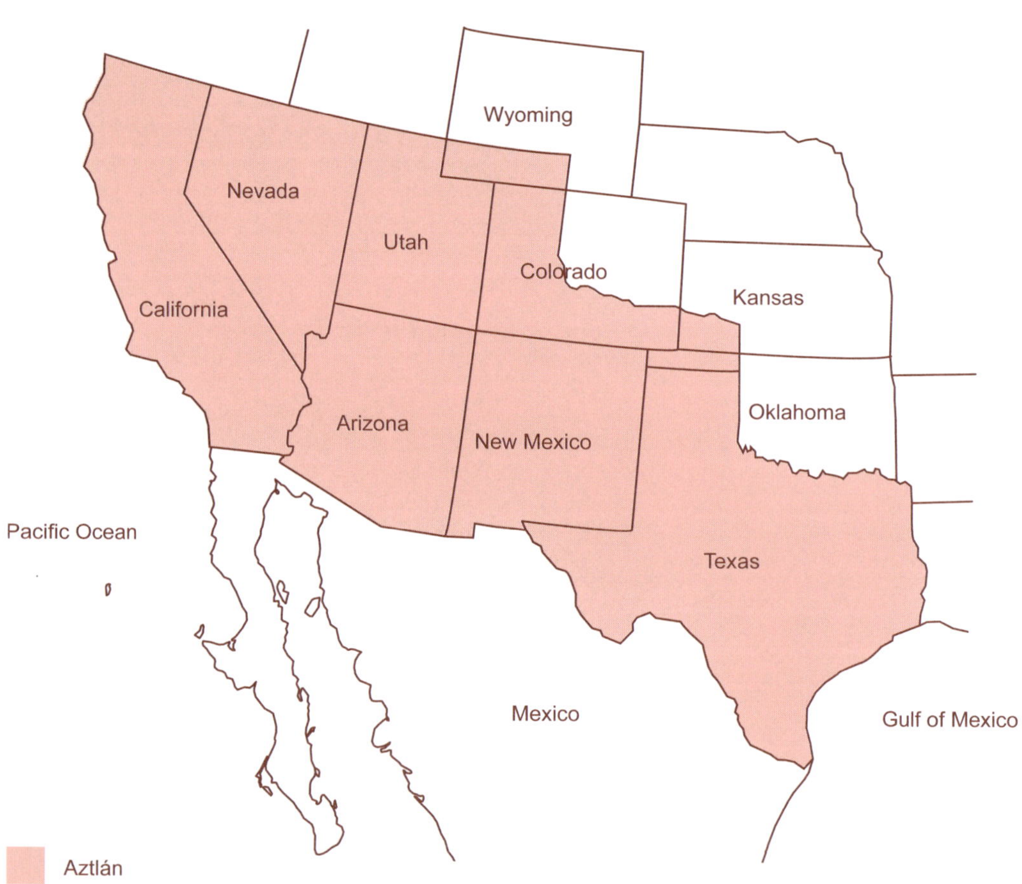

The civilisation of Aztlán, which underlies the current US territories, can be found surfacing in the work and life of millions of Chicanx.

Although my work is in dialogue with the idea of global souths, the idea is not embedded in my work. While I was born, raised, and educated in Argentina (until I departed for the global norths of France and the US), the ideas that became embedded in my praxis of living were borderlands and borderlines. Borderlands and borderlines (geo-historical, racial, sexual, linguistic, religious, national, epistemic, hermeneutic) are all over, dividing the world into global souths and global norths. I first read Gloria Anzaldúa in 1987, and in that encounter I learned that my discomfort from living came from dwelling in the borderland.[1] Society, education, modernity, and normalities of all sorts kept telling me that I should live in the territory—the global norths, global souths, eastern hemisphere, western hemisphere or whatever—but not in the border. Once one begins crossing borders—physically, legally, or illegally—dwelling in the border is the question, the existential question you continue to engage. Here is Anzaldúa:

> The US–Mexican border *es una herida abierta* where the Third World grates against the First World and bleeds. And before a scab forms it haemorrhages again, the lifeblood of two worlds merging to form a third country—a border culture.[2]

It is not just about the US–Mexican border.[3] The US–Mexican border is but one of the many instances and consequences of global linear thinking constitutive of Western modernity and the economic, political, epistemic, aesthetic, subjective (racist, sexist) context of Western Civilisation. Dwelling in the border is a global experience and it's shaped and reshaped by different local histories: where, when, and by whom (Spain, Holland, England, France, or the US) was the local history to which you belong interfered with?

1   Gloria Anzaldúa, *Borderlands/La Frontera: The New Mestiza* (San Francisco: Aunt Lute Books, 1987).
2   Ibid., 3.
3   For other articulations of living on the border see Aníbal Quijano, "Coloniality of Power, Eurocentrism, and Latin America," *Nepantla: Views from South* 1, no. 3 (2000); and Maria Lugones, "Heterosexualism and the Colonial/Modern Gender System," *Hypatia* 22, no. 1 (2007).

Border cultures are not the happy merging of two equal meanings or entities. There is a power differential because borders are created by classifications, and classifications are neither ontological nor made by some transcendental creator. Furthermore, there is no question of a particular borderland that is embedded in Anzaldúa's life. It is all over the global Third World, grating against the global First World and bleeding the blood of colonial wounds.

Anzaldúa's borderland is in the West of the East (the Middle East in the Western imaginary) and the norths of the souths (e.g., Maghreb), and the souths of the norths (Greece, Italy, Spain, Portugal). It is here in the borderland where modernity grates with coloniality and bleeds. Modernity/coloniality: the slash being the sign for all kinds of borders. Borders between the "democratic and just" norths (the US, the European Union) and the "diabolical and authoritarian" norths (Russia); between the West (the US, the European Union) and the East (China).

And there is more: the global souths presuppose the global norths (and hence the borderline) at the same time that the global norths are *in* the global souths through investments, military bases, corporations, media, and NGOs. Moreover, there are global souths in the global norths: the south of Europe is in a global north, and the south of the US (the Land of the Confederates) and the south-west (the Land of Chicanx, also called Aztlán) are in a global norths.

The global souths (at least in some ways) are geo-political partitions. However, considering them solely as such disregards corpo-political configurations like sexism and racism. Anzaldúa's borderlands are both geo- and body-political. Geopolitically speaking, there is the border between Mexico and the US. The body-political refers to the borderlines of being a woman, lesbian, and Chicana.[4] The global souths could hide sexism and racism only insofar as those who promote geopolitical partitions could

4   Cherríe Moraga and Gloria Anzaldúa, eds., *This Bridge Called My Back: Writings by Radical Women of Color* (New York: State University New York Press, 1981).

hide or disguise the hegemony of whiteness, masculinity, and heterosexuality.

All kinds of energies flow from the borderlands, from people whose praxis of living is shaped by their dwelling in the border. And the one who senses that they are dwelling in the border is the one who has been classified—never the one who classifies. The Third World is not an ontological planetary partition. It is an invention of individuals and institutions dwelling in the First World.[5] And there are scales also among those of us who are classified and of course ranked. Anzaldúa continues: "Borders are set up to define the places that are safe and unsafe, to distinguish *us* from *them*."[6]

To be conscious of dwelling in the border means to be aware of colonial wounds—of your own, as well as those of the people to whom you relate because of the common experiences of colonialism. Colonial wounds require decolonial healings. This is a route being taken by decolonial artists, curators, critics, and thinkers in general, including the contributors of *Future Souths,* who are working with curators and institutions—be they museums or departments of art history and visual studies (as the dictum goes) in different universities.

What is to be considered is that decolonial thinking is required not only in the global souths but all over the planet, since racism and sexism cannot be contained in hemispheric partitions. Coloniality is all over, and so must be decoloniality.

5   Walter D. Mignolo, *The Darker Side of Western Modernity: Global Futures, Decolonial Options* (Durham, North Carolina: Duke University Press, Durham, 2011).

6   Anzaldúa, *Borderlands/La Frontera,* 3.

Dialogue
Dialogue between Walter D. Mignolo, Dylan A. T. Miner, Carla Macchiavello,
and Zoe Butt, with Comments by Salote Tawale and James Nguyen

WALTER D. MIGNOLO (WM) Good afternoon, evening,
morning. The approach to the conversation is as follows.
I will formulate a question for Zoe, Dylan, and Carla
to respond to, and in that order. After each of your
responses, I will open up the conversation for you to
extend your comments or to ask me a question. We will
proceed like this until the end of the hour allocated to
this dialogue.

How do each of you think of border dwelling,
thinking, and doing, especially with regard to
concepts of futurity, as it is formulated by Verónica
for *Future Souths* (*FS*):

A particular concern of *FS* is to acknowledge
the historical symbolic and developmentalist
relegation of the souths to "backward,"
"derivative" cultural locations, while turning
attention toward contemporary theory and
aesthetics that conceptualises the souths as sites
of futurity.[7]

VERÓNICA TELLO (VT) Thanks, Walter. That statement
is a provocation for sure :)

ZOE BUTT (ZB) The *FS* proposal initially jarred me to be
honest, Walter and Verónica. I've never placed terms
like "backward" or "derivative" into my practice
or thinking, or in relation to my locale — Saigon
(and broader Asia for that matter).[8] If anything, I've
sought to be based where I am because, here, I see
new ways and means of talking and thinking about
time and space with my communities. Communities
here read as heavily diasporic, deeply affected by

7   This statement appears on the *Future Souths*   8   Zoe Butt is based at the Factory: https://
     website: http://futuresouths.org.   factoryartscentre.com/.

years of "occupation" but also offering many ways to rethink and delink from how art is valued by the English language, for example, or rethinking the role of the copy, of the need to "circulate," of the need to be "mobile." I guess you could say that yes, I believe that these communities represent the future I am wanting (but the terms we use need to resonate on the ground).

DYLAN A. T. MINER (DM) Thinking from and in Indigenous spaces and knowledges, I do not understand time to be linear. As I mentioned in the previous conversation, "Futures," I have been working extensively with this notion of *anikoobijigan* (or *anikoobijiganag* in the plural) and how ancestors/descendants, who others might see as representing past and future, are actually intimately linked through us. Using concepts like *anikoobijigan*, or Indigenous knowledge more generally, is not for me a marginal way of thinking. In many ways, I am an Indigenist and position Indigenous epistemologies at the centre of my practice. And this practice is always communal. And always engaged with contestations of the settler-colonial nation-state. And it is always engaged with futurity, but one that is couched in non-linear notions of temporality and spatiality.[9]

CARLA MACCHIAVELLO (CM) The concept of being behind, below, and/or backwards with regards to Europe (and then the US) has been constantly present in discourses of Latin American art.[10] Since the 1960s, conscious efforts have been made to subvert this geopolitical baggage.[11]

---

9   Dylan A. T. Miner, *Creating Aztlán: Chicano Art, Indigenous Sovereignty, and Lowriding Across Turtle Island* (Tucson, Arizona: University of Arizona Press, 2014).

10 See, for example, Nelly Richard, "Latin American Cultures: Mimicry or Difference?," in Leon Paroissien, ed., *The Fifth Biennale of Sydney: Private Symbol: Social Metaphor* (Sydney: The Biennale of Sydney, 1984).

11 Beyond the theories of dependency and liberation that gained traction in the 1960s and 1970s (Enrique Dussel), some examples from the art scenes of Latin America that discussed dependency and proposed new categories, or even the abandonment of the notion of Latin America, are Marta Traba, "La Cultura de la Resistencia," in *Mirar en América, selección y prólogo de Ana Pizarro*

However, the notion of dependency is still somehow very much a part of the present state of play.[12]

WM　Let me first respond to Dylan and then to Zoe and Carla. I am not Indigenist, nor Indigenous, but I am working with Indigenous intellectuals, some of them are my students, and I agree with Dylan's points above.[13]

Coloniality embedded the souths in me: I grew up intellectually as a person from the Third World who goes to France to study and becomes a *Sudaca*, and then to the US and becomes a Latino.[14] These experiences shaped my diasporic praxis of living.

(Caracas: Biblioteca Ayacucho, 2005); Gerardo Mosquera, "El arte latinoamericano deja de serlo," *ARCO Latino* (1996); Mari Carmen Ramírez, "Tactics for Thriving on Adversity: Conceptualism in Latin America, 1960–1980," in *Global Conceptualisms: Points of Origin, 1950s–1980s*, ed. Luis Camnitzer, Jane Farver, and Rachel Weiss (Queens, New York: Queens Museum of Art, 1999); and Luis Camnitzer, *Conceptualism in Latin American Art: Didactics of Liberation* (Austin: University of Texas Press, 2007). One might even call this a canonical history, since there were numerous local and transnational discussions on the topic over the years.

For an interesting critique of the relations of art history and Euro/North America, see Laura E. Pérez, *Eros Ideologies: Writings on Art, Spirituality, and the Decolonial* (Durham, North Carolina and London: Duke University Press, 2019), 28. As Pérez argues, "If we employ current art history categories for understanding contemporary art, or art since the historical avant-garde period of the first four decades of the twentieth century, we are left without useful categories by which to understand Chicana/o and other US Latina/o art as anything other than 'political art,' a way of minimising both the conceptual and the aesthetic projects in this diverse body of art as it emerges in the 1960s and continues through the present. Within Western art history, developed as part of a cultural evolutionist discourse, there is a catch-22 described well by intellectuals and artists in late 1990s publications like *Beyond the Fantastic* (edited by Gerardo Mosquera, 1996) and *Santería Aesthetics in Contemporary Latin American Art* (edited by Arturo Lindsay, 1996). This conundrum—that of being judged as always playing catch-up, ostensibly without the originality or the training environment of the 'First World' capitals (Paris, New York City), or of not being authentic enough (i.e., recognizably 'ethnic,' 'folkloric,' 'exotic,' 'fantastic,' 'primitive,' etc.)—remains the culturally disciplining 'place' of minority art and its scholarship today: always other, always marginal, and, at best, a flavor of the month."

12　It could be argued that the discussion continues and becomes even more complex through the lens of coloniality and anticolonial thinking. See for example Pedro Pablo Gomez et al., *Arte y Estética en la Encrucijada Descolonial II* (Buenos Aires: Del Signo, 2014); and the catalogue book *Memorias del Subdesarrollo: El Giro Descolonial en el Arte de América Latina*, curated by Julieta González for the Museo Jumex (2018).

13　My book, *The Darker Side of the Renaissance*, is about just that: languages, memories, and space. Walter Mignolo, *The Darker Side of the Renaissance: Literacy, Territoriality, and Colonization* (Ann Arbor, Michigan: University of Michigan Press, 2003).

My specific diasporic experience is that of the immigrant: born into a large family of Italians from the north in the south of America, going to the north (France), becoming a *Sudaca* as I say, and then a Latino in the US where I live now.

I found in non-European Indigenous epistemologies a way out of the Indigenous European epistemology that was implanted in me.

And yes, once more, dependency (on European and North American epistemologies) is not over because it is part of the coloniality of power, and coloniality is all over.

DM   May I add that in the settler-colonial context, we must foreground the Indigenous (knowledges, struggles, sovereignties). Here in Turtle Island/North America, this needs to happen in intentional ways. Of course, this is all conjoined through capitalist and colonialist contexts, which we can collectively contest. Anzaldúa, of course, began her important text, *Borderlands/ La Frontera* (1987), with Indigenous notions.

ZB   Dylan, since you cite Anzaldúa, do you think of yourself as a border dweller? To quote Walter (writing with Madina V. Tlostanova):

> Theorising from the borders is, in our view, a way of dwelling, being, and thinking in the borders … That is, dwelling in the borders means rewriting geographic frontiers, imperial/ colonial subjectivities, and territorial epistemologies.[15]

---

14   Pejorative term for South Americans deployed by Spaniards in Europe, and thus other Europeans. The term "sudaca" is a racialised, ethnic label that likely derives from the Spanish pronunciation of SUDA-meri-CA-no (South American). The term is mostly applied to Spanish-speaking South Americans, excluding those from Portuguese colonies such as Brazil. Urban Dictionary, https://www.urbandictionary.com/define. php?term=SUDACA.

15   Madina V. Tlostanova and Walter D. Mignolo, *Learning to Unlearn: Decolonial Reflections from Eurasia and the Americas* (Colombus, Ohio: Ohio State University Press, 2012), 26, 72.

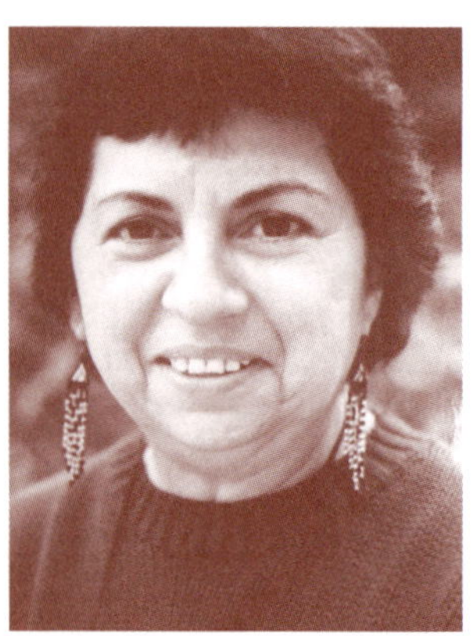

Gloria Evangelina Anzaldúa (September 26, 1942–May 15, 2004), a Mexican American/Chicana feminist, author, poet, scholar, and activist. Shown in 1990 at Smith College. Image courtesy K. Kendall (Creative Commons).

DM I am a bit conflicted. My family was forced from an island in the Great Lakes and across Lake Huron after the War of 1812 because they had resisted the US nation-state. But does this make me a border dweller? I might follow Eve Tuck and K. Wayne Yang's argument that decolonisation is not a metaphor: Is border dwelling a metaphor?[16]

WM Border dwelling is what has been embedded in me, that is that. And I act on that feeling; emotioning, reasoning, doing. At the same time there is not just one experience of living in the border and responding to coloniality. There are many ways of dwelling in the border. I am a white privileged man of European descent in South America, next to Indigenous people and people of the African diaspora. I am seen by the other whites (in Europe or the US) as a deficient South American.

ZB I agree with Walter that border dwelling is about experience—something that many of the theories concerning the souths were not privy to.[17] And I might add that many of the participants in this chat are also not living in the souths (even if they are from the souths, part of what Verónica describes as the "mobile souths," after Ramaswami Harindranath).[18]

WM There are two theories about the souths, one comes from the south of Europe (de Santos) and the other from the south of the British Commonwealth.[19] I am from the south of the hemispheric partition, living in the south of the north, the land of the

---

16 "The metaphorization of decolonization makes possible a set of evasions, or "settler moves to innocence," that problematically attempt to reconcile settler guilt and complicity, and rescue settler futurity." Eve Tuck and K. Wayne Yang, "Decolonization is Not a Metaphor," *Decolonization: Indigeneity, Education & Society* 1, no. 1 (2012): 1.

17 For example, Comaroff and Comaroff, *Theory from the South*.

18 See "Introduction."

19 Boaventura de Sousa Santos, *Epistemologies of the South: Justice Against Epistemicide* (London: Routledge, 2014); Connell, *Southern Theory*.

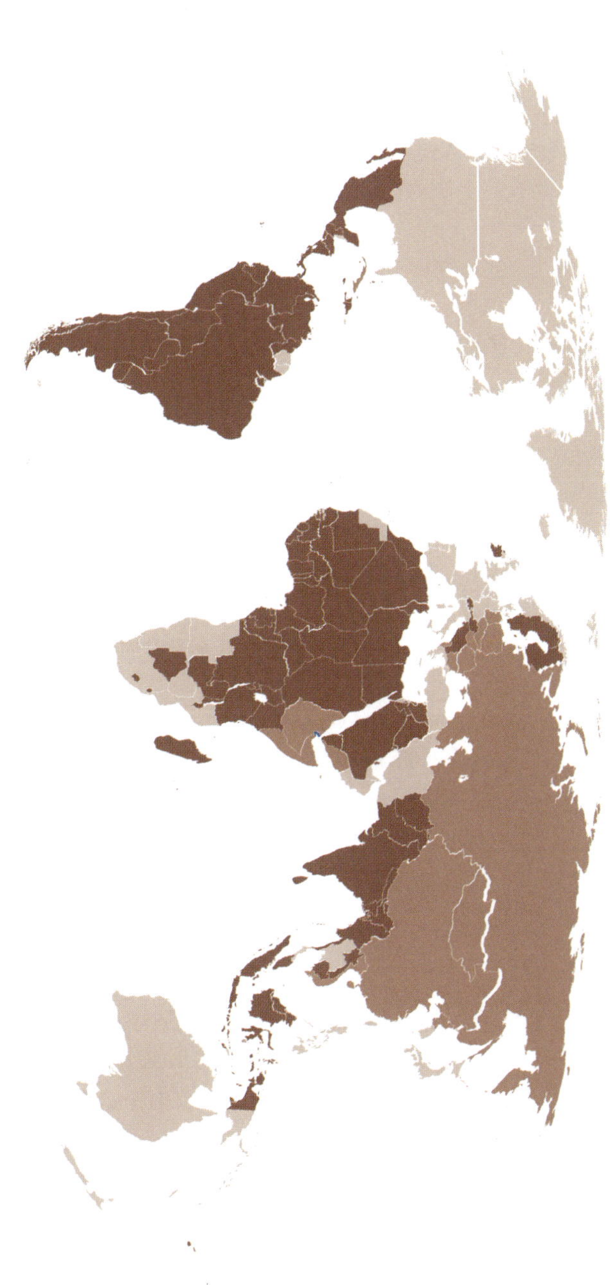

The "Three Worlds" of the Cold War era, April–August 1975

First World: Western Bloc led by the USA, the UK, NATO, Japan and their allies;
Second World: Eastern Bloc led by the USSR, the Warsaw Pact, China and their allies;
Third World: Non-Aligned Movement (led by India and Yugoslavia) and other neutral countries.

Confederates and the Black plantation slavery. I am working in a university (Duke) that was founded by a plantation owner.[20]

DM I wonder how the Fourth World—and the Third World—play out in relation to contemporary discussions of norths and souths.

ZB How do you define "Fourth World," Dylan?

DM Fourth World meaning the global Indigenous world.

WM I do not define the Fourth World; I start from how people define themselves. George Tinker made a brilliant distinction between Latin American liberation theology, which is an off-white project, and Native American theology of liberation, which are in different boats, having in common theology and liberation but separated by racial configurations.[21]

SALOTE TAWALE (ST) I find the terminology of First to Fourth Worlds quite jarring.

DM Salote, the First to Fourth World categories have a numerical and therefore linear relationship tied to earlier notions of capitalism and the nation-state.

WM Classifications are made by those who control knowledge. The Third World was not invented by people of the Third World but by people of the First World. The "First World" has the privilege of being the only classifier while being only one member of the classified.[22]

---

20 For the history of Duke University's ties to slavery, see Marianne Twu, "Slavery and Segregation," Duke Human Rights Center, accessed May 1, 2020, https://humanrights.fhi.duke.edu/who-we-are/history-of-human-rights-at-duke/slavery-and-segregation/.

21 George Tinker, *American Indian Liberation: A Theology of Sovereignty* (Maryknoll, New York: Orbis Books, 2008).

22 Walter Mignolo, "The Enduring Enchantment (Or the Epistemic Privilege of Modernity and Where to Go from Here)," *South Atlantic Quarterly* 101, no. 4 (Fall 2002).

This represents tremendous epistemic power. Same with the Fourth World.

CM Does this notion of the border allow us to move beyond these classifications? Or does it become an empty term?

DM That is a good question, Carla.

ST It is a good question. Can we discuss?

WM For me, it is not an empty term because it is embedded in my praxis of living. For other people who do not dwell in the border it may be empty. For me it is non-negotiable.

CM The border seems to be a concept to which we can all relate, yet as was mentioned earlier, positionality or direction—where we come from/have moved/are going—is central to thinking about it.

WM Well, I cannot live and think otherwise than dwelling in the border. Others dwell in the territory; Hegel for example.[23]

ST Borders are also moveable, Walter.

WM Not only that, but they are also all local. Whoever dwells in the border in Vietnam, South Africa, or France (immigrant refugees) are not living in an empty space

---

23 "Hegel—as I read him—was well grounded in the territory…I learned from indigenous cosmology what I couldn't learn from Hegel and Western cosmology. However, I was trained (in body and mind) in the latter. Learning from what Western modernity had disavowed, and not observing and describing what modernity disavowed, opened up new dimensions of the border to me. Sensing that border is not a mental or rational experience, I sensed it, and sensing is something that invades your emotions, and your body responds to it, dictating to the mind what the mind must start thinking, changing its direction, shifting the geography of reasoning." Walter D. Mignolo, "Foreword: On Pluriversality and Multipolarity," in *Constructing the Pluriverse: The Geopolitics of Knowledge*, ed. Bernd Reiter (Durham, North Carolina: Duke University Press, 2018), xi–xii.

but in the full memory of the border modernity/coloniality. That is crucial for us, the ones engaged in this particular cultural praxis of decoloniality (notice the difference between praxis of living and cultural praxis).[24]

DM   I wonder how "border dwelling" and "border crossing" exist in relationship to Tuck and Yang's notion that decolonisation is not a metaphor. I actually argue, quite intensely, for the dissolution of borders.[25]

Two days ago, Canada celebrated 150 years of their nation-state and tomorrow the US celebrates "Independence Day." The violence of this border, not to mention others, is real for me and my family and our ancestors. I cannot escape thinking about the function and role of the nation-state, as well as capitalism, in all of this.

WM   Agreed. There are two dimensions of the border: one is the enunciated border, and the other is the border we inhabit. You can study the border from the territory. But when you dwell in the border you do not study.

I agree, of course, that the nation-state is already a border because the state was built in correspondence with one ethno-nation. The settler is just that: a reproduction of the nation-state (bourgeois, Christian, European, and perhaps, I will add, masculine).

I'll just add one more thing: This morning I have been listening to a lecture by Jean Casimir, a Haitian scholar, explaining how Haitians organised themselves as a sovereign nation without the state, which has

24   Walter D. Mignolo and Catherine E. Walsh, *On Decoloniality: Concepts, Analytics, Praxis* (Durham, North Carolina: Duke University Press, 2018).

25   Dylan A. T. Miner, "*Gaagegoo Dabakaanan miiniwaa Debenjigejig* (No Borders, Indigenous Sovereignty)," Decolonisation (blog), October 1, 2015, https://decolonization.wordpress.com/2015/10/01/gaagegoo-dabakaanan-miiniwaa-debenjigejig-no-borders-indigenous-sovereignty/.

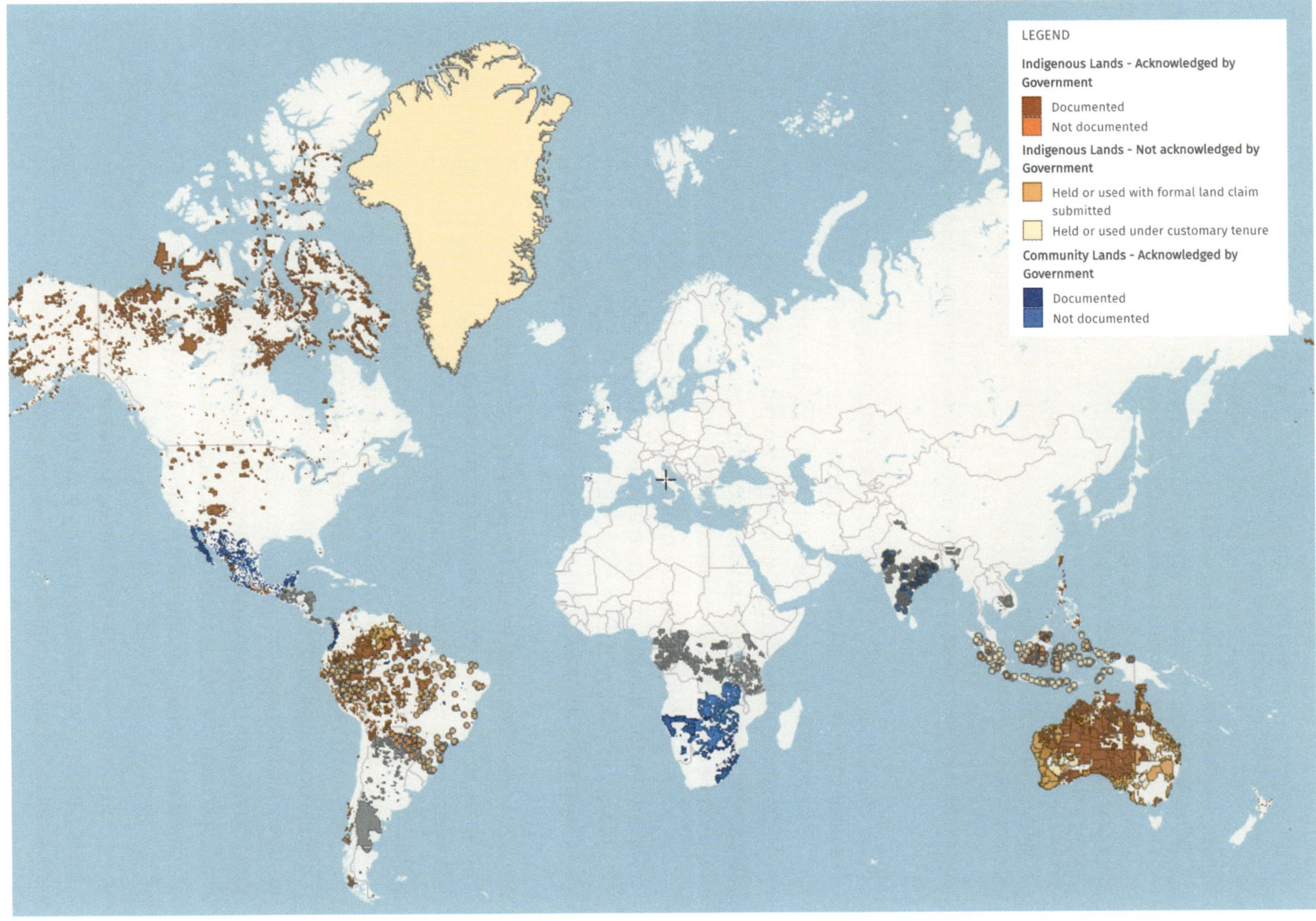

Indigenous and community land maps, *LandMark, Global Platform for Indigenous and Community Lands*.
Image source: Landmark, https://www.landmarkmap.org.

allowed their survival till today.[26] This is perhaps what Leanne Simpson, a First Nations scholar from Turtle Island, means by "resurgence."[27]

ZB Walter you just wrote, above, "when you dwell in the border you do not study." I'd like to know more about what you mean by "study" here. I feel the time required to process ideas here (in Saigon) is subject to a different state of play than, say, Durham/Duke University; we don't have the formulas and the systems and the disciplinary knowledge and lingo to "enter" into study…but perhaps I'm getting stuck in the formal reading of the word…because if I ask myself "what is study?," I would say, study is living.

WM To study means that you think you are the subject who studies an object or domain or field of study. This concept is at the heart of modern epistemology that divides the subject from the object.[28]

Thinking, on the other hand, is embodied. There is no separation between the knower and the known.[29] Anzaldúa didn't study; her thinking progressed through her body (and not from the "mind," as modern and secular, Cartesian if you wish, academia will have you do).[30]

---

26 On Jean Casimir's work on this topic see Jean Casimir, *The Haitians: A Decolonial History* (Chapel Hill, North Carolina: University of North Carolina Press, 2020).

27 Leanne Betasamosake Simpson, "Indigenous Resurgence and Co-resistance," *Critical Ethnic Studies* 2, no. 2 (2016).

28 Mignolo, *The Darker Side of Western Modernity*.

29 Walter D. Mignolo, Marc Woons, and Sebastian Weier, "Interview with Walter D. Mignolo," in *Critical Epistemologies of Global Politics*, ed. Marc Woons and Sebastian Weier (Bristol: E-International Relations Publishing, 2017.

30 As Walter Mignolo elaborates: "*Borderland/La Frontera* is border thinking in action. Anzaldúa is not 'studying' borderlands. She inhabits them…Studying the borderland means that whoever does the study places themselves outside the borderland while whomever dwells in the borderland *reflects* on themselves and their experiences of living in the border. All these thinkers are un-disciplinary: They do not study, they think and their thinking is border thinking because they think from their body and not from the 'mind', as modern and secular (Cartesian if you wish) disciplines do. Disciplines separate the known from the knower." Mignolo, Woons and Weier, "Interview with Walter D. Mignolo," 13, 22.

ZB   Yes exactly, one "thinks" (in an embodied, situated mode); and I think living in this largely Buddhist land has taught me that "study" is a labour that posits "us" and "them."

WM   You are right. In South America we grew up writing essays; in the norths, the academy undertakes study. So decolonial thinking is returning to the essay, and in the essay, you just think.[31]

ZB   In Buddhist thought "thinking" is about embodying the present—this state of being is a form of thinking. This concept of study is what is problematic for me, especially in working in trying to empower my community.

WM   That is the point. Indigenous people and communities of Afro-Colombian peoples of the Pacific are like the Buddhists (for whom "thinking" is about embodying the present) and that is what I meant when I said that Indigenous epistemologies inform my border thinking (and my critique of territorialising, colonising, epistemologies).[32]

31   For further thinking on this topic see Walter D. Mignolo, "Epistemic Disobedience, Independent Thought and Decolonial Freedom," *Theory, Culture & Society* 26, no. 7–8 (2009).

32   Mignolo, "Epistemic Disobedience." Mignolo elaborates: "Not everyone inhabits the border, and it is not necessary to do so. Not everyone inhabits the territory; those who inhabit the borders do not. But borders (they called them 'frontiers' in the advance of civilisation) were traced by actors inhabiting the territory and guarding it from 'foreign' forces. The problem is that modern Western epistemology is territorial, and territorial epistemology presupposes 'the frontier' rather than the border. On the other side of the frontier exists the void, namely space to be conquered or civilised. Territorial epistemology (modern and postmodern) cannot be decolonial; it is an imperial epistemology. Modern epistemology was built precisely to make sense of, justify, and legitimise coloniality. Post-modern epistemology is an in-family critique of modern epistemology but remains within the rules of the game. Decolonial thinking is always-already border thinking; although not all border thinking is always already decolonial thinking. Furthermore, decolonial border thinking implies epistemic disobedience and delinking from modern and post-modern epistemology, including Marxist post-modern versions." Mignolo, Woons, and Weier, "Interview with Walter D. Mignolo," 13–14.

As Indigenous thinkers, including Dylan, have said, the past and future do not exist. Only the present. So, shall we rethink *Future Souths*?

ZB   Does the title posit time as linear?

WM   Should it be *Futures, Souths*?

DM   Can we imagine futures that do not always imply linear temporalities?

WM   That is true, the only thing that the plural does is to multiply temporality. But again, the Indigenous think in terms of spiral circularity.

ZB   I like "spiral circularity."

DM   Yes. For me the concept of *anikoobijigan* does that.

WM   In Nahuatl Ollin (Aztec) there is the constant, united movement of space and time.[33] Kant, on the other hand, divided time/space.[34]

ZB   On the topic of Indigenous cosmologies, I wanted to raise that in reviews of two recent large-scale exhibitions, Venice and documenta, critics have argued that the exhibitions handle "First Nations" conditions with an exoticism that smacks of 1990s identity crisis.[35]

DM   Zoe, the recent issue with a Sam Durant sculpture at the Walker in Minneapolis is similar.[36] Here,

33   James Maffie, "Aztec Philosophy," Internet Encyclopedia of Philosophy, accessed March 1, 2022, https://iep.utm.edu/aztec/.

34   Immanuel Kant, *Critique of Pure Reason* (London: Penguin, 2008).

35   Paula Clemente Vega, "The 2017 Venice Biennale and the Colonial Other," Third Text Online, November 1, 2018, http://thirdtext.org/vega-2017-venice-biennale. Further, see

T. J. Demos, "Learning from documenta 14: Athens, Post-Democracy, and Decolonisation," Third Text Online, accessed March 1, 2020, http://thirdtext.org/demos-documenta.

Durant made a public sculpture invoking the gallows built to execute thirty-eight Dakota Indians. The local Dakota community demanded that it be removed, with intentions to ceremonially bury it.

WM   I am listening and thinking about the limits of modern thinking. Modern epistemology only knows the reason of the master because the slave has no reason.[37] As border thinkers we know the reason of the master and the reason of the slave.

JAMES NGUYEN (JN) Jumping in here: By existing on the border, are you forced to always question your position and to reposition, rather than taking your position for granted? Is this actually an increasingly powerful position to be in, in a world that is shifting and evolving at a phenomenal pace? Does this mean border people have the muscle memory and tools for resilience and resistance that makes them more equipped than people at the historically stable centre?

WM   James, that's a lovely series of propositions to end on. To the many questions on border dwelling left unanswered here, I'll just say: this is the way I live and do in this world…

36   Susan L. Allen and Amy B. Weisgram Engstrom, "Inclusivity in Contemporary Art: Assessing the Walker's Scaffold Controversy," *Sua Sponte* 44 (2018).
37   Mignolo, *The Darker Side of the Renaissance*.

Networks

3

NETWORKS: MAPPING KNOWLEDGE AND ALLIANCES UNDER PRESSURE
Zoe Butt

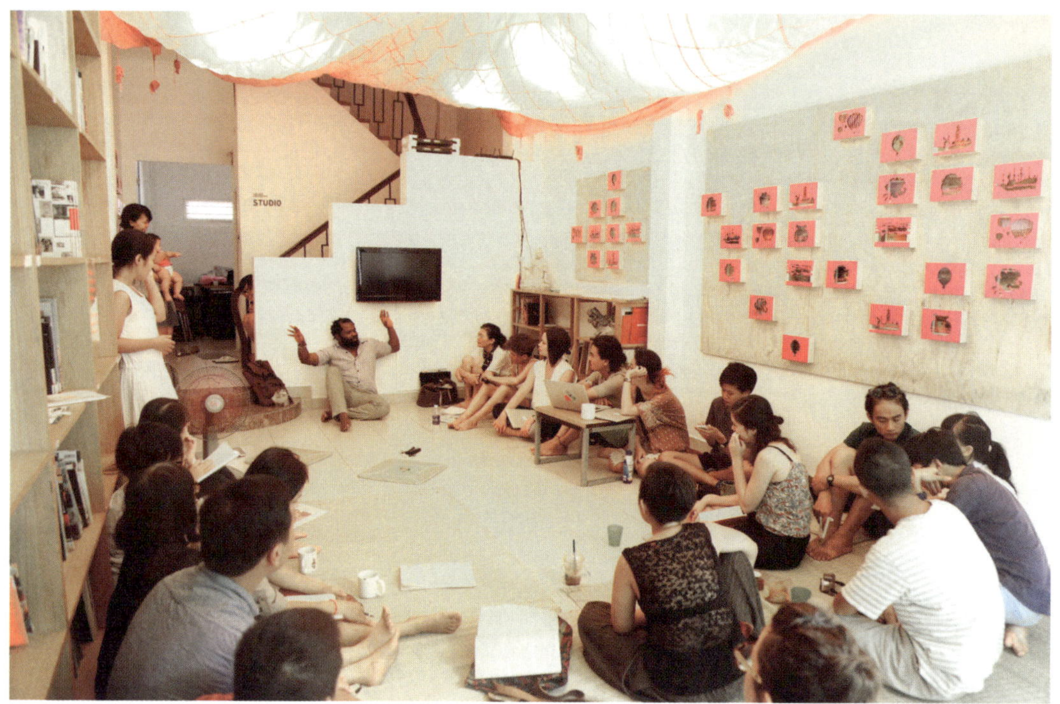

Ntone Edjabe speaking as a guest of *Conscious Realities*, 2015. Hosted by Hoa Sen University, organised by Sàn Art. Image Courtesy Zoe Butt.

I live in a country called Vietnam, which translates as "the Viet people of the south" ("*Nam*" meaning "south").[1] South of what? South of China.

Vietnam is also a political north. Our youth preen like Korean popstars, while our civic infrastructure is dependent on foreign investment. Meanwhile, Japan builds the country's first subway line and our restaurants are rife with menus in Russian.

The local production of art in Vietnam takes place in a parallel universe to the exhibition circuits of the (Western) "art world." In Vietnam, "art" must negotiate the conflicting forces of nationalistic narcissism, myopic (or blind) consumption, and (censored) political activism. These forces are in turn modulated by a form of postcolonial neoliberalism marked by cultural defensiveness (see Vietnam's long, fraught relationship to China), corruption (bribery is endemic), and fear of the "other" (e.g., no foreigners teach in the state educational system).

As such, like much of the artistic landscape across Southeast Asia today, it is the foreign NGO or diplomatic mission that programs "contemporary" culture as a vehicle for soft diplomacy. Feigning care of culture and community through mandatory "collaboration" between locals and Westerners, such operations and operators often run on institutional rhetoric, residual colonial guilt, and bureaucratic apathy. In such a compromised/ instrumentalised landscape of art, the contextualisation of artistic intent is sadly rare.

As a cultural worker operating in Saigon, I want local artistic production to speak to its own cultural underpinnings and historical consciousness, its own journeys of spiritual introspection and material memory. As a curator, I find it necessary to map and remap our cultural and social alliances, to seek the experiential errantry of hearts and souls that resonate with the way *we* measure *our* time and space.

1   This dialogue was first held in 2017, and since then Butt lives and works acriss Chiang Mai (Thailand) and Ho Chi Minh City (Vietnam).

In 2013, I developed *Conscious Realities*, a curatorial and educational program comprising a series of dialogues and residencies taking shape at Sàn Art (where, until early 2017, I was executive director and curator). Initially, this project's geographical scope was the "global south," but over the program's four-year span I came to realise the serious shortfalls of such a term as it is anchored in the geopolitical frameworks of neoliberalism, and is a term that dangerously assumes a universality in human systems of value and interpretation. Contesting this false universality, the invited guest speakers (curators, writers, and artists) from South Asia, Southeast Asia, Latin America, and Africa pivoted their voices towards the ideas of diaspora and voluntary and involuntary migration, and the importance of forming networks of southern knowledge and experience on their own terms. These latter forms of networking and exchange were vital for empowering our youth to sense alternative narratives and epistemological formations not otherwise available in local popular media and ideologically controlled curriculums and modes of consciousness; it also prompted them to have a deeper awareness of that which structures, with cause and effect, their present realities.

Dialogue
Zoe Butt with Carla Macchiavello, Katherine Carl, Srdjan Jovanović Weiss,
and Walter D. Mignolo, with Comments by Rachel O'Reilly

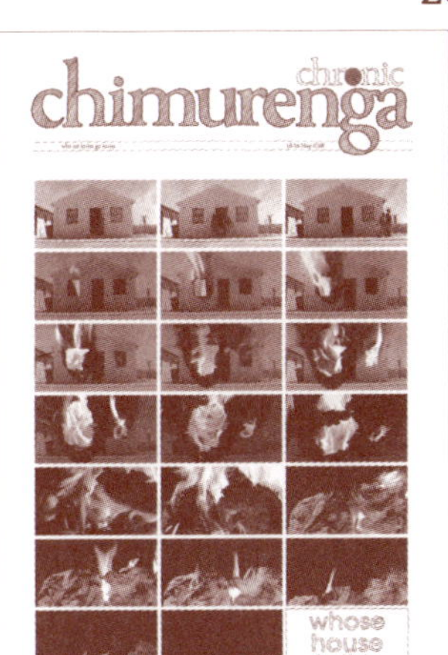

Chimurenga Journal 16 (October 2011) "The Chimurenga Chronicle" ("The Chronic"). "The Chronic" is a one-time only edition of *Chimurenga Journal* which takes the form of a speculative newspaper. Backdated to May 18–24, 2008—the first week of the xenophobic violence across South Africa three years ago, "The Chronic" (2011) is an opportunity to provide the depth of reporting and analysis that should have appeared during this period. The newspaper also looks outward— covering events, scenes, and situations from around the world during this period. By imagining the newspaper as a low-tech time travel machine, the aim is not only to reanimate history, to ask what could have been done–but also to provide a space from which to re-engage the present and re-dream the future. Image courtesy *Chimurenga*.

ZOE BUTT (ZB) How and why should we think and create networks of exchange that build and critique shared histories common to the lived experiences of a debatable "south"?

I'd like to start by describing a scene from one of the workshops I ran in conjunction with *Conscious Realities*. In April 2015, I invited Ntone Edjabe to Saigon. Edjabe is a musician, writer, and editor from Douala/ living in Cape Town, who in 2002 founded a platform for pan African art and writing called Chimurenga.[2] We agreed that Edjabe's visit would focus on one aspect of Chimurenga's work, *The Chronic*, a broadsheet launched in 2011 which explores the act of remapping "Africa" according to differing measurements of facts. In *The Chronic* Edjabe asked: "What if maps were made by Africans for their own use, to understand and make visible their own realities or imaginaries?"[3]

As theoretical accompaniment, we discussed Edouard Glissant's text "Transparency and Opacity" from *Poetics of Relation*.[4] This was a tough exercise as much of Glissant's language is very difficult to translate into Vietnamese (some of Glissant's words do not translate). Ntone encouraged participation with the text and embraced confusion and storytelling in order to do away with the insecurity he could see reflected in the workshop participants (seventy percent of whom were Vietnamese and educated within Vietnam).

2   Ntone Edjabe, "Diagnosing the Chimurenga Chronical," Sàn Art, April 9, 2015, https:// san-art.org/education/the-chimurenga-chronic/.

3   "The Chimurenga Chronicle," *Chimurenga* 16 (October, 2011).

4   Édouard Glissant, *Poetics of Relation*, trans. Betsy Wing (Ann Arbor, Michigan: University of Michigan Press, 1997).

During the workshop we attempted to remap Vietnam using Ntone's methodology, as described above, but found that participants didn't have the skills or resources to do so—most alarming was the endemic self-censorship of their minds. This situation forced me to think harder about the practicalities of knowledge production in a country with extreme censorship of culture and education (particularly literature, film, and the visual arts), and where resources are thin, often leaving only the study paths of international aid and neoliberal opportunity.

For me, it was the artists around me who emboldened my commitment to try and find space for a deeper engagement with critical geographies and histories beyond the assumed, prescriptive money flows of global capital, beyond the red (political) tape and national borders of our archives. Many of these artists have taken great risks to dig deeper into their cultural consciousness, with the presentation of alternate realities and by picturing futures of dense dystopic wonder. Think, for example, of *The Island* (2017) by Tuan Andrew Nguyen, or *Tropical Siesta* (2015) by Phan Thảo Nguyên—two Vietnamese films that have been met with critical acclaim in the West but which have had little circulation within Asia. Beyond the artists and writers I named above, how do we broadly sustain and make visible our re-reading of maps and history, and related theories; how can we give our communities in this south the chance to experientially respond when the structures of engagement exclude them (via language, educational structure, curricula limits, etc.)? Is the "global" exhibition circuit traversing across and through museums and biennales developing communities of care? How are our international educational institutions, with scholarship in this arena, thinking of these communities as engaged participants/actors of their research?

To kick off, I'd like to ask Carla to respond.

CARLA MACCHIAVELLO (CM) Different options of educational institutions have been opening up to address these issues;[5] beyond traditional institutions, sometimes even art programs like yours are supplanting larger institutions in this role.[6]

ZB But do we generate enough affect to change the dominant systems of thinking? We have so much informal education but too little of it seems to enter official coursework.

WALTER D. MIGNOLO (WM) I'll jump in. One strategy— or thing to do—is to change the system within the system, and the other is to delink from the system.

CM I am not sure if informal education has affected dominant (institutional) systems of thinking yet, but it is certainly having effects in local arenas.

WM Yep, I agree with Carla. This is what we are doing now at this moment in the Decolonial Summer School in Middelburg, and there are many such programs.[7]

ZB Yes, I've been thinking very hard about how to delink from the system, which means not taking its money, and not circulating in its structures of visibility.

WM That is one way to think: to use the system rather than let the system use you. Of course, you would have to make concessions, but that is a tricky matter.

CM The question of survival makes it hard not to "take the money" or make strategic alliances.

5   For example, Ensayos, the collective Carla Macchiavello is a part of: http://ensayostierradelfuego.net.

6   For a fairly Eurocentric analysis of this phenomenon, see Sam Thorne, *School: A Recent History of Self-Organized Art Education* (Berlin: Sternberg Press, 2016).

7   Decolonial Summer School Middelburg: https://decolonialsummerschool.wordpress.com.

ZB	What strikes me is that the formal educational and art world systems in the souths adopt colonial/capitalistic models of space and time. How to challenge that formality with the strategy of delinking…how to stop the "brain drain" and flow towards the presumed centre.

WM	On the question of stopping the brain drain: let's not waste time stopping it, but instead devote all our efforts to creating ways of living, and preserving what we want to preserve, and creating what we want to create.[8]

CM	Indeed, but a main issue is how to practically strengthen informal educational settings.

ZB	Yes, and the need to strengthen them internally, even if in dialogue with other similar spaces elsewhere, is incredibly important and what makes me commit to Southeast Asia, in particular to Vietnam.
	I want our museums and our biennales to care more for the communities of knowledge that they showcase. I'd like universities to change their "study" habits and see their subjects as living, animate, shifting, dynamic (in other words, to shift from studying to thinking, as discussed in the "Souths" dialogue, chapter 2). I sound idealistic, but I continue with my tirade, begging for outreach programs to be the centre of the museum.

WM	Zoe, in regard to creating communities of knowledge, what do you say is a key strategy for shifting the geography of sensing, knowing, doing, thinking, and believing?

ZB	Walter, you came here to Saigon, and I wonder what reflections you have on the context here. You are anchored in a critical scholarly university and me in a grassroots environment in the south. How do you see your capacity to assist here?

8	Creating in this way relates back to discussions in chapter 2, "Souths."

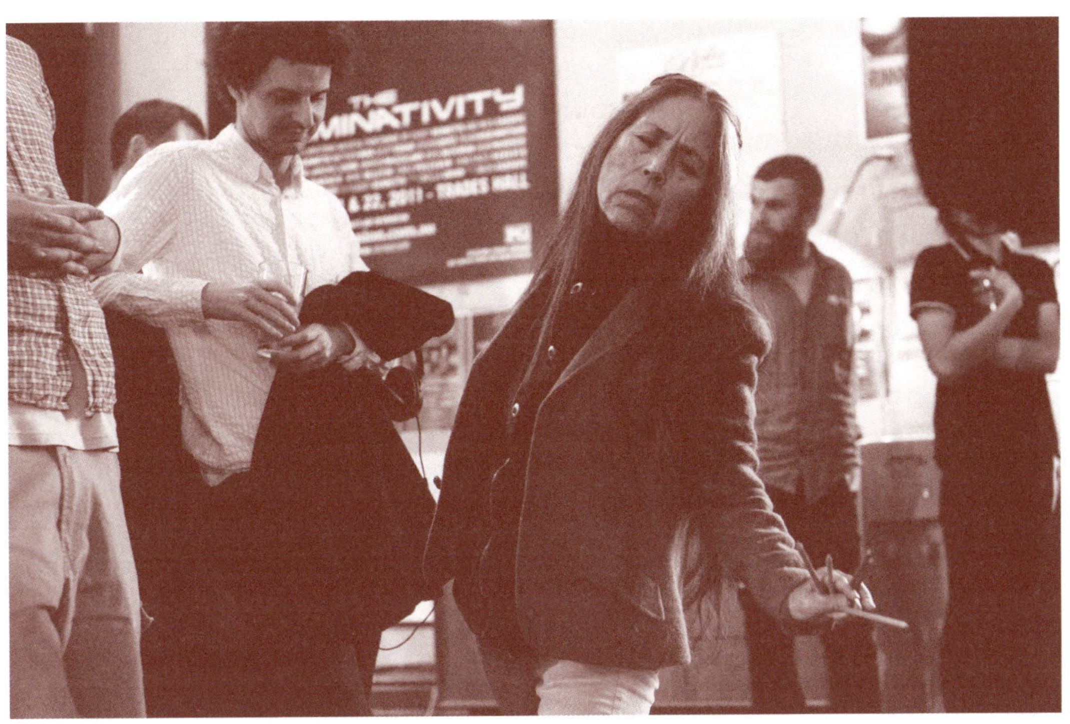

Cecilia Vicuña, *Artist as Poet*, 2016. Performance. "The Artist As…" series, Ensayos, Monash University and Institute of Modern Art. Liquid Architecture, Melbourne. Photograph by Keelan O'Hehir. Image courtesy Liquid Architecture.

WM Well, in a way I am working across both;
I am active in a university and in grassroots
communities. The Maria Lugones Decolonial
Summer School (formerly the Middleburg
Decolonial Summer School) is situated across both.

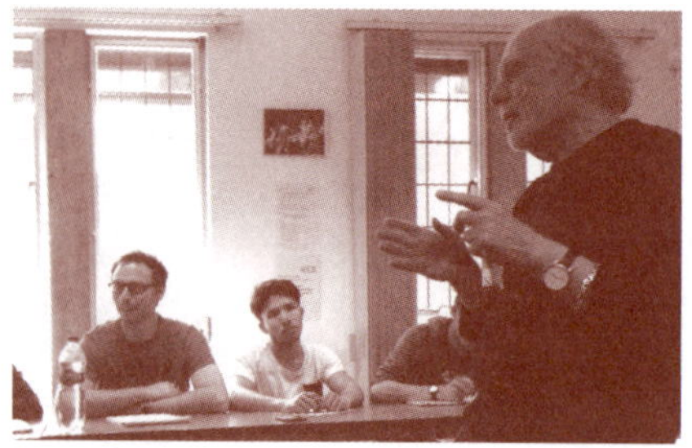

Walter D. Mignolo, Maria Lugones
Decolonial Summer School (formerly the
Middleburg Decolonial Summer School),
2014.

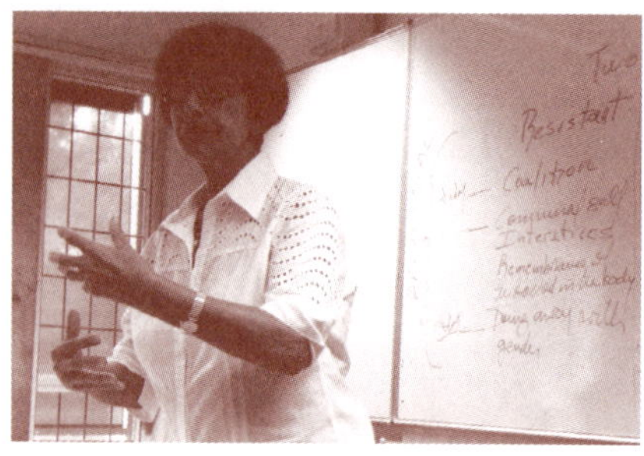

Maria Lugones, Maria Lugones
Decolonial Summer School (formerly
the Middleburg Decolonial Summer
School), 2014. Images courtesy the Maria
Lugones Decolonial Summer School.

CM I think there are border zones and
crossings worth emphasising here, doing
academia while creating other platforms.
Perhaps we need to find and create more
of these borders and crossings.

WM As for Vietnam, and your other
questions Zoe, what I saw in a few
days chatting with your people
was precisely what we are talking
about. I sensed that all of you are
border dwellers (see definition in
the "Souths" dialogue, chapter 2)
because your praxis of living is
always shaped by the struggle to
delink rather than the work to
conform and succeed in the existing
dominant system.

CM Zoe, I was thinking about your leading
question for this dialogue: How do we
avoid becoming yet another source
of extraction (or exoticism) for larger
international networks organised from
the norths to feed a system in which we
do not yet have sufficient agency? Perhaps
both regional and "southern" networking offers ways
to support, strengthen, and create a parallel universe.[9]

ZB Very nicely put, Carla, thank you. Much of the
research initially fuelling that discourse is just
suddenly visible in the norths.

9   This notion of southern collaboration is
further discussed in chapter 7, "Global Art."

KATHERINE CARL (KC) Yes, I agree. Only now are Western/northern universities beginning to engage. This is somehow unfortunately new for them.

WM I insist on the distinction between border zones (the enunciated, what you see) and border dwelling (the enunciation, from where you see).

ZB Exactly, and meanwhile the universities in this south seem intent on feeding technique over concept; and thus, once again, regional locations do their utmost to operate as networks of independence (for so much of our education is still caught up in "nation" building).

But it is true, we still do not have sufficient agency to both operate and influence these dominant narratives; however, I want to think that the future is about a continued delinking, as Walter puts it…and that this creates a critical mass down the line that swells new systems of learning.

SRDJAN JOVANOVIĆ WEISS (SJW) The question for me is: What is the missing knowledge that is in plain sight?

ZB The knowledge is there, it's just the way that we learn it that makes us place hierarchies around it.

KC In terms of survival, is there a way to share resources across norths–souths and East–West, where any unevenness can be turned into advantage?

ZB Linking between "artists as agents," "teachers as resources," and "entrepreneurs as capacity" is something we could do more of and with—lack of expertise and resources are critical to delinking.

I say "entrepreneurs as capacity" because, recently, I've noticed that more local people with foreign educations are returning, and they bring with them an understanding that the systems of capital cannot move here as the norths expect; they are innovators and they connect two differing economies.

KC I agree, Zoe. In my contexts—New York and Belgrade—students are pushing the doors open wider, and some of us within the university (at the CUNY Graduate Center) are trying to locate resources to support widening research and networks (including connecting with Belgrade, historically part of the Third World).[10]

Working in tandem outside the university setting, and outside established art networks, is crucial for sharing art-making strategies and imaginative research.[11]

WM I agree with Katherine—that is important. I agree with all the strategies being described, but what would be the goal? What for?

ZB The goal would be to give access to expanded forms of education and to have awareness of the need to delink. I agree with Katherine that working in tandem between practices and time zones is where the experience can enter the learning.

SJW How does one teach that which is at stake? Is there a way to call teaching something else?

WM We could distinguish schooling from education.

KC We had a wonderful producer who helped us with developing the School of Missing Studies (SMS),

10 For a history of Belgrade and its positioning as a Third World country, see Ivana Ancic, "Belgrade, the 1961 Non-aligned Conference," Global South Studies, accessed February 28, 2022, https://globalsouthstudies.as.virginia.edu/key-moments/belgrade-1961-non-aligned-conference.

11 For an account of the School of Missing Studies, see Srdjan Jovanović Weiss and Katherine Carl, *Lost Highway Expedition Photobook* (Ljubljana: Centrala Foundation for Future Cities, School of Missing Studies and Škuc Gallery, 2007).

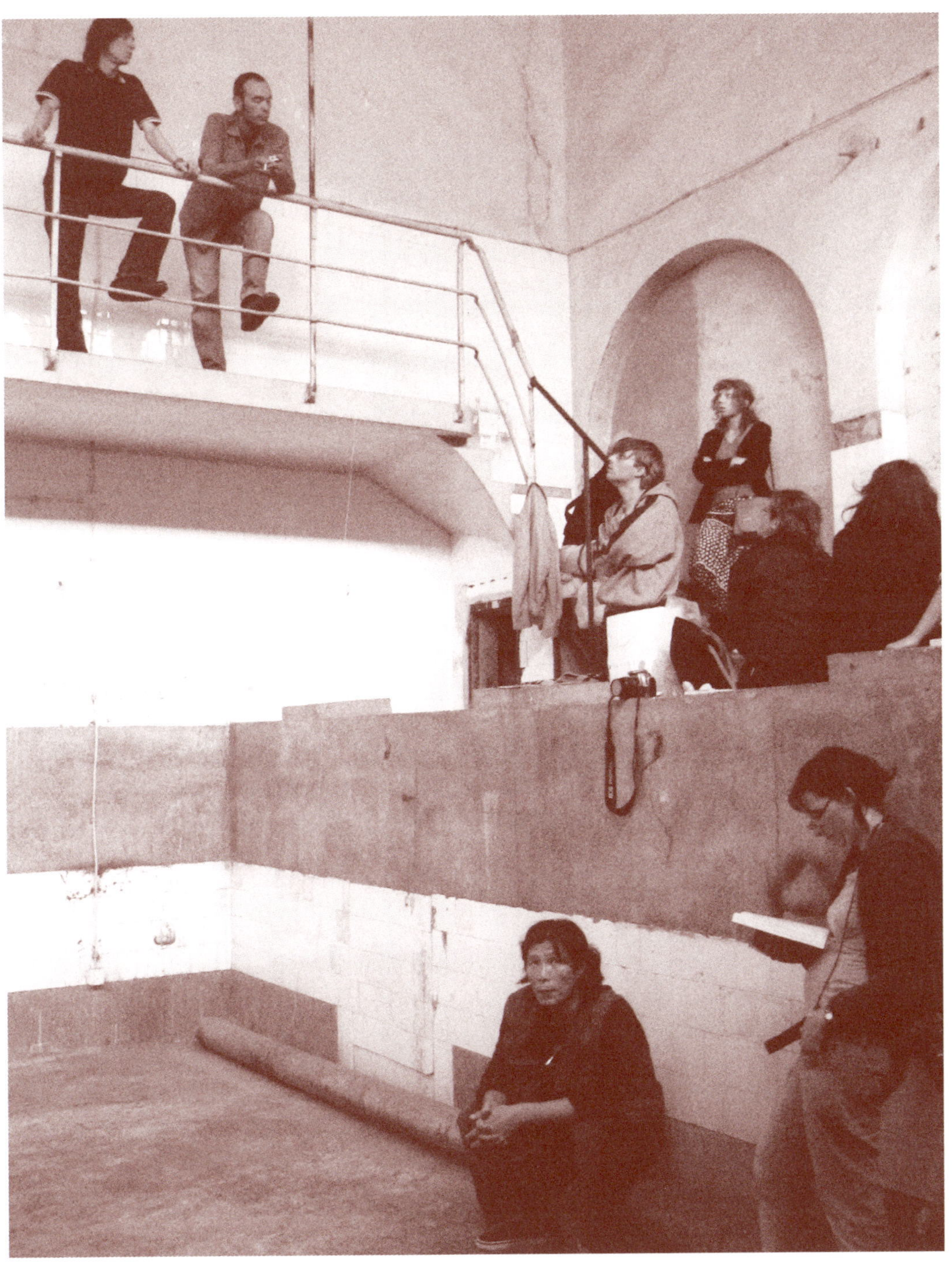

Belgrade, former Turkish bath. Kyong Park at the bottom. Photograph: author unknown. School of Missing Studies. Image courtesy Srdjan Jovanović Weiss.

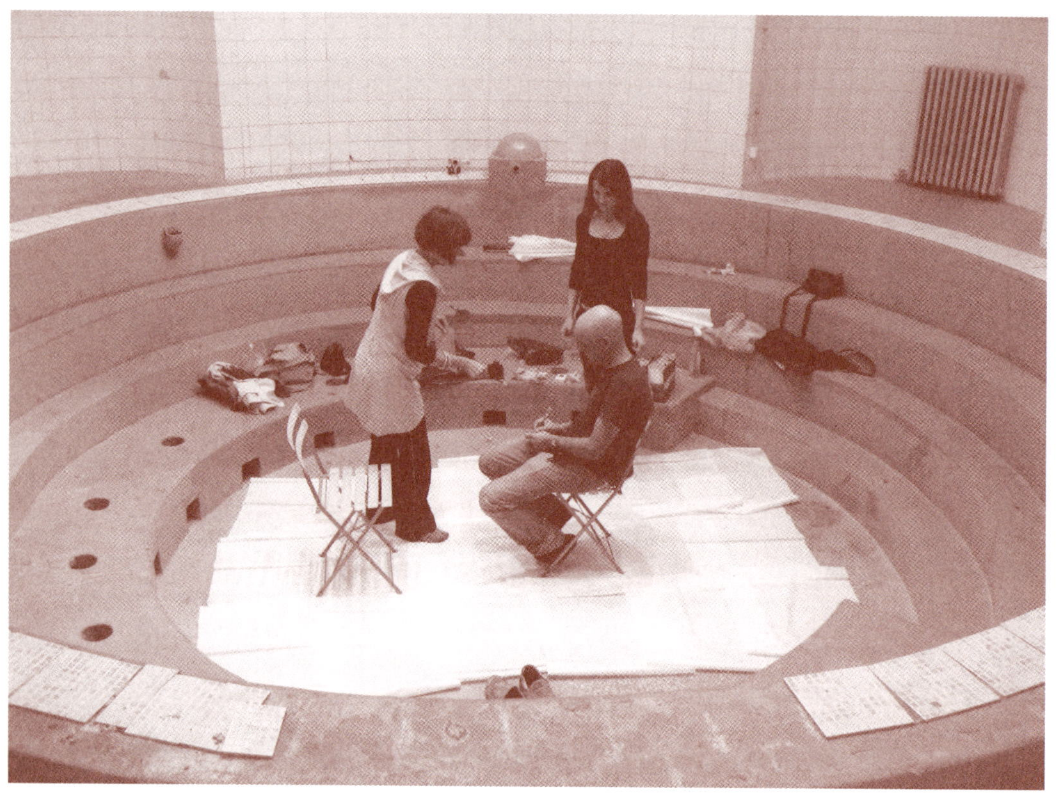

Belgrade, former Turkish bath. Kyong Park at the bottom. Photograph: author unknown.
School of Missing Studies. Image courtesy Srdjan Jovanović Weiss.

which I initiated in Belgrade with Srdjan. We wanted
to develop the SMS's film production capacities. This
producer was a new Belgrade entrepreneur—one with
open eyes.

sjw For him learning was like a soft power operating
     laterally.

kc We were learning together across different incomes,
    areas of expertise, categories that would not normally
    come together.

zb I think so much of our knowledge and access
    comes from the money flows to which we are
    indebted, and it is this "learning together" which
    has made my practice incredibly interdisciplinary
    and made a huge impact on the artists with whom
    I live and work. So perhaps the key is to ask our
    sharing and listening to be wider in its reference
    points and to take the site of that learning away
    from the assumed citations.
        Katherine and Srdjan: Are there particular
    programs in NYC that you wanted to initiate but
    instead found hesitancy/prevention? If yes, can
    you share? By "programs" I mean activities that
    link this north (New York) to a south (Belgrade).

sjw Working with NYC-based universities proved to
    be impossible. Thus, we went for non-profits such
    as the Van Alen Institute. However, this was a while
    ago; things may have changed. NYC schools hesitated
    because they saw what we were doing as being too
    far outside the fixed curriculum, and thus non-
    scientific.

kc In the university I found a large funder who
    was very eager, however there was not enough/
    any interest and expertise from the university
    itself. So, over time, I have found that it's better
    to do things in the name of art, and everything

else—research, commissions, dialogues, social science research—can be smuggled into that name/container/catalyst.

SJW   Rather than rely on universities, we could do projects with much lighter funding, but with shared interest and curiosity, and not worry about measuring achievements. In universities everything is monetised and bound to a grading system.

KC   Formally, such tactics mean working on the margin, the margins of educational systems, though within such systems at the same time.

ZB   There is a very big gap between the educational models of scholarship within universities and the practical/ visual landscape of art- and exhibition-making; and so, perhaps we can turn to art-making for a little bit of this conversation. I feel that it is in the investigatory character of much contemporary art in the souths that the systems of knowledge are being challenged.

CM   Not only investigative projects, but I am also thinking of the turn to the pedagogical in art practices, perhaps countering institutional resistance to more experimental modes of education.

ZB   Yes, Carla, I totally agree. The lecture performance mode is fascinating me right now. For example, Tiffany Chung is a Vietnamese artist who has been doing research on the Vietnam Exodus post-1954. She has collected and amassed a huge amount of data on the movement of Vietnamese refugees. In the context of the current European migration crisis, she found herself thinking, "Oh, this world has really not felt its statistics," and so she developed a way of performing this data. She presents hand-drawn maps and statistical data, blending fact and fiction to deliver a lecture, which she delivers in the tone one might expect from a government authority or NGO, much

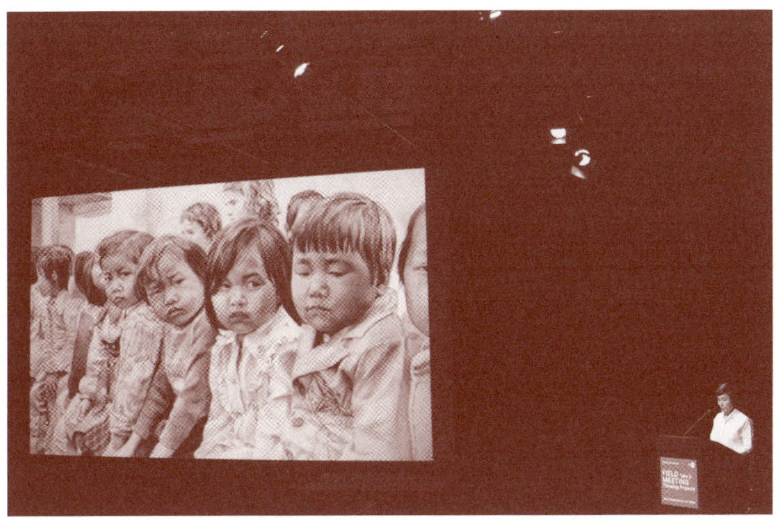

Tiffany Chung, *Remapping History: The Unwanted Population*, 2017. Performance lecture, *ACAW FIELD MEETING Take 5: Thinking Projects*, November 15, 2017. Hosted at SVA Theatre. Image courtesy the artist.

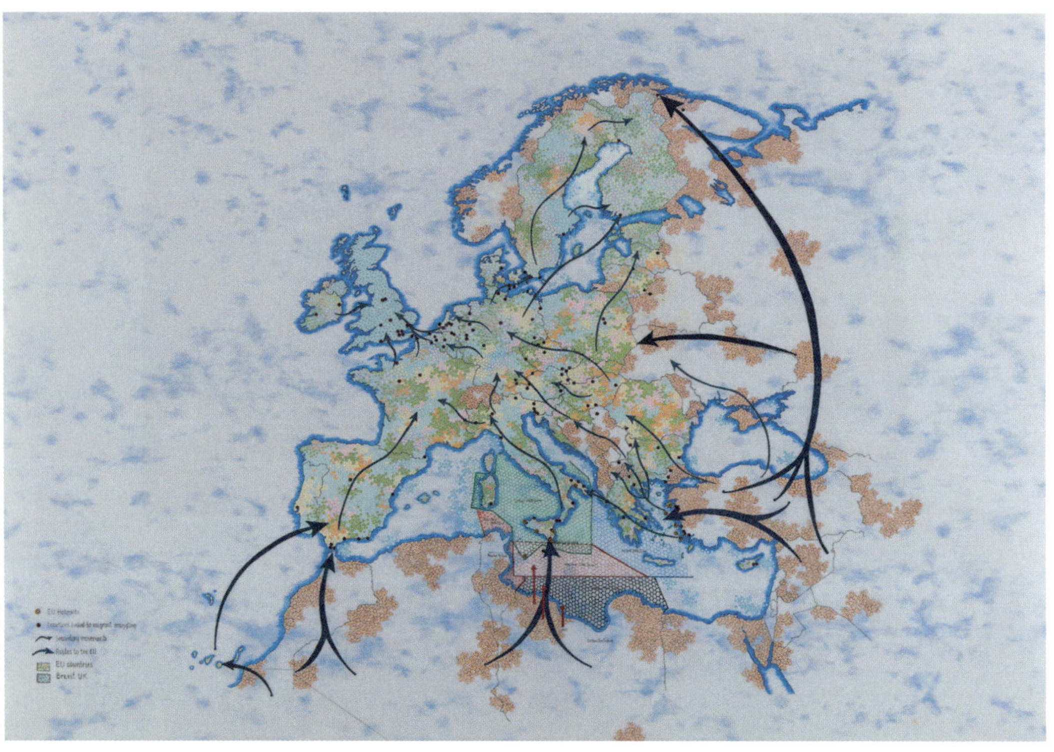

Tiffany Chung, *Europol, UK Parliament: Tracking Migrant Smuggling Routes to and Within the EU*, 2017, acrylic, ink and oil on vellum and paper 77 x 100 centimetres. Image courtesy the artist.

like Walid Raad does.[12] What I find compelling with this method is the role of performativity in knowledge transmission. The idea that a lecturer is an artist, acting a role that deliberately mimics an assumed power, has a different impact on the listener; it is distinct from just listening to a basic oral presentation as is typically the academic experience of learning. Such performativity, I find, has an experiential effect on the listener that brings all knowledge into doubt/question.

KC   The quasi-fictional approach, via the lecture performance, still holds power, I think (even though it has been performed a lot).

RACHEL O'REILLY (ROR) Chiming in as listener, and as someone who once curated Southeast Asian art and now, after moving to the norths (Germany/Netherlands), teaches and also lecture performs anti-colonial aesthetic politics (through non-aligned movement, the globalisation of settler-colonialism), I would like to say that I tend to observe a general decreasing literacy, or never-literacy, in art history and cultural aesthetic politics from outside Europe *except* in the lecture performance mode. I understand Zoe's point about the investigative (via the lecture performance) to be very much focused on the contemporaneity of deep cultural and mythopoetic continuities and survivances. That is why the lecture performance continues to appeal and questions which knowledges we can value.

12   See, for example, Walid Raad, *Scratching on Things I Could Disavow*, 2015, performed at the Museum of Modern Art, New York, https://www.moma.org/calendar/events/1465. On the blending of fact and fiction in performance, see Carrie Lambert-Beatty's canonical essay, "Make-Believe: Parafiction and Plausibility," *October* 129 (Summer 2009).

WM I am hearing a lot here about strategies of animating or networking knowledge, but I would like to hear once more: Strategy and networking for what? What do we want to achieve?

ZB I want to achieve more awareness in my geographies of care, and to achieve a delinking from Western/northern art flows. I want these things because so little of this south affords a space for any option.

CM I want to locate ways for mapping ourselves, and to find ways to juxtapose different maps, too.

WM Maps are crucial since they control our geopolitical imaginary.

KC Walter, can you say a bit about what *you* want, and what has been generative for you?

WM Many things. Blurring the distinction between art and scholarship, or naming a common goal: decolonial aestheSis[13]. Bringing together different people—you see and you hear, and you talk, and you think and all the distinctions in the academy vanish.

KC So decolonising, as articulated and felt by many, is common ground?

WM Well, yes, because the colonial matrix of power is a complex set of domains, levels, and flows, and that is what controls us.

ZB Walter, I can't tell you how many epiphanies I've had since my community sat down to think about the decolonial with you. The conversation continues, and the threads of work are appearing,

13 For more on Mignolo's concept of "decolonial aestheSis," see Chapter 6, "Species(isms)."

and you find a new option—a "decolonial option," to use your term. So much of the practical side of making new networks is also about finding new enunciations, differing terminologies.

WM Changing the terms of the conversations—that is my goal and the goal of the people I am working with. It is crucial because it is the vocabulary that controls us. We cannot escape, but we can do a lot of thinking with it once we begin to delink.

ROR Re: new enunciations, or shared vocabularies— I can't help but be suspicious of assumptions of commonality that are not actually intersubjectively negotiated through incommensurable experiences such as "truth" and "decolonial." How do contemporary uses of the decolonial track against neoliberal aesthetic distortions of common interest, etc.? I'm also suspicious of the role of language in relations of capitalisation and speculative valuation, too.

CM Language is a map…

ZB Before we abruptly end, I'd like to say thank you to all in this little chat room. I learnt a lot and hope one day to be able to chat in person. For me, this conversation highlights a crisis within the presumed structures of learning in our neoliberal world; it is evident that we need to undertake our own mapping of knowledge, dreaming, and needing, and to continue to insist on the recognition of our own terms of reference for how we see, think, and act.[14]

14 For a history connected to this dialogue, see Zoe Butt, "Spirit of Friendship: Artist Groups in Vietnam Since 1975," *Southeast of Now: Directions in Contemporary and Modern Art in Asia* 2, no. 1 (2018).

Contracts

4

CONTRACTS I (COLONIAL LAW): EXPLOITATION AND ORDER WITHOUT PROGRESS

Edgar Alejandro Hernández
and Rolando López

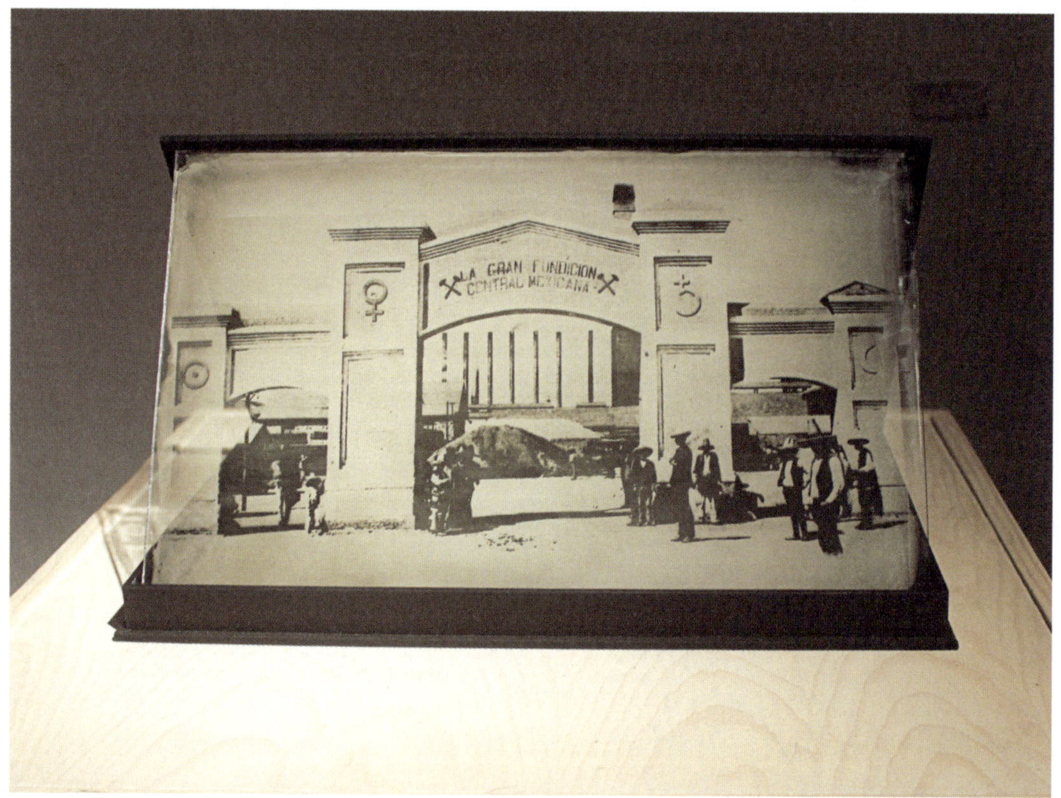

Rolando López, *Gran Fundición Mexicana façade*, 2015, from the project *Guggenheim Museum Aguascalientes* 2013–, wet collodion, silver on glass, 22 x 35cm. Replica of image from historic archive (ca. 1905). Image courtesy the artist.

For the last nine years, Mexican artist Rolando López has been developing *Guggenheim Museum Aguascalientes* (2013–). This project has as its subject the ten hectares of industrial toxic waste situated in Solomon Guggenheim's old mining estate in Aguascalientes, in central Mexico, established in 1894. Guggenheim's operations in Aguascalientes were legalised via a contract signed by the then state governor, Alejandro Vázquez del Mercado. The contract gave Guggenheim extraordinary privileges during a period of economic development led by Mexican President Porfirio Diaz. Deployed under a façade of positivist ideals of order and progress to legitimise the Mexican state to the outside world, Diaz's economic development policies catalysed the plunder and systemic exploitation of local territories and peoples by foreign investment—a method common to practically all of Latin America.

The contract between Guggenheim and Vázquez del Mercado was signed on April 12, 1894. According to the document, at the time Guggenheim was also president of the Great Mexican National Foundry of Monterrey (located in Nuevo León) and, in order to expand the mining industry, he created the Great Central Mexican Foundry in Aguascalientes, which operated from 1894 to 1924. In exchange for a deposit of 4,000 pesos and an infrastructure investment of 200,000 pesos, the industrialist was licensed to exploit the mining operation, or hacienda, at the rate of 180 metric tons daily, and was exempt from paying taxes for twenty years. Guggenheim was also eligible to receive, free of charge, any property or natural resource owned by the state.

The exploitation of resources and populations by nineteenth-century colonial investors continues into the contemporary era. Today, for example, the state of Aguascalientes promotes foreign investment, especially to the automobile industry, echoing the ways in which it accommodated Guggenheim. In 1894, the Guggenheim contract established social, economic, and environmental norms that shaped the contemporary condition in Aguascalientes.

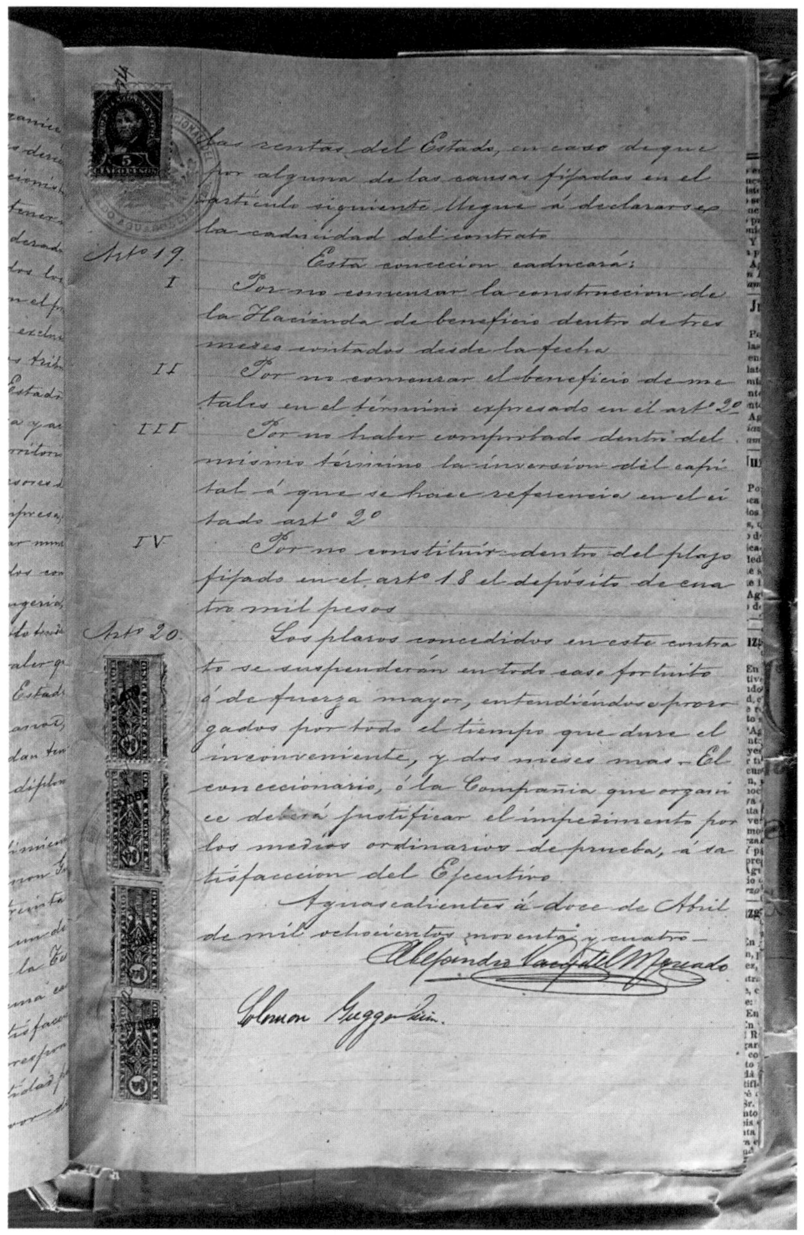

Contract between Solomon R. Guggenheim and Vázquez del Mercado, Governor of Aguascalientes, Mexico, 1894. Published in the newspaper *El Republicano*, in the state of Aguascalientes, Mexico, April 22, 1894. Image courtesy the artist.

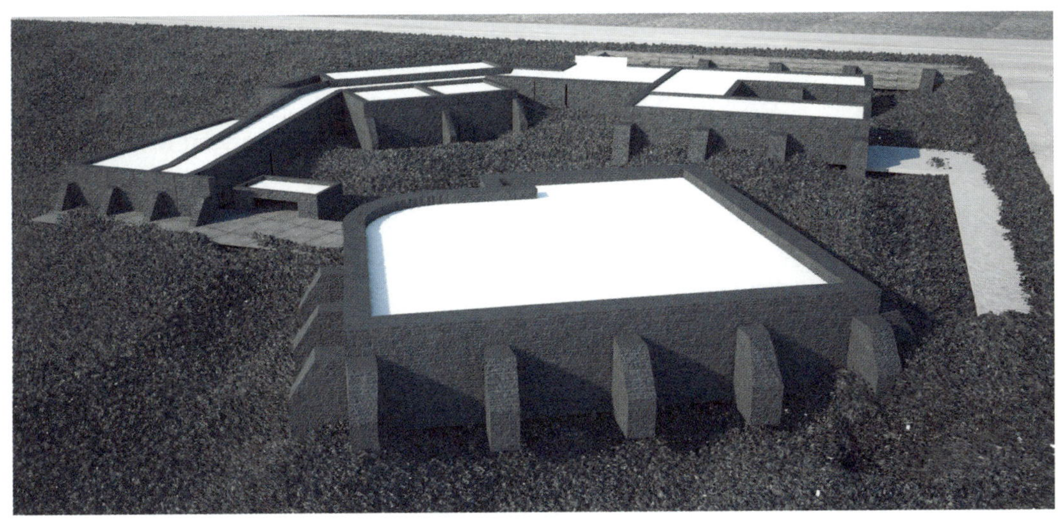

Rolando López, *Museo Guggenheim Aguascalientes* (model), 2013, from the project
Guggenheim Museum Aguascalientes 2013–. Image courtesy the artist.

Article 5 of Guggenheim's 1894 contract states that he could set up stall shops in the mining hacienda.[1] The stores sold goods at prices that far exceeded the income of the workers. Their debt grew exponentially: as a consequence, their children or relatives inherited their debt in a cycle that has come to be considered a sort of latter-day slavery because it gave rise to debt servitude (the children or relatives subsequently having to continue working in the mining hacienda). Article 7 expressly states that Guggenheim could utilise or appropriate any amount of land owned by the state for the establishment of the smelter and its buildings, works, and dependencies. Article 8 makes a similar allowance for the indiscriminate use of water and, in fact, for any type of natural resource (further, Article 8 entitles Guggenheim to request the expropriation of private property). Here it should be noted that the operations of Guggenheim's mining hacienda were a chief cause for the San Pedro River to run dry in Aguascalientes. Article 15 proposed that the mining hacienda would employ students from state universities and schools. This same phenomenon happens today: public universities in Aguascalientes structure their curriculum to promote technical careers catered to automobile manufacturers installed in the state to the detriment of humanities-focused careers.[2]

López has constructed the *Guggenheim Museum Aguascalientes* by critically engaging with Guggenheim's legacy, from the foundry in Aguascalientes to the Guggenheim Museum in New York. López's project is a proposition for a museum to be built on the site contaminated by the old foundry, whose walls will be built with slag (an industrial waste material). The museum exists as a concept, which

---

1   This and the following articles are found in the contract between the governor of Aguascalientes Alejandro Vázquez del Mercado, and the representative of the Mexican National Foundry, Solomon R. Guggenheim. Published in the newspaper *El Republicano*, in the state of Aguascalientes, Mexico, on April 22, 1894.

2   For a detailed analysis of the political economy of the automobile industry in Mexico, see Alejandra González Jiménez, "Entanglements: Volkswagen de México and Global Capitalism" (PhD diss., University of Toronto, 2017).

materialises, however ephemerally, each time López activates the *Museum* on the site of the foundry. He initiates processes of collecting the foundry's remains (pillars, doors, and objects from the land such as stones, tree branches, flowers, and feathers) and archival documentation (of workers, politicians, Guggenheim's contract). Via performances and museological experiments, López transforms the site momentarily as well as our encounters with land, history, and art. In such moments, the museum exists, without the need for walls or sophisticated façades, much less immaculate white cubes. *Guggenheim Museum Aguascalientes* is a site-specific artwork, structured by a constant tension between memory and oblivion.

Dialogue
Led by Edgar Alejandro Hernández with Rolando López, Carla Macchiavello,
Rachel O'Reilly, and Verónica Tello

EDGAR ALEJANDRO HERNÁNDEZ (EH) I want to begin
by clarifying that the work of Rolando López, and
specifically his work with the contract between
Guggenheim and the Governor of Aguascalientes,
is not focused on the future but on the present. This
present catastrophically seems to have no remedy.
It is structured to, again and again, repeat the effects
of centuries-old coloniality.

Rolando's work offers a critical means to
address problems that are not limited to Mexico
or Latin America, but which are global and open up
the possibility of a south (or souths) that generates
its own narrative. These (alternative) narratives are
always born out of the archives we have (I am thinking
of the Guggenheim contract in particular). With this
in mind, I'd like to pose a question to all of you. Even
though archives might be partial, they are a key means
we have to understand our present. Or at least, if put
to a use other than they were originally intended, they
can be vital tools to forge an alternative to colonial
narratives and infrastructures. What do you think?

CARLA MACCHIAVELLO (CM) I found it really interesting
how in Rolando's work the Guggenheim contract
was "mined." That is, he mines the contract to make
a museum that in turn mines the other museum
(Guggenheim), that is "mined" in the sense that
Lucy Lippard thinks of this term—something
like digging deeper into the underlying issues of
land use.[3] Mining is another way to think about
decolonising museums.

---

3   Lucy R. Lippard, *Undermining: A Wild Ride
*Through Land Use, Politics, and Art in the
Changing West* (New York: The New Press,
2014).

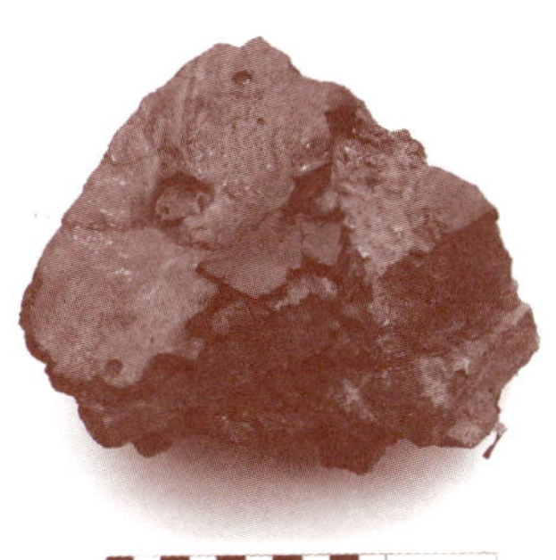
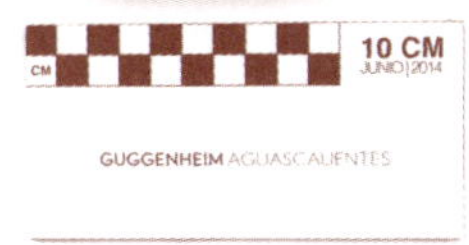

Rolando López, *Guggenheim Museum Aguascalientes* (collection Ayeres), 2013–. Image courtesy the artist.

RACHEL O'REILLY (ROR) Yes, the contract, despite being immaterial in itself, offers up the deep time structure of a situated material history. The contractual form naturalises an investment in a particular kind of futurity, while the artist is working in temporal directions other than this.

It is a particular form of archive—an archive of the feudal firm. It gives literacy and acknowledgement of the deep history of private firms and financing before and beyond the model of the nation that usually binds our thinking about museums and, in doing that, it gives a lot of analytical purchase to the multiple unfolding crises of social and planetary reproductions of today.

ROLANDO LÓPEZ (RL) For me, the archive has the possibility of revealing aspects of our subjectivity that are hidden; it reminds us where we are; it contextualises our current situation, as artists and researchers accessing the archive.

EH The *Guggenheim Museum Aguascalientes* is, in essence, the negative—or underbelly—of the project promised by the twentieth century (that is, we are mining the false promises). Because of this, it does not aim to be a skyscraper or monumental "starchitect" building but digs deep into the earth and its toxic industrial waste.

VERÓNICA TELLO (VT) It's worth remembering that the history of Guggenheim in Aguascalientes is not only a vertical one, where we are digging or mining, but a horizontal one, where we are tracking it across disparate lands. The foundry in Aguascalientes was just one part of Guggenheim's larger industrial enterprises across the Americas, spanning Alaska, Mexico, and Chile (and other places), forming syndicates with other empire builders such as J. P. Morgan and Jacob Schiff. In this light, I see the Guggenheim foundry as an exemplar of large-scale industry mobilising

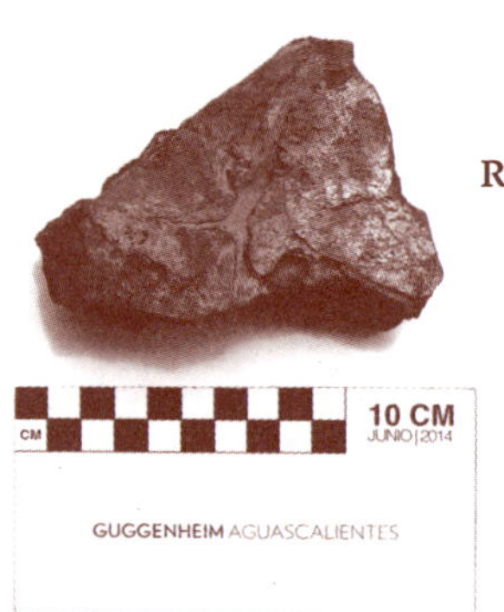

Rolando López, *Guggenheim Museum Aguascalientes* (collection Ayeres), 2013–. Image courtesy the artist.

capitalist enterprise—but Rachel, before, you referred to it as a feudal firm. Can you elaborate?

ROR　Yes. Corporations, financial vehicles used for the development of large-scale colonial/extractive industries, precede the state (Mexico, the US, etc.), and have full continuity with the model of a feudal firm, where we have a householder managing private business dealings based on the model of a properly productive household—i.e., the model assumes there is no welfarist or protective state for labour identifications, etc., apart from labourers' dependent attachment on the householder.

CM　The feudal image is interesting, since one thing that caught my attention is that in the contract and all its clauses and articles, there is almost no mention of the inhabitants of Aguascalientes; they keep getting "mapped out" and so does the history of the region, including its earlier colonial history.

VT　I had the same thought! And I came across a quote in my research for this dialogue worth sharing. The quote is from the *American National Biography*, which is a "database of historically significant American figures."[4] It has an entry on Solomon Guggenheim and briefly mentions his business activities in Mexico (unsurprisingly, his activities are narrated as a distinguished triumph of modern enterprise):

> Possessing considerable personal charm as well as shrewd business sense, he [Guggenheim] succeeded in persuading Mexican politicians to

4　Lillian B. Miller, "Guggenheim, Solomon Robert," in *American National Biography*, ed., J. A. Garraty, M. C. Carnes, and American Council of Learned Societies (New York: Oxford University Press, 1999), https://doi.org/10.1093/anb/9780198606697.article.1300666.

grant concessions with respect to customs duties, land acquisition, and taxes; and he skilfully fended off the protests and obstructions of Mexican competitors.[5]

What is striking here is that even the "protests and obstructions" of local business—let alone other anti-colonial anti-capitalist protests, which are not cited—are narrated as little more than hurdles that Guggenheim expertly managed.

ROR   Yes precisely! The art/istry of governance personified, through the use of particular regimes of finance and capital navigation.

VT   I wonder if the *Guggenheim Museum Aguascalientes*—as a "counter-museum project," if we can call it that—has recorded any other histories of "protest and obstruction"; that is, any histories that remain invisible or outside the language of the contract and the neatly constructed histories of the *American National Biography*. And I guess by "counter-museum project" I mean one that operates beside, and in critical dialogue with, a colonial museum, recording and maintaining histories of the underbelly of that museum.[6]

RL   The research work that I have developed as a counter-museum, which is a term I connect with, has allowed me to record stories that are in tension with the capitalist narratives promoted by the Guggenheim family in our country. These stories, maintained through oral traditions in Aguascalientes, mainly come from workers and their families who were forming unions at the time the foundry was active, their ideological

5   Miller, "Guggenheim, Solomon Robert," https://doi.org/10.1093/anb/9780198606697.article.1300666.

6   Verónica Tello, "Counter-Memory and and–and: Aesthetics and Temporalities for Living Together," *Memory Studies* 15, no. 2 (2022), https://doi.org/10.1177%2F1750698019876002.

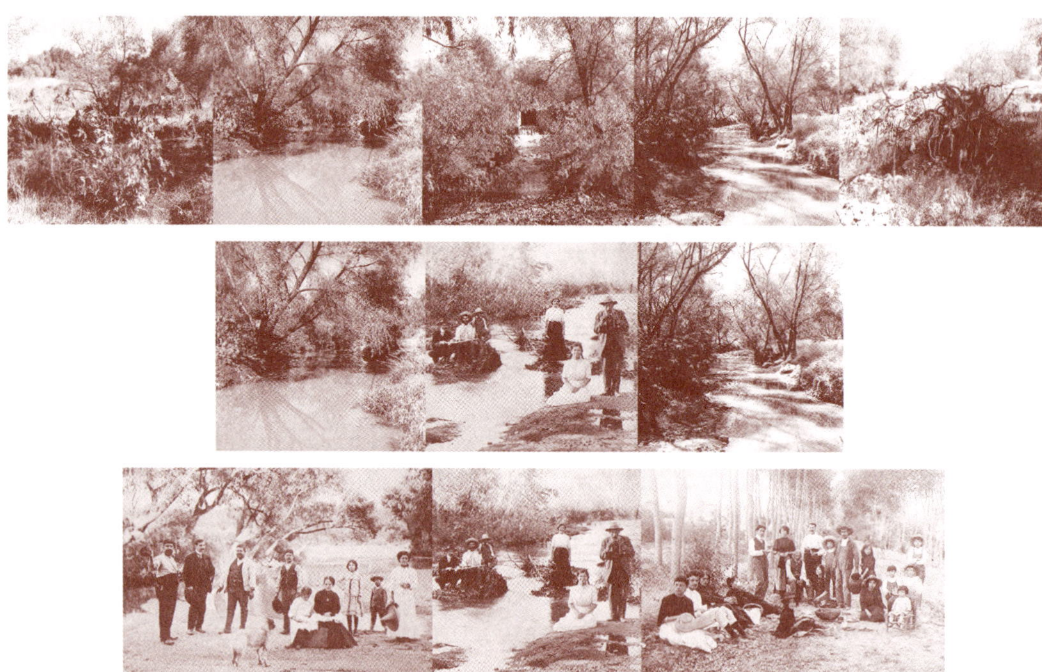

Rolando López, photomontage that shows the river of black waters that run over the bed of the dying San Pedro River in Aguascalientes in relation to archival images of families visiting the river at the beginning of the 20th century, 2020, from the project *Guggenheim Museum Aguascalientes*, 2013–. Source images: Historical archive of the city of Aguascalientes, anonymous author. Image courtesy the artist.

perspectives shaped by the Mexican anarchism of the early twentieth century.[7]

For me, thinking with and through an archive has to go beyond the documents that may be held therein, or the documents we may or may not have access to. The archive is an expansive concept; anything can be read as a trace or a remain of history (Earth itself is an archive). As I said above, an archive reminds us of where we are, where we stand.

The archive that I work with is born out of a very specific setting: the Guggenheim foundry/Aguascalientes. Like all archives, the one I work with contains an enormous variety of documents/artifacts, which together offer me/us the possibility of understanding the deep time of planetary extraction and colonial violence through the lens of a specific context.

ROR   On this question of whether there is a counter-archive: there may be no archive that lies "under" the corporate archive that is legible to it, but a method of counter-memory does aid a certain counter-locative attention to what is there, what has never been destroyed, and what has been remembered aside from all corporate intent to the contrary, etc.

VT   This returns us to the point Edgar made earlier regarding the archive—or the contract more precisely—being a document of the future.

ROR   Yes, a future so duplicitous, never arriving etc. Not caring about the difference between the promise of "future performance" of the investment versus the actual material consequences and metabolic scripts of the (minimally languaged) contract…

7   For a history of Mexican anarchism, see Barry Carr, "Marxism and Anarchism in the Formation of the Mexican Communist Party, 1910–19," *The Hispanic American Historical Review* 63, no. 2 (1983).

VT That's an interesting juxtaposition, Rachel.

ROR Yes. The counter-museum is the museum's consequence.

RL The *Guggenheim Museum Aguascalientes* project is a counter-museum made up of a collection of thousands of toxic waste residues that make us sick daily. Each residue is an archive that tells us about colonial arrogance. By "colonial arrogance" I mean the distorted image that the coloniser has of himself as a totalising force in spite of his limited perspective.

VT We all have a partial view, as Adrienne Rich or Audre Lorde remind us, only some of us don't (want to) register that.[8]
Guggenheim Museum Aguascalientes does not generate a counter-narrative for an alternative present or future. Instead, *Guggenheim Museum Aguascalientes* is conceptualised as a museum of a negative promise, where there is no future (only a present shaped by colonial trauma).

RL The future is denied. There is the latent possibility of dying tomorrow from a lead-related illness by simply breathing in Aguascalientes. It is a counter-museum because it seeks to expand the limits of what we have thought that this institution (the museum) is and has been. It seeks to emphasise the strategies we can invent from our precarious condition.

8   Adrienne Rich, *Blood, Bread, and Poetry: Selected Prose 1979–1985* (New York: W. W. Norton & Company, 1994); Audre Lorde, *Zami: A New Spelling of My Name—A Biomythography* (New York: Crossing Press, 1982).

ROR How much does it matter that the *Guggenheim Museum Aguascalientes* is built or unbuilt? Given the role of speculative finance in cultivating attachment to things that don't exist anyway, or that materially exceed their nominal conception, isn't the point to be "entertained" by "imagining" the full toxicity of the proposed Guggenheim museum, whether it gets built or not?[9]

CM The project risks imagining something beyond existing normative modern structures.

ROR Yes, it is maybe an annihilation of modern structures at the level of the imagination—an attempt to annihilate the toxicity of modernist museological infrastructures, and the relations of capital through which these are built.

RL The project is conceived not as a construction of cement and steel, but a very fragile construction generated from similarly fragile subjects and human interrelations. It is a structure under pressure; as such, it may fall tomorrow and possibly rise again…as we have learned to do in our context.

ROR I imagine, perhaps, this fragile structure (trying to picture it) speaks not only back to the Guggenheim legacy, but also to that which otherwise needs *or* wants to be produced or made locally…

EH The *Museum* exists only as long as the actions that Rolando proposes occur, and it disappears as quickly as everyone leaves the situations (in galleries, museums) he creates (through installations, performances).

---

9   For a discussion on the role of speculative finance in cultivating attachment to things that don't exist, see Marina Vishmidt, *Speculation as a Mode of Production* (London: Brill, 2018).

Returning to my introductory remarks,
I want to insist on the negative of modern
promises, since the *Guggenheim Museum
Aguascalientes* does not seek to be a functional
precinct, nor to be innovative or productive.
On the contrary, it emerges from industrial
waste and happens in a site that is legally lost
in nothingness.

VT   Other than the negative being the necessary "other"
of Western modernity, which allows the West/norths
to exist, why is the negative promise fundamental to
your thinking of the Guggenheim project, Edgar and
Rolando?

RL   For reality to manifest, it must have a positive and
negative side; this is the basis for my understanding
of the world—as shaped by my Indigenous past.
The *Guggenheim Museum Aguascalientes* reveals the
shadow that accompanies the system of art at a
global level.

EH   While the Guggenheim franchise is built upon majestic,
modernist, and postmodernist structures and
museums, the *Guggenheim Museum Aguascalientes* starts
from the opposite: it is dark, dirty, and toxic. Its sheer
existence bothers.

VT   Rolando and Edgar, since we are touching on the
global, modern art institution that is the Guggenheim, I have to ask: How important is it for you
to think of the *Guggenheim Museum Aguascalientes*
project in relation to what is happening in Abu
Dhabi with migrant labour (as the Gulf Labour
Artist Coalition has brought to the fore)?[10] The
Guggenheim Museum Aguascalientes is built on
the landscape where capital (via mining) made

10   Gulf Labor Artist Coalition, https://
gulflabour.org.

the Guggenheim art empire possible, which continues to proliferate through the construction of global art museums.[11]

RL   What is happening in Abu Dhabi reflects the arrogance of coloniality. I am concerned about what can be done under the guise of art. Ultimately, art in its modern phase embodies the vices of the institutions that sustain it and prolong its existence. We have to dare to imagine beyond these outdated systems.

ROR   "I am concerned by what can be done under the guise of art": yes, agreed.

EH   All the protests that take place in Abu Dhabi arise out of the capitalist logic that structures the Guggenheim empire/Foundation, and echo the promises of order and progress that brought Solomon Guggenheim to Mexico a century ago.

ROR   I was just thinking (in this repetition of our questions re: "What is the museum you are making?"): For me, global art's idea of the museum is a (bourgeois) infrastructure that at best can be occupied to do certain things other than how they are normatively done, but there is often little continuity in that performance of differential production. Museum space can give legitimacy and can disseminate visibility for a critical project (to varied effects, including none). But at its most locally and regionally productive, the museum tends to lose its internationalist modularity and look much more like other kinds of social architectures, fabrics or something.

11   Global Ultra Luxury Faction (G.U.L.F.), "On Direct Action: An Address to Cultural Workers," *eflux journal* 65 (May/August 2015), http://supercommunity-pdf.e-flux.com/pdf/supercommunity/article_1213.pdf.

I grew up in a port town (Gladstone, Australia) in which about seventy-five percent of capital flow is connected to a major miner, Rio Tinto, and where the local Rio Tinto–sponsored art prize has exhibited relatively critical practices in the small city. My Indigenous friends there continue to struggle over basic rights to fish in the toxic harbour. I never assume in advance that the museum is going to inherently matter or feel safe to people most affected by extractivist capital. That doesn't mean local people can't get something out of it or demand much more from it ordinarily.

RL   Undoubtedly, the experience at Gladstone shows us, once again, how large corporations exercise their power over life. We in Aguascalientes share with the inhabitants of Gladstone a toxic inheritance and the experience of having our art and ideas hijacked by death peddlers.

Eduardo and I agree with Rachel that the infrastructure of the art system, as well as, of course, that of the museum, are bourgeois institutions that impose their regimes on the thinking and feeling of all those who accept their privileged point of view without hesitation. We consider that the production of class, racial, sexual, and gendered difference is unlikely to occur in museums. The production of difference occurs in environments and situations where there are fewer rules and more capacity for play and experimentation.

From our perspective, the one privilege of living in the shadow of the great cultural industry called the Guggenheim is this: it allows us to observe its "light." It manifests itself spectacularly, but we assure you that it uses its light to attempt to blind us to the economic, historical, and social facts that shape it. Can we hope that the individuals who lead these institutions will acquire sufficient historical awareness one day so that we may enjoy their art?

CONTRACTS (AND COLONIAL LAW) II:
THE GAS IMAGINARY
Rachel O'Reilly

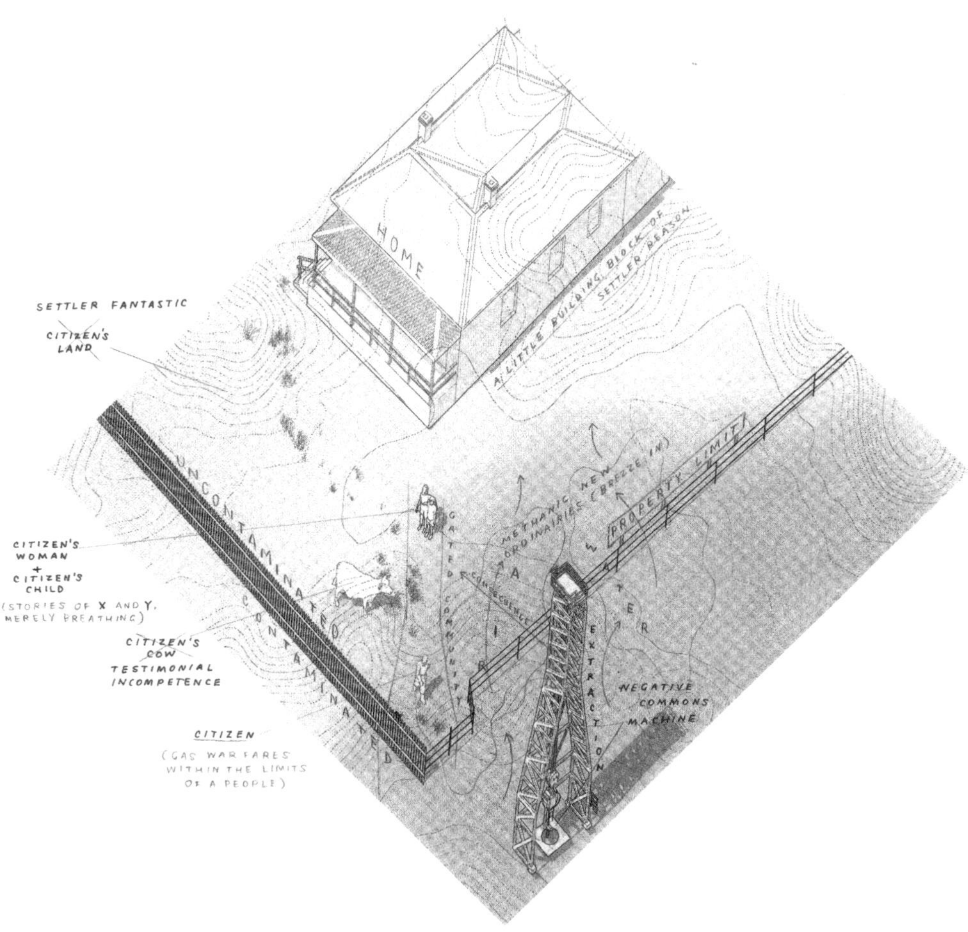

Rachel O'Reilly, *Citizenship Topsoil*, from *The Gas Imaginary*, 2014, produced in collaboration with Rodrigo Hernández and Pa.LaC.E (Valle Medina and Benjamin Reynolds), limited edition series of unique 3 x 9 Risograph prints on paper, ink, pencil, 279 x 315mm. Images are part of the long-term project, *The Gas Imaginary*, 2011–2020. Image courtesy the artist.

The Gas Imaginary (2013–2020) is a multidisciplinary artistic project which has been developed in dialogue with Gooreng Gooreng Elders and women environmental activists (located in Queensland, Australia). It uses poetry, collaborative drawings, installation, moving images, and public lectures to explain the colonial, legal, aesthetic, and technical conceits of "unconventional" gas mining (aka fracking), from its role in the US New Economy to its spread across Australia since 2009. Within *The Gas Imaginary*, fracking is read as a rhizomatic territorial formation and corporate installation project, or land art, that conceptually cuts the late liberal imagination of mining and citizenship, while being entirely continuous with the settler-colonial project, as capitalism reaches the limits of land use.

Especially in its early phases, the project has tried to mediate the clear analytical challenges that unconventional extraction poses to late liberal conceptions of place and territory, property, and governance, both materially and at the level of the imaginary. While invested in the analytics of the global fracking industry, I also talk about *The Gas Imaginary* as site-specific and site-generalising artistic research. On the one hand, it has been very committed to producing a polyvocal counter-image of the industry's installation within, and material transformation of, the colonial port and harbour ecology of Gladstone, Queensland—unceded Gooreng Gooreng Country and a former capital of a colony of Northern Australia, where four generations of my family grew up. Gladstone, named after the British "home rule" prime minister, has an ongoing and prominent but under-documented role in the export of mineral wealth from the north of Australia. Simultaneously, I am interested in tracking the repetitive aesthetic tactics of a cross-border industry through specific forms of legal innovation, pseudo-scientific imaging regimes, and financialised language for ecosystemic and cultured worlds.

Early works from the project included two series of Risograph prints, which I produced in collaboration with the artist Rodrigo Hernández and Pa.LaC.E, an architectural design collaborative (Valle Medina and Benjamin Reynolds), using 3D software and hand-drawn lines from my poems.

The first series (*The Gas Imaginary*, 2014) traces the difference between the modernist imagination of underground mining versus contemporary fracking regimes; the second gives a deep time and horizontal social image to the privatised drama of approvals surrounding the expansion of the port of Gladstone into a gas export hub for Queensland (*Gladstone, Post-Pastoral*, 2016).

In Gladstone, despite traversing World Heritage-protected, UNESCO-listed terrain, the liquefied natural gas (LNG) developments and destructive harbour dredging were made possible through legal innovations and special economic zonings. Environmental impact assessments of the infrastructure itself have since been proven to have lacked critical information on groundwater and well locations, while the process of approval has been subjected to state and federal government inquiries.

In this project and across other recent research (for example, in my writing on the contradictions of artistic autonomy in the settler colony), my sensitivity to relations between language and political economy has led me to pay increased attention to the aesthetics of the contract. The contract contains futurity in a continuum of asymmetrical obligations. It is the main fulcrum of negotiation around which contemporary powers of accumulation and resistance—through negative stake-holding—meet and move and struggle.[1] If you look at this historically, the power of the contract seemed more prominent in the feudal era since colonial modernism naturalised liberal democratic regimes of rights and redistributions for some citizens (enabling protection from the full force of global capital, especially for British property owners). However, now the power of the contract in disabling settler/modern democratic resistance to corporate state power is becoming more and more apparent. The museum, of course, is caught up in this, not only at the level of sponsorships (as discussed in the previous chapter).

1   Angela Mitropoulos, *Contract and Contagion: From Biopolitics to Oikonomia* (Wivenhoe, New York: Minor Compositions, 2012).

So, attention to the contract enables financialised power to be given its history. In the long *durée* of colonial securitisations of land, genocidal innovations of fungibility are inseparable, still, from contemporary wars of accumulation.

In *The Gas Imaginary*, the more conceptual and psycho-analytic work of the drawings in particular aims to point to the role of contractual form in the intimate, oikonomic reproduction of extractive industry investments and the social licensing of extinction-oriented developments.[2] This is the long story of fossil capitalism, which has been upscaled since the 1970s, producing the most extractive era in human history by far.

2   I engage with Mitropoulos's *Contract and Contagion* in D. Butt and Rachel O'Reilly, "Infrastructures of Autonomy on the Professional Frontier: 'Art and the Boycott of/as Art'," *Journal of Aesthetics and Protest* 10 (2017), https://www.joaap.org/issue10/oriellybutt.htm.

Dialogue
Rachel O'Reilly and Angela Mitropoulos, with Comments by
Edgar Alejandro Hernández and Rolando López

RACHEL O'REILLY (ROR) It might be good to begin by explaining where/how I began research on *The Gas Imaginary*, also because there are so many connections with Rolando's lines of inquiry in the "Contracts I" dialogue.

My research began in the wake of the 2008 global financial crisis, during the peak of the Australian mining boom. During this period, mega-mine licenses (for gas but also for new coal mines) were being approved at unprecedented scales all over the country, licensed almost solely by the promise of (fictitious) job creation. The harbour of my hometown was being dredged to make way for the installation of the fracking industry in Queensland, the contract for one of the main companies was being socially licensed through state arts infrastructure, and there was a major ecocide event from the dredging. The main legal case put together around that dredging event aimed to compensate the commercial fishermen for loss of income, while other attempts to allocate responsibility for the actual ecocide hardly figured so prominently.

ROLANDO LÓPEZ (RL) Indeed, Rachel, there is so much systemic violence sustained and advanced under the pretext of art.

ROR I do not think it is possible to separate aesthetic experience from some broader material sense of responsibility to extramural culture. The opposite of Guggenheim! Of course, European art theory has more often been concerned with a notion of the environment that has played out apart from infrastructure's (gendering) shadow.

In any case, from the paternal side of my family I had absorbed some literacy in the history and political economy of those industrial geographies

and the corporate privileges they hold. My uncle
was Federal Commissioner for Taxation during
the 1980s "Bottom of the Harbour" schemes, and
throughout the 1970s and 1980s era of "Northern
Development" between Western Queensland and
Gove, my grandfather organised with the Federated
Iron Workers. The commodities port of Gladstone
changed a lot during this ongoing mining boom, and
I was thinking a lot about what it means for a feminist
cultural worker interested in art and politics, who grew
up with a fully industrialised sense of the harbour
already, to engage with that acceleration as research.
But it all really only became artistic research after
I went to a local community harbour meeting in 2011.
I was disturbed by the way in which the development
approvals that rationalised the destruction of the
harbour were actually destroying people's vocabularies
and literacies in even talking about the materiality of
what was being destroyed. I wrote a long poem that
night that later became *Rue Methanic* (2013), the first
work element of *The Gas Imaginary*.

   The Gas Imaginary is picking up on all of the
diagrams, linguistic tools, and fictional plans of
securities that the industry uses, in order to think
through production and a counter-poetic. I guess that
would be the summary.

   I should also say it has taken me a long time to
produce these things since it was mostly unfunded
for the first few years. My uncle, who was depressed
by the current state of trade union politics in Australia,
basically fed and housed me in the beginning when
I wanted to do local research. Things have changed
now that the project has legibility, but I am basically
committed to returning to do more work around the
history of the harbour, and its connections to the north
of the country, which is leading me more and more
to think through present scales of port and pipeline
development elsewhere, and the current phases of
large-scale industrialisation of the desert and ocean,
based on older frontier geographies.

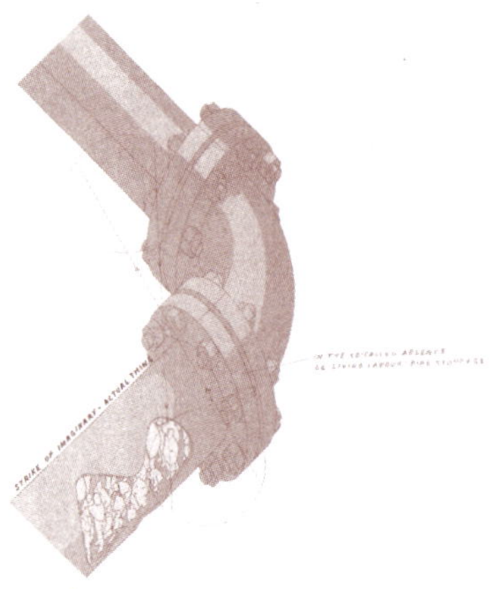

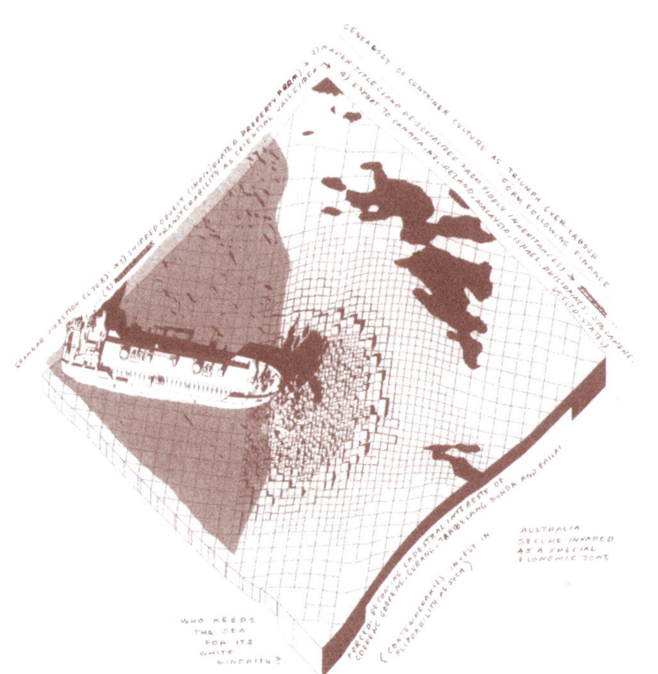

Rachel O'Reilly, *Flow Stoppage* (Virtual) (top) from *The Gas Imaginary*, 2014, and *Torrens Title Redacted* (bottom) from *Gladstone, Post-Pastoral*, 2016, produced in collaboration with Rodrigo Hernández and Pa.LaC.E (Valle Medina and Benjamin Reynolds), limited edition series of unique 3 x 9 Risograph prints on paper, ink, pencil, 279 x 315mm. Images are part of the long term project, *The Gas Imaginary*, 2011–2020. Images courtesy the artist.

ANGELA MITROPOULOS (AM) Both series of drawings in *The Gas Imaginary* are remarkably dense bundles. Contractual assemblages, as it were. The use of topography and axonometric projection—both of which refer to design and mapping techniques, but which (for me at least) compel the viewer to linger on the use of non-linear perspective. Really, amazing work.

I was also struck by the commentary on depth–surface relationships that proceeds through-out the series. As in one of the works in the series *Orthodox Value (Limited Edition)*—a lot in that series made me smile.

So I am interested in the conjunctures between cartographic techniques, logical-semantic systems and contracts. And I'm also interested in how others see keeping open a divergence between recomposing perspective (and affect) and operationalising these systems. How do we, as Rachel says, pick up the diagrams and tools that the industry uses, so as to think more about production and a counter-poetics? An exploded diagram is not, in terms of its treatment of perspective, a Noel Counihan Christ-like painting of a miner in a yellow helmet, or Fred McCubbin's bush pioneer triptych, or Turner's landscapes—and I would say more interesting for all that. It interests me because it denaturalises the processes and techniques that gave rise to the geometric construction of an instantaneous and singular perspective by introducing more than one plane, highlighting the dependencies on perspectival angles, and so on. (Side note: Rio Tinto's lawyers once sent me a "cease and desist" letter).

ROR Hah. Amazing. Regarding depth surface: I have been wondering more lately if these are even different materialisms that are not just scaled or layered. The European left still struggles to think beyond the labour point of view towards land as something that is being destroyed in a kind of offset way to their own imaginary (but also biogeochemically in movement and relation).

AM　Right, because European materialisms are not very good at understanding the depth of property law, e.g., *terra nullius* ("empty land"). Which, to link it back to the brief discussion of a counter-aesthetics (via counter-monuments), is a question of perspective and affect, not transcendence or phenomenology. The idealisation of the commons (and "commonwealth"), the bounteous open frontier, and the labour theory of right is the charter of Europe's social democratic Eden, limited by its elision of colonisation and the generalisation of property rights—not least in the techniques of mapping, measuring, and evaluating territory and representing an abstract space of equivalence.

ROR　Yes, this is the other part of the conversation. I really started this project because it was a great opportunity to teach and research against settler equanimity with property/possession and against what is ahistorical in settler environmentalism.

　　For example, it's taken years for me to find the archives and also the scholars who have theorised Torrens title, the model of landed property designed for Australia's parcel-by-parcel dispossession project (building on Chapter 1's discussion of scattered and fragmented archives). Torrens title moved across the British Empire and is now the preferred land registry system of the International Monetary Fund, used to dispossess peasants across the souths, etc. So this is a globally significant conceptual innovation.

EDGAR ALEJANDRO HERNÁNDEZ (EH)　What also interests me about your work, Rachel, is how it combines the aesthetics of cartography and contractual information. Your assemblage here is, I think, a very interesting way of making manifest the contract as an image, while being grounded in the politics in which it came to be. We, Rolando and I, have not yet succeeded in visualising the Solomon Guggenheim contract within the context of the mining at Aguascalientes, at least to the extent you have.

ROR Edgar, in my experience it takes some time to subtract and organise information. *The Gas Imaginary* started as a failed literary non-fiction project. I had a grasp of the politics at play in Gladstone but only in the form of gossip. None of the information on the approved plans, nor the processes corrupted, were accessible when I began. The approval process was finally whistle-blown three years later, by a senior woman scientist working on the environmental impact assessment, and only then was the empirical scale of onshore unconventional gas verifiable. Before that, one had a sense of obvious power differentials and qualitative local change only. The fishermen observing the construction and dredging up close, comprehending risks of damage in a way desktop assessments don't, were the most vocal. That set in motion a kind of justice dramaturgy that was all about settlers' traumatised rights to the harbour, particularly given the absence of First Nations voices which were being channelled into commercial in-confidence native title negotiations and Indigenous land use agreements at the time.[3]

So I "failed" to write a literary narrative attempting empiricism then, but was doing studio visits as part of the first residency that supported the project and was essentially "drawing" an argument about

3   Gooreng Gooreng Elders address this
     silencing in the feature documentary
     INFRACTIONS 2019, the final work of
     The Gas Imaginary that connects Gladstone,
     Queensland approvals and pipelines to
     shale as struggles in the Northern Territory.
     See www.infractionsdocumentary.net.

power and different forces in play across different kinds of montaged elements of the plot. Those drawings I realised were key; I showed them to my architect collaborators (Pa.LaC.E) and they worked with me to materialise them in 3D software. It is clunky on purpose, because it is precisely about violently "bad" modelling of the complexity of what is there.

In my earlier museum curating work I had been tracking Indigenous new media art practices that interrogated mathematical universals in the early 2000s,[4] so it was really discomforting for me to be using 3D software to make this argument. But it is also the over-determined aesthetic that I'm showing. It's dumb. The plans of these projects are so deeply unscientific, and that is also the point: the amateurism of the corporation, and the extinction-oriented stupidity of its plans.

The work also pays respect to all of the different oppositions to the contract, and it is somewhat unorthodox on this point I think, in so far as unconventional extraction creates unconventional politics (and aesthetics). The multiplicity of the drawings is also a kind of tribute or modelled appreciation of all of the different positions of activist groups that add up to a totality of positions of refusal negating the naturalism of the mine or development contract. There is also a distribution of credit for unpaid labour and grassroots thinking that is about undoing hegemonic ideas of justice, to get at the non-transcendental reality of First Nations claims (and others) as planetary mattering.

In the *Orthodox Value Theory (Limited Edition)* diagram, the little person there in the middle was the main and often the only full-time activist working against the installation of the gas in her hometown. She was a retiree whose island-edged property happened

---

4   See *Place: Local Knowledge and New Media Practice*, ed. Danny Butt, John. Bywater and Nova. Paul (Newcastle, England: Cambridge Scholars, 2008).

to be near the gas developments. Her relationship to Indigenous sovereignty has changed over the years we have talked, as a result of a late-in-life overexposure to corporate power over land.

AM	That is kind of what I mean by keeping open the space between perspective (or the kinds of positions art invites) and the operationalisation of those asymmetries or systems. Lingering on the moment between diagrams—or mathematical descriptions, which assume the correlation of dissimilar bundles of information through symbolic formulations and processing—and a concept of the diagram as more or less adequately representational of something else, makes the diagram into the object (of our gaze), bringing to the fore the ways in which the diagram generates an aesthetics of objectivity or truth.

Your work makes me think of the ways in which CAD—the programs you use for the diagrams—is both the art of technique and also non-linear, in that it goes against the realism/naturalism of European art.

Beyond the use of CAD, I'm interested in the use of montage in *The Gas Imaginary*. Can you talk us through some of the ways in which you put together those montages? That is, the way you approach assemblage, or de-assemblage, which is, as a viewer, how I respond to those drawings. I mean, they force me to linger on the construction of the montage.

ROR	I was reading a lot of work psychoanalysing modern mining, for example the writings of Laurence Rickels.[5] He reads the petro/carbon imaginary through German modernism and psychoanalysis as a demonic infrastructure of secular romanticism, and also labour resistance (the ability to stop mine productivity being

5	For example, Laurence A. Rickels, *The Devil Notebooks* (Minneapolis, Minnesota: University of Minnesota Press, 2008).

obviously an assertion of labour power against slavery and the firm, etc.). To my mind, paternal modernity treats the mine as a kind of "daddy" investment. It reproduces classed patriarchies and traffics in a very neo-feudal image of nuclear family happiness and wealth.

Rickels writes about the beginning of romanticism and the hetero-couple form in the undergroundness of the mine worker and the necessity of the wife to reproduce him/the mine through her imagination. So romantic love begins there, in his absence and her longing in reproductive labour (which is contractually not dissimilar to today's mining marriages except the wages to danger ratios are very different).

But let me return to the question of the aesthetics of fracking. The verticality of modernism is coal. And I was thinking about that because with fracking, the industry images were being sold as vertical (virtuous) despite involving the lateral rollout of tens of thousands of mine heads — a horizontal revolution (counter-revolution) that isn't just about depth but lateral fracturing and movement of toxins, waters, subjectivity, wayward women defaulting from marriages/settler property lines to join mine fights, etc.

Citizenship Topsoil, also part of the *Gas Imaginary*, is about the limits of justice in settler property trauma. In the first years of the fracking rollout, white farmers mobilised around a kind of negative commons created by toxic water on private property. Formerly quite conservative and otherwise politically inactive people became suddenly much more literate in neoliberal governance of the ground, that is, through water destruction, lucrative gag orders, and privately negotiated mine jobs. It is very hard to romanticise this kind of mine work, which is mostly about construction, securitisation, and remote desktop monitoring.

Flow Stoppage (from the *Gas Imaginary*) tries to explain that resistance is only possible or useful before the moment of installation (here I'm thinking through my previous writing about installation art in relationship to the installation of extractivist infrastructure).[6] There is no such thing as a gas labour strike with any anti-capitalist efficacy (unless you risk explosions). The flow stoppage must happen before installation and be imagined as stopping pipelines, etc. The last image is a bit intense and uninterpretable, about swallowing the politics of the good enough father, or industrial patriarch, illiterate in environment as a value question.

The second series hones much further in on the specific images and administrative decisions that destroyed Gladstone Harbour. I won't go through it except to mention my favourite images. I guess the main findings of the work in relation to the aesthetics of the industry, and what I probably sought out by studying it, are:

1   The industry's tactical continuity with the very earliest forms and strategies of land speculation and land law innovation (i.e., Australia was essentially settled as a "special economic zone" of Empire, so the notion of a "corporate invasion" that appears as a problem for settlers on stolen land only in the neoliberal era is deeply problematic).

2   The sheer difference in scale of current energy infrastructural developments that are not even trying to have welfarist/redistributive payoffs any longer, and therefore will find it more difficult to normalise extractivism via logics of compensatory "protection" in the late liberal imagination.

3   The possible role of artists in cultivating literacy around these aesthetic, linguistic, and design tactics that, as Rolando was mentioning, point to an underside of material "aesthetic" activity.

6   Rachel O'Reilly, "Dematerializations of the Land/Water Object," *e-flux journal* 90 (April, 2018).

I can't actually read/track one line of production/
ontology (including valuing Indigenous artistic
positions) without also attending to attempts
at destruction that make full use of aesthetic
infrastructure to normalise extraction (not only
through sponsorship) "elsewhere." I think that
it has become rather non-ambiguous that the
marriage of Art/Culture and mining industry
benefits was a key part of the state's successful
legal defeat of Indigenous land rights demands,
across the majority of the country, after the Mabo
and Wik cases. Native title in that sense freed up
much of the land base for many more kinds of non-
Indigenous speculative "rights to development."

AM   There's a parallel here with frontier warfare, i.e.,
appropriation at the threshold of contracts. I was
thinking of Jomini and the war of manoeuvre.

ROR   Yes, I agree. The frontier never stopped. Through
the work of people like Denise Ferreira da Silva, I've
realised how crushed/incompetent we can be when we
only critique the coloniality of form without retaining
hold of what is being missed out on by staying so
attached to destruction—or what is even more
common, when we curate the negative away entirely
in the spirit of a reconciliatory idealism (I feel like
there is a certain division of labour here, too, but since
Euro-American art history almost never talks about
the coloniality of form, it is important to name where
it appears, banally). Cultural production/poetics is also
about the richness of everything that has resisted being
encrypted by hegemonic concepting, including that
done by the cultural industry. (I miss curatorial work
for that constant exposure to practices of differential
worldly production other than what I can manage to
see from levelling out this destructivity, I guess.)

7   Mitropoulos, *Contract and Contagion*, 51–53.

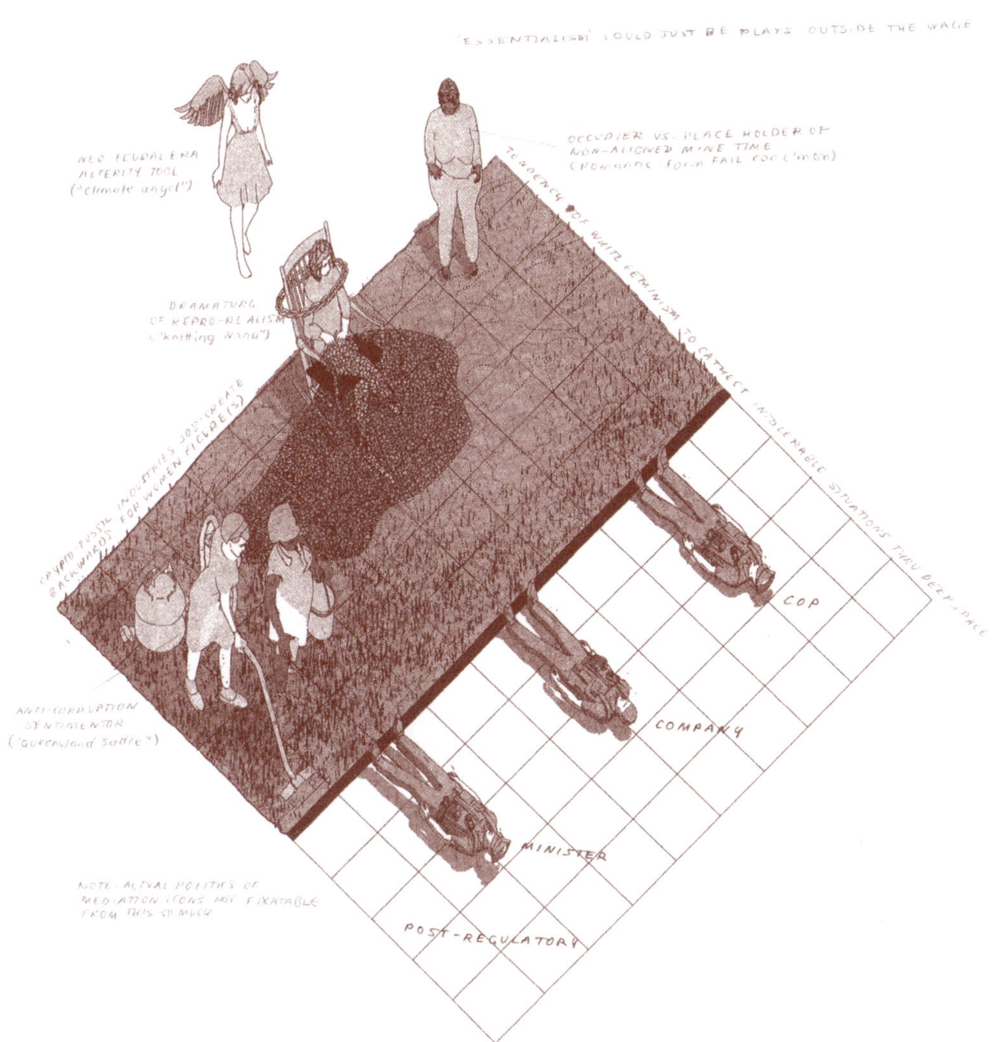

Rachel O'Reilly, *Post-Contractual Surrealism*, from *Gladstone, Post-Pastoral*, 2016, produced in collaboration with Rodrigo Hernández and Pa.LaC.E (Valle Medina and Benjamin Reynolds), limited edition series of unique 3 x 9 Risograph prints on paper, ink, pencil, 279 x 315mm. Image is part of the long term project, *The Gas Imaginary*, 2011–2020. Image courtesy the artist.

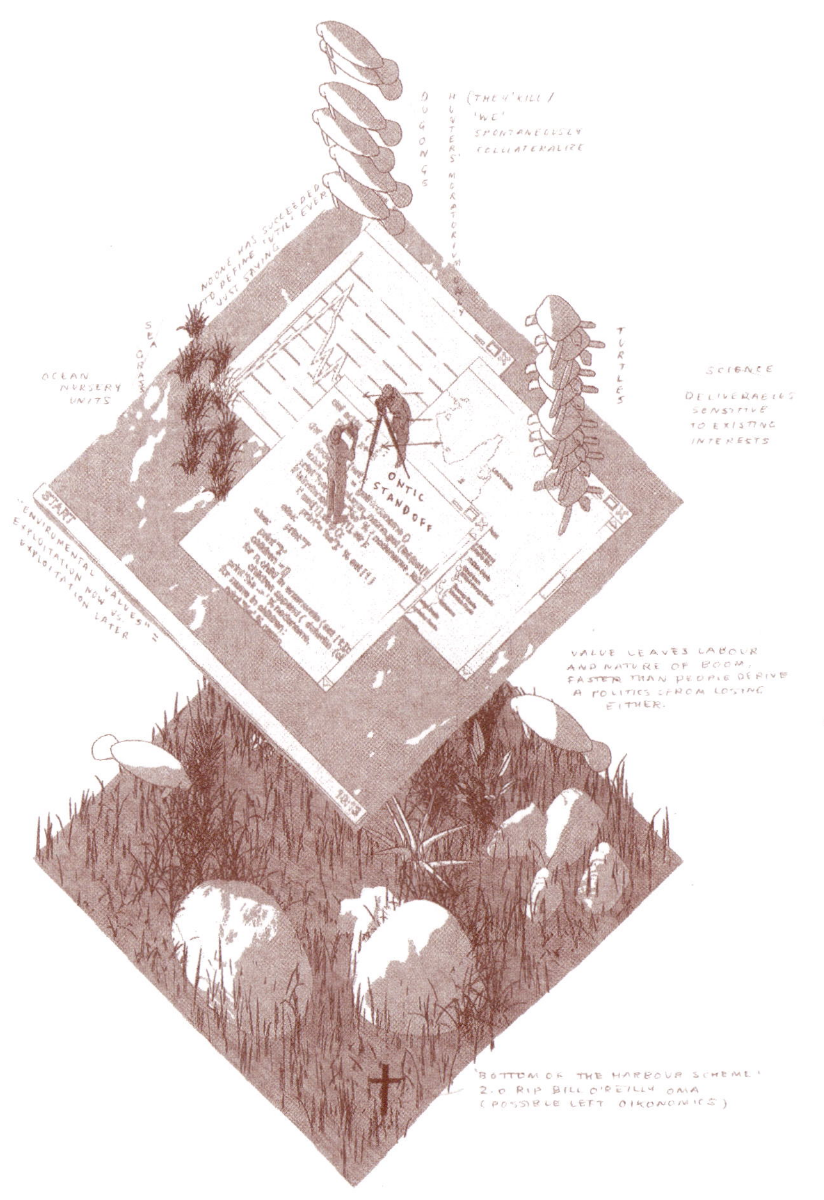

Rachel O'Reilly, *Orthodox Value Theory*, from *Gladstone, Post-Pastoral*, 2016, produced in collaboration with Rodrigo Hernández and Pa.LaC.E (Valle Medina and Benjamin Reynolds), limited edition series of unique 3 x 9 Risograph prints on paper, ink, pencil, 279 x 315mm. Image is part of the long term project, *The Gas Imaginary*, 2011–2020. Image courtesy the artist.

Angela, can you say more about how you deal with this in your own work/practice? Actually, your writing on the Ancients is really key, isn't it?[7]

AM I tend to push history as far as I can, to the point where I know (and feel) that nothing ever stays the same. I like to read as far back as I can, to situate the circumstances in which a concept was invented, had a very different meaning, or did not exist so as to break through either the archaism that attaches to what is treated as self-evident, or assumed to be immutable, or has become encoded as an abstraction or in the logical procedures it implies. It is a technique of estrangement or, the term I think I prefer, defamiliarisation.

ROR Yes.

AM I've also calmed my allergy for Hegelian dialectics by emphasising just how incomplete every logical-semantic (and historical) system is.

ROR How does that calm the allergy?

AM Well, in the sense that you mention: that the negative is also a protocol within a system. Studying risk taught me that downside and upside risks are still values. Risk management systems are predicated on the incorporation of the accidental or negative. So, if no map is complete because the process of abstraction is also one of subtraction, then there is no closure. I prefer this way of thinking to trying to locate a fixed point of resistance, because being able to imagine or locate such a point presupposes a connection to what already exists, a process of representation to which it is linked, and which narrows the range of the foreseeable.

Species(isms)

6

SPECIES(ISMS)
(AND HUMAN/NON-HUMANISMS)
Carla Macchiavello

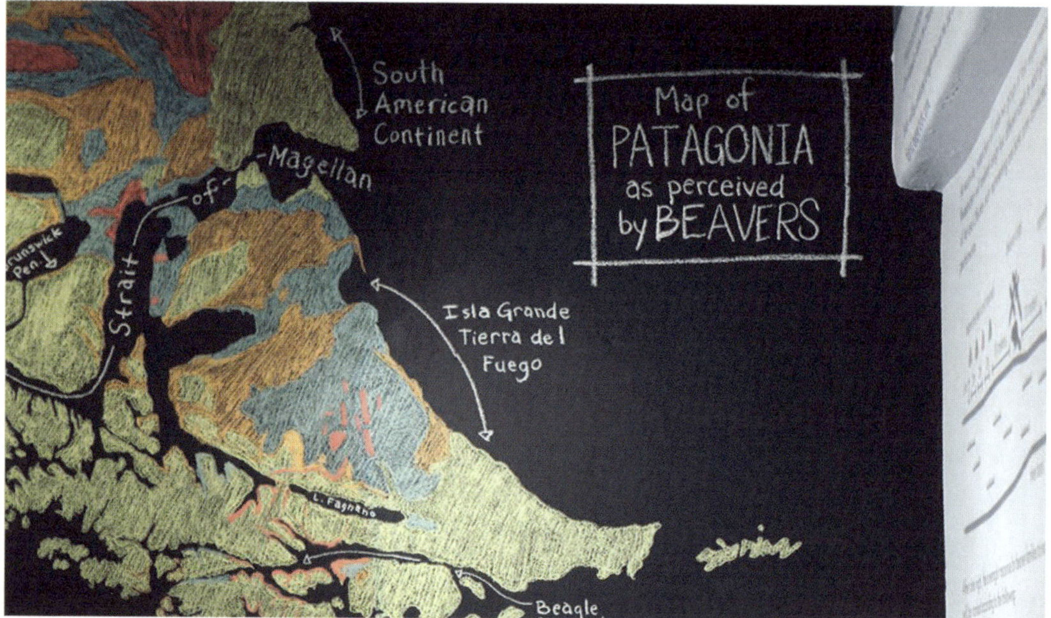

Installation view of *Dear Enemy* exhibition at the Institute for Art and Olfaction in Los Angeles, 2015.
Ensayos contributors: Christy Gast, Camila Marambio, Derek Corcoran, Giorgia Graells.
Photograph by Christy Gast. Image courtesy Carla Macchiavello.

What do care, communication, and collaboration among heterogenous species look and feel like within and beyond an "extreme" location? Can the margin, the periphery, even the antipodes be rethought as an extremity turned centre? Perhaps this is not so hard to imagine: as I have increasingly found in Tierra del Fuego, the more one excavates the particular history of this archipelago off the south of South America, the more interwoven it becomes with other places, the more it grows laterally.

Can the end of the world, the *finis terra*, provide something more than an inverted image of its (colonial) other and, instead, catalyse affinities (*ad finis*) among kinds? Can speculation coming from/at the end of the world move away from the emphasis placed on vision at the root of our species, and our speculative logocentrism, to a form of seeing-understanding that is thinking-feeling—that thinks-senses? Might interspecies communication be finding ways to arrive at a common sense (*sensus*, from the Latin, *sentire*: to feel, to know, to find one's way)—a common ground beyond the human? Could this process be understood as a decolonisation of the senses? What if *to know*, as poet and artist Cecilia Vicuña has suggested, is *to be with* ("*conocer, con o ser, ser con*")?[1] Can one identify with one's opponent, care for the "enemy," even perhaps become it?[2]

For the past few years, I have been thinking-feeling-dreaming with Ensayos, a nomadic collective research practice and ecofeminist collective founded in 2010, comprising writers, poets, and activists.[3] Ensayos, which mostly takes place in Tierra del Fuego, resituates thinking about "the end of the world" (whether that is the human[ist] world, life on

---

1   Cecilia Vicuña, *PALABRARmas* (Santiago: RIL editores, 2005), 87.

2   Macchiavello is referring here to the concept of the "dear enemy": "In ethology, dear enemy recognition is a situation in which a territorial animal responds more strongly to strangers than to its neighbors from adjacent territories. This phenomenon may be generally advantageous to an animal because it minimizes time and energy spent on territorial defense, and reduces the risk of injury during territorial encounters." "Dear Enemy Recognition," Encyclopedia. co.uk, https://www.encyclo.co.uk/meaning-of-Dear_enemy_recognition. For further reading see F. Rosell and T. Bjørkøyli, "A Test of the Dear Enemy Phenomenon in the Eurasian Beaver," *Animal Behaviour* 63 (2002).

3   About Ensayos, https:// ensayostierradelfuego.net/ensayos/.

earth as we humans know it, or a geographical end of the world at the south) as a sensorial/aesthetic engagement (thinking-feeling) with multispecies collaborators ("co-labourers" in Donna Haraway's terms).[4] It seeks to imagine and put into action (*"imaginación, imagen en acción,"* according to Vicuña) different ways of being with and in the world.[5] Ensayos is/is not a thing (a residency, an idea, a curatorial vision); it works as a temporal, shifting assemblage of practices that try out ways to create common grounds and listen to other beings speak.

Ensayos (which translates into English as "rehearsals, inquiries") has been a sensual, deeply sensorial, place-based research practice focused on the ecopolitics of Tierra del Fuego (and increasingly in archipelagos beyond it). It learns by walking and moving with, being moved and guided by, those who live (and died) in the land—its caretakers, its inhabitants. It learns by listening to land, water, animate and inanimate beings, their stories and songs; by smelling, sometimes reeking; by vibrating as much as observing. It delves into mystery, too—the uncertain, the invisible, and at times the oracular. As a rehearsal, it opens itself to fail, to falter, to not know.

I tend to think of Ensayos in theatrical terms, as acts of staging, performing, experimenting, practicing, and learning (acts that also define scientific practices) from and with Tierra del Fuego: from its history, strata, and layers of corporal and immaterial memory, present, movements; from the localised and migrant practices of her inhabitants, colonisers, and visitors; from a variety of practices that meet in its varied spaces (including biological sciences, social sciences, sheep businesses, tourism, and art, among others); and from body to body across and within different worlds. Ensayos sets up spaces for dialogues as much as misunderstanding, like a shelter (precarious, temporary, resistant)—yet these do not occur necessarily through words. Dialogue in Tierra del Fuego has historically

4 Donna Haraway, *Staying with the Trouble: Making Kin in the Chthulucene* (Durham, North Carolina: Duke University Press, 2016).

5 Vicuña, *PALABRARmas*, 83.

been a matter of signs and their performance: from the smoke interpreted as fire that gave it its European name (as opposed to *Karukinka*, the name given to it by the Selk'nam people); to the words and gestures of Fuegians in canoes directed towards incoming ships that were read by Europeans as desperate begging (as described by Charles Darwin);[6] to the interpretation of pigments, body paint, costume, sound, and song as the re-enactment of a spirit world; to the movements of water, sky, and earth as confiding gestures speaking in the tongues of wind, wafts of odour, touch, ancestors. Ensayos might thus be thought-felt as a practice of learning to listen and communicate differently, across diverse ways of experiencing the world.

It was the work of Ensayos in its playful weaving of art, science, and everyday life that caught the attention of Verónica. She invited me to share these ideas as a provocation, a starting point for an exchange with other artists, anthropologists, and thinkers who have been, in their different practices and within varied territories, engaged with coloniality, heterogeneous worldings, ceremony, embodiment, and undoing the nature/culture divide. They have been cultivating the power of the imagination and deep attention to do differently, away from colonial frameworks. What ensued was an encounter of our differences and a starting point for more conversations to come.

6   Charles Darwin, *The Voyage of the Beagle*
     (London: Penguin, 1989).

Dialogue
Carla Macchiavello, with Dylan A. T. Miner, Fernando do Campo,
Jennifer Biddle, and Walter D. Mignolo

CARLA MACCHIAVELLO (CM) Greetings to all. To begin our dialogue, I will propose some ideas, and would like to hear your thoughts. We could start with Fernando, Jennifer, Dylan, and Walter. We can then let the conversation grow and criss-cross in different directions from there.

The title of this dialogue, "Species(isms)," was suggested to me by Verónica as a provocation, and for a while I felt uncomfortable with the term, until this troublesome aspect became attractive. Did it mean that the discussion should focus on what makes a species particular while critiquing speciesism? Did it allude to a queering or making strange of these distinctions? Could it help us think of points of difference?

Overall, it made me think about the need to revise terms, the language used, and the relation of naming to coloniality when thinking of ecological matters, from the more popular idea of the Anthropocene and the critiques it has been subject to, to notions of us/them (whatever those terms are filled in with): nature/culture, centre/margin, remote and extreme.[7] Revision itself is an interesting concept in relation to species and speciesisms, since the root of the word "species" is "to see" or "a way of seeing." Therefore it may allude both to the sense of sight and to an ampler idea of vision; to revise as a way to see again in the sense of seeing differently, to take a different viewpoint.

This viewpoint might be one from the ground or under it—submerged, aquatic, airborne, microscopic—but it might also be a vision, as in a dream. Perhaps this widening of the term can help us change the way we see and connect to powerful forms

7   T. J. Demos, *Against the Anthropocene: Visual Culture and Environment Today* (Berlin: Sternberg Press, 2017).

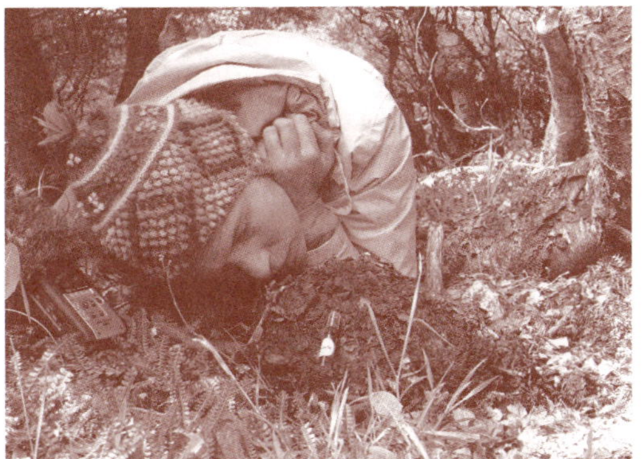

Camila Marambio field testing *Dear Enemy* scents at beaver site in Tierra del Fuego, 2016. Photograph by Christy Gast. Image courtesy Carla Macchiavello.

of visuality and awareness, beyond the naked eye, beyond the human, and beyond one way of knowing. Much discussion concerning aesthetics and ethics, aesthetics and ecology, today dwells on sensing, sensation, embodied ways of seeing, perceiving beyond what we can see with our eyes, attending to the invisible and nonhuman, and sharing sensations across species so as to see beyond capitalist thinking, colonial divisions, and normalised forms of violence.

In Ensayos—a collective research program that joins artists, scientists, activists, policymakers, local agents, and their inquiries—different points of view are rehearsed and experimented with. Some of these connections have been attempts at so-called interspecies communication.[8] Oftentimes these have involved playacting, performing as other—a very serious practice, though.[9] I was involved in a theatrical experiment in Paris where each participant interpreted an agent in Tierra del Fuego, including beaver, lenga trees, sheep estancia owners/workers, sun, water, moss, a hunter (which I interpreted), among others.

Other examples have included (to mention a few): scientists and participants wearing beaver suits (including beaver heads) while performing their everyday activities; filming across surfaces, such as water and mud; listening sessions of Arctic glaciers crackling and wind recordings in Tierra del Fuego; listening to whales and seafaring people sing; developing a coastal curriculum; call and response practices with the sea,

8   Haraway, *Staying with the Trouble*.

9   See for example, *Fortunes of the Forest: Divination, Dance, and Story* (2020): "A livestreamed, participatory performance incorporating plant knowledge through ritual, movement and conversation." https://ensayostierradelfuego.net/field-notes/fortunes-of-the-forest-divination-dance-story/.

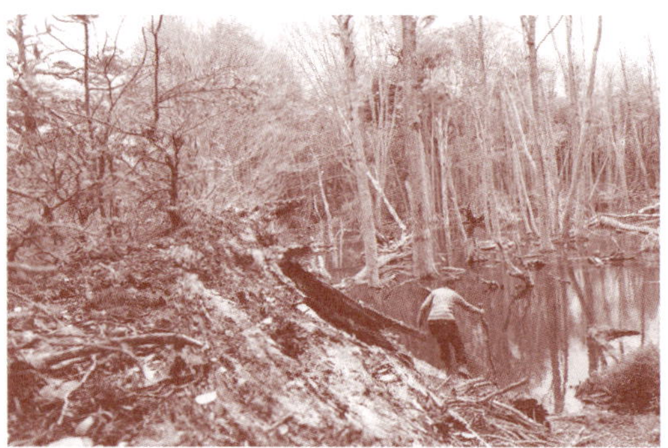

Christy Gast collecting field recording in Tierra del Fuego, 2016. Photograph by Camila Marambio. Image courtesy Carla Macchiavello.

forests, and land; and scientific experiments based on olfaction, like *Dear Enemy* (2015), an exercise in communication in Tierra del Fuego through scent mounds.[10]

I worry, though, that these performative attempts are not enough, in the sense that they might repeat the colonial gestures/disposition, reinscribing under other forms of hierarchical thinking or human exceptionalism. But then I am reminded that mimesis—to imitate and become like the other—can be a life and death thing, a strategy of survival found in different species. And while I might not experience the world as a plant or animal or rock, or know it fully, I might still approach its sensible experience, and that an exercise not only rehearses, it also creates.

How do you approach some of these issues in your own work and practice? We could start with Fernando, then Jennifer, Dylan, and Walter.

FERNANDO do CAMPO (FdC) Thanks Carla. Much of what you've brought up I think of constantly in relation to "seeing" house sparrows. I've been a birdwatcher for some years, and this requires a particular way of seeing. A few years ago I was living in New York City, and I realised that I had an affinity to this species, and that this affinity was quite complicated.

CM   What kind of affinity?

FdC   The presence of the house sparrow in Brooklyn made me feel at home, because I had encountered

10   Ensayos, *Dear Enemy* (2015), https://ensayostierradelfuego.net/programs/dear-enemy/.

them in all the places I had lived: Buenos Aires, Tasmania, Sydney, New York. As a species that wasn't indigenous to these lands, its colonial agency made me feel as if we were bedfellow colonisers, and that was complicated. Interestingly, this affinity—this sensing of the sparrow's colonial presence and affect, if you like—constitutes a form of meeting with a non-human which performs the colonial affection for this species that the old-world colonisers intended to elicit by way of introducing it.[11]

Since then, I have been making work about the history of this species and my relationship to it, often using archival documentation and fiction as a way to make the human notice the presence of other species within urban spaces, and the colonial agency they carry. A recent work, *The Archive of We* (2020), made during the editing phase of these dialogues, presents a series of correspondence between modernist painter Barnett Newman and a group of house sparrows in the 1960s, presented as a series of slides and letters.

CM   How do the birds speak in your work?

FdC   In this work, the birds write to Newman to ask about his zip paintings (e.g., *Onement I*, 1948) and whether or not these could signify pictorial spaces to be entered by non-human species. Newman is excited at first to think through his zip paintings as landscapes, but becomes quite defensive of the potential for an entity to be present therein. The sparrows tease Newman back, alluding to their own species history, alongside that of nineteenth-

11   For a brief history of the introduction of the sparrow in Australia, see "House Sparrow," Australian Museum, accessed March 1, 2022, https://australian.museum/learn/animals/birds/house-sparrow/.

century colonialisation, and the endless landscapes in which they go unnoticed.

CM   Yes, but how did you let the animal speak?

FdC   Actually, I share the worry implied in your question: My gestures do repeat a somewhat colonial gesture by speaking for/with the sparrows through verbal forms of language. But I do also think that in these moments something new is being created, and the non-human is part of that in a new way. I've also been developing a lot of new work based on listening. This is mainly based on my practice as a birdwatcher entering my art practice more directly, and in these works I speak with different species through non-verbal forms of communication. For example, with a body of work I'm developing on the laughing kookaburra, I've been thinking about laughter, whereby a narrative form is not necessary, but rather allows for a corporeal and sonic way for humans and non-humans to encounter each other and to perhaps co-create.[12]

CM   I am interested in this—practices that locate ways to listen in other ways.

FdC   That is forever changing. In many ways, the human flaw is to assume the permission to speak for/with, but at the same time I find it so important

12   Fernando do Campo, *The colours of federation (WHOSLAUGHINGJACKASS)* (2017), "NSW Visual Arts Emerging Fellowship 2017," Artspace, Sydney, November 8–December 9, 2017, https://www.artspace.org.au/program/exhibitions/2017/2017-nsw-visual-arts-emerging-fellowship/; Fernando do Campo, *The Jackass laughed all the way to Kolkatta* (2018), "The 1818 Project," Newcastle Art Gallery, NSW, September 8–November 4, 2018, http://nag.org.au/Exhibitions/Current/Archives/2018/THE-1818-PROJECT; Fernando do Campo, *The Kookaburra Self-Relocation Project (WHOSLAUGHINGJACKASS)* (2020), MONA FOMA, Launceston, Tasmania, January 17–19, 2020, https://contemporaryarttasmania.org/programs/the-kookaburra-self-relocation-project-whoslaughingjackass/.

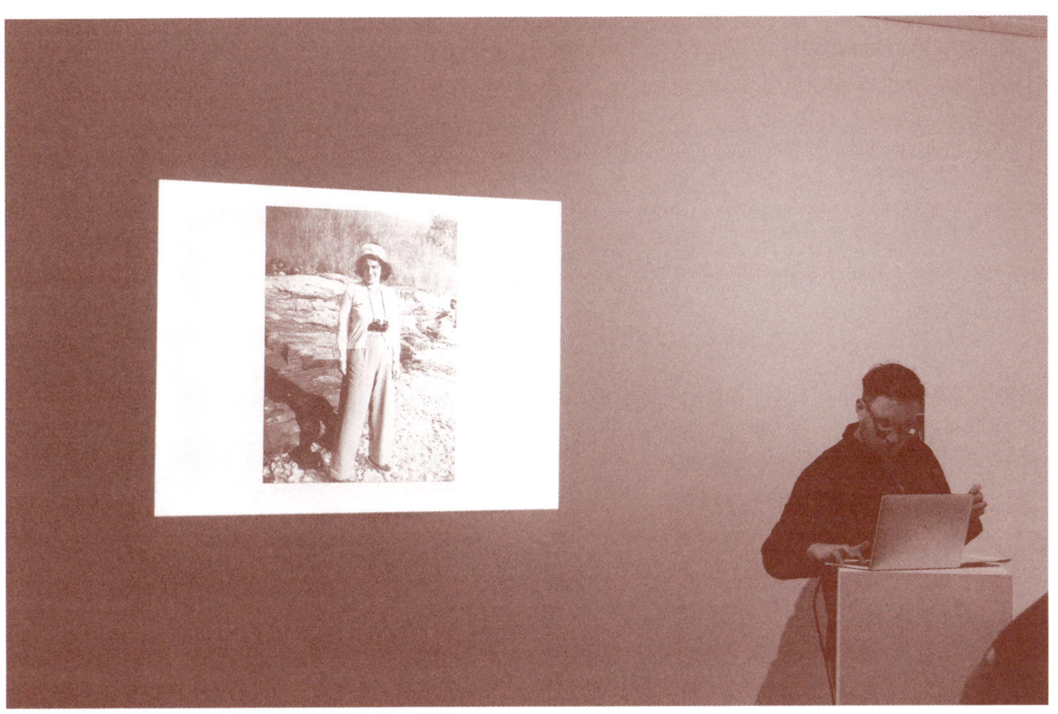

Fernando do Campo, *The Archive of We*, 2021. Performance lecture, UNSW Galleries, Sydney/Gadigal land. Working as an amateur volunteer historian for the entity HSSH (House Sparrow Society for Humans), Fernando do Campo shares a box of slides and correspondence from the 1950s between the HSSH and the Abstract Expressionist American painter Barnett Newman. Image courtesy the artist.

to continuously attempt to locate ways to firstly listen and then somehow respond anew; to meet halfway at least.

CM Jennifer?

JENNIFER BIDDLE (JB) Greetings to you all. Like you, Carla, I am also uncomfortable with the term "species," though for differing reasons maybe. I have the privilege to work with societies/ life worlds as a long-term collaborator and anthropologist with First Nations Warlpiri (and other First Nations artists and communities) in the Central and Western Desert. Here, human/non-human distinctions are not bordered or bounded in such ocular or univocal ways, and the capacities of so-called interspecies communication are on the one hand everyday and normal, but on the other not available in the same ways to anybody or everyone—they are instead highly restricted, hierarchical, and regulated, both internally and externally. Highly differentiated capacities to hear, to know (in sensory-perceptual terms, or what you, Carla, call "thinking-feeling"), and differentiated responsibilities to hold and to share (or not) such understandings and knowledges make for a very different kind of communicative economy than the terms and expectations of Western colonial sign systems and their meanings—such as, for example, the code of English literacy and its purportedly neutral and universalising *logos*, the alphabet. In contrast, there are critical capacities and restrictions in First Nations contexts that tie response to responsibility, to put it crudely, and make for inalienable relationships between mark and sign, Ancestor and human—what Tuscarora artist and curator Jolene Rickard means, I think, by her concept of "visual sovereignty."[13] This is why it

13 Jolene Rickard, "Sovereignty: A Line in the Sand," *Aperture* 139 (1995).

matters that and First Nations people are authors artists and writers of histories and knowledges on their own terms, because it ensures against the forms of extractivisms that would breach—and have breached, historically—such primacies of relationality.

DYLAN A. T. MINER (DM) In this moment I am thinking about Anishinaabemowin, the language of the territory I live, and which I am a learner of. In Anishinaabemowin, species are not divided in the same way as in Western systems, and neither are they gendered—we categorise species as animate and inanimate. There is a well-known story about some rocks being animate and others not. To know whether one rock is animate, you must have an intimate relationship with place. Otherwise, you do not have the knowledge to determine if rocks, for instance, are animate.[14]

One more comment on animacy/inanimacy. For a number of years, I have been engaged in a project collaborating with medicinal plants.[15] In Anishinaabemowin, the term for medicine is *mshkiki*, which in English is something like "strength of the earth." There is always a reciprocity with the non-human in ways that are intimately linked to ecological and ontological systems.

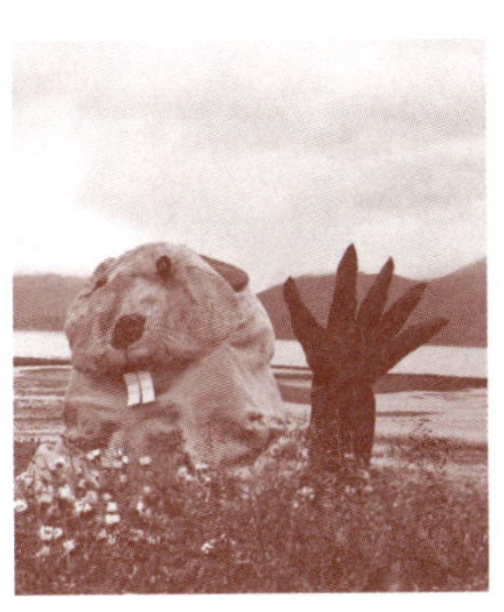

Beagle Channel.
Photograph: Christy Gast.
Image courtesy Carla
Macchiavello.

14   "What is considered animate or living does not directly correspond with Western categories. While most rocks are animate, some are not. If something is made of stone and is living, one would say *asiniiwi*. Inversely, if it is inanimate, then the word *asiniiwan* needs to be used. To understand all of this, a complex and intimate knowledge is needed. Accordingly, one needs a profound knowledge of the natural world to be able to extrapolate if and when an object is *aawi* (animate) or *aawan* (inanimate). As artists, we may make an *aawi* or an *aawan*. As we work with community partners to build and make things, we should know whether or not they are animate." Dylan A. T. Miner, "Mawadisidiwag Miinawaa Wiidanokiindiwag // They Visit and Work Together," in *Makers, Crafters, Educators: Working for Cultural Change*, ed. Elizabeth Garber, Lisa Hochtritt, and Manisha Sharma (London: Routledge, 2018).

15   See, for example, Dylan Miner, "Michif–Michin (the people, the medicine)," August 5–28, 2016, Gallery Gachet Vancouver, http://gachet.org/2016/08/02/michif-michin-the-people-the-medicine/.

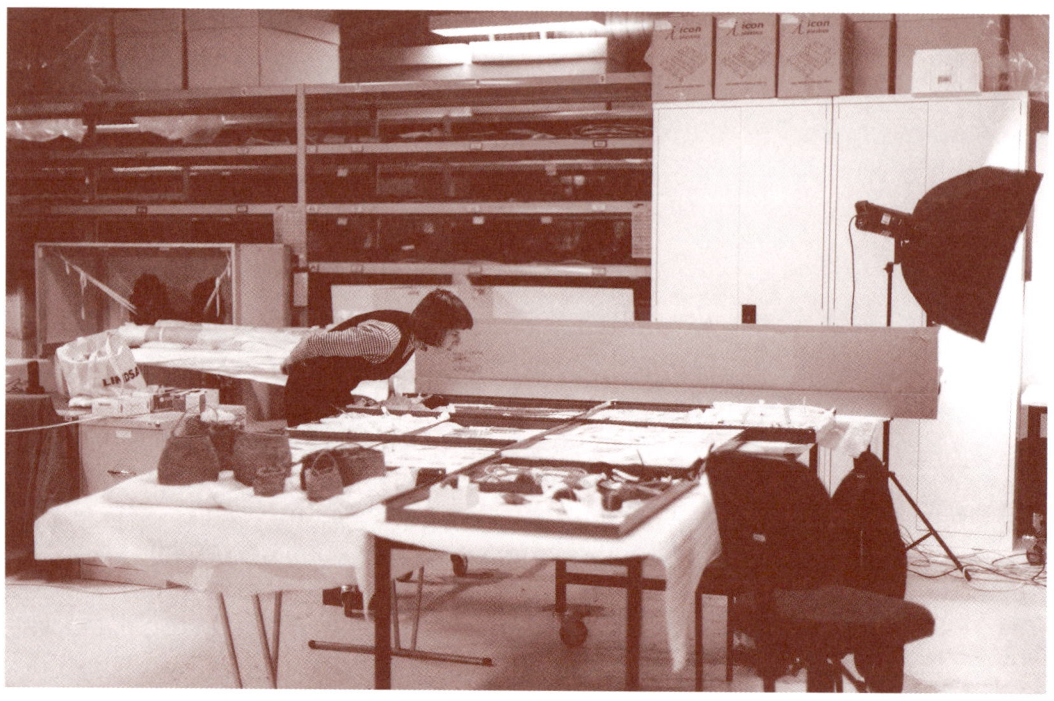

Camila Marambio reviewing and photographing Yaghan collection in Melbourne Museum, Australia, to take inventory back to Yaghan community in Isla Navarino, Tierra del Fuego, for possible repatriation, 2018. Photograph by Jacqui Shelton. Image courtesy Carla Macchiavello.

JB That is indeed the kinds of differentiations of the so-called human to the geos, to other species, I was trying to refer to above: relationships to place/species are tied to capacities to hear and sense and be responsible for—not a universal literacy or a neutral code, nor one that can be learned by anyone or everyone as the "modern" democratic idealised Western sign system and "human" mode of communication or aesthetics suggests.[16]

CM Walter, would you like to join us?

WALTER D. MIGNOLO (WM) Yes indeed, very interesting conversation. To start with, nature is a Western concept, so I prefer to avoid it and talk to Land, in the way Indigenous peoples—from the Mapuche to the Anishinaabe—talk to Land and Earth. Non-Indigenous people (including myself) do not have the same relationship to Land, but every living organism comes from and returns to the Earth during a life cycle...

DM Just yesterday, in a course I am teaching on art and ecology in the Great Lakes watershed, we had this very conversation about Land as understood in Indigenous epistemologies. Our conversations echoed the recent writings of Anishinaabekwe scholar and poet Leanne Betasamosake Simpson, particularly her notion of Land as pedagogy. For Simpson, Land is reclaimed through pedagogy; that is, the process of telling Nishnaabeg stories cultivates Nishnaabeg intelligence, culture, and nation-building across generations.[17]

WM Simpson's concept of Land as pedagogy reveals a major fallacy of Western epistemology: the primacy of

---

16   See Jennifer Loureide Biddle, *Remote Avant-Garde: Aboriginal Art under Occupation* (Durham: Duke University Press, 2016), especially part 1, "Biliteracies."

17   Leanne Betasamosake Simpson, "Land as Pedagogy: Nishnaabeg Intelligence and Rebellious Transformation," *Decolonization: Indigeneity, Education & Society* 3, no. 3 (2014).

vision, or "seeing," over all the other senses, including listening (in all kinds of ways). Perhaps in discussing the importance of listening or of Land as pedagogy we are also discussing our struggle to delink from Western epistemology and aesthetics (broadly, sense perception). One way to delink is through "decolonial aesthesis," an embodied consciousness that registers "the wound of coloniality hidden under the rhetoric of modernity, the rhetoric of salvation."[18] As I've said elsewhere, with my collaborator Rolando Vázquez:

> Decoloniality is at once the unveiling of the wound and the possibility of healing. It makes the wound visible, tangible; it voices the scream. And at the same time decolonial aestheSis moves towards the healing, the recognition, the dignity of those aesthetic practices [and ways of knowing] that have been written out of the canon of modern aestheTics.[19]

CM   I'm glad you brought up this term, Walter, for even though "aesthesis" may have been colonised it is, after all, still able to hold the idea that perception occurs through all our senses. As your concept of decolonial aestheSis suggests, an expanded form of sensory perception can not only reveal the wounds of colonialism but heal them.

JB   I'm thinking here of Cheryl L'Hirondelle and her articulation of *nêhiyawin* (Cree worldview), which is made manifest in her work through the use of language, narrative, song, the sound of the drum, VR, immersive new media, and other forms of embodied

---

18   Walter Mignolo and Rolando Vazquez, "Decolonial AestheSis: Colonial Wounds/ Decolonial Healings," *Social Text Online*, July 15, 2013, https://socialtextjournal.org/ periscope_article/decolonial-aesthesis- colonial-woundsdecolonial-healings.

19   Ibid.

and performative practice.[20] What is vital in her work as I experience it is a palpable sentient imperative; it gleans and glimpses something of the dynamics of the complexity of *nêhiyawin*.

It seems to me that it is these kinds of capacities to know and experience the world in Indigenous-specific terms (of the kind Dylan and Walter are referring to) that are under occupation. Such capacities are precisely what get abnegated, denied, ignored, and refused in the move to make bodies and experiences compliant, colonised, and normative bodily experiences.

WM The issue here for me is the following: There is a kind of living organism (species) that can name itself as species and classify other species. Among these kinds of animals—species that engage in languaging and classification—there are many different cosmologies. Western cosmology dominates. First Nations peoples around the world know and sense according to their cosmologies, and all of us who have been educated in Western cosmology sense and think accordingly. Now we non-Indigenous people are realising that we've been trapped and, as Jennifer says, schooled to devalue all other cosmologies.

CM What kind of agency or place do you see art as having in this discussion? This is a general question for all.

WM The problem is art, the concept of art. I have been writing and teaching and talking about the need to decolonise aesthetics to liberate aestheSis, including from art. For me the question is what

---

20   Cheryl L'Hirondelle, "Codetalkers Recounting Signals of Survival," in *Coded Territories: Tracing Indigenous Pathways in New Media Art*, ed. Steven Loft and Kerry Swanson (Calgary: University of Calgary Press, 2014); and "Cheryl L'Hirondelle," Artists Corner, accessed June 11, 2021, www.cheryllhirondelle.com/about.

do we want, first; and second, how can we work toward these goals through what is named "art"?

DM   I wonder if, following Leanne—who is following her teachers, who are following ancestral knowledge, who articulate Land as pedagogy—I wonder if we can think, similarly, of art as pedagogy. I am still interested in art. I am quite interested in the ways that contemporary Indigenous artists have used global infrastructures to connect in horizontal ways Indigenous to Indigenous, at times using settler-institutions or creating Indigenous-led ones.[21]

CM   A strategic form of using art?

JB   Yes, really important. Strategic ways of keeping alive at-risk languages—as well as ways of knowing and doing, being and sensing otherwise—in more horizontal intra-Aboriginal assemblages or "virtual reservations" in Michelle Raheja's terms.[22] For example, we could look at the globalising networking by First Nations artists and community members actively taking shape in Jason Edward Lewis's *Aboriginal Territories in Cyberspace* or Julie Nagam's *The Space Between Us*.[23]

DM   Yes, Jennifer, exactly. And Carla, such projects represent a strategic form of using art. I think of art as a shapeshifter similar to *Nanaboozhoo* that can be many things. (In NYC art is a capitalist monster, but it doesn't need to be. Think of Indigenous artists

---

21   Beyond those led by Jason Edward Lewis and Julie Nagam, mentioned by Jennifer Biddle in this dialogue, also see Brook Andrew, *NIRIN*, Biennale of Sydney 2020, Sydney, March 14–November 15, 2020, accessed February 27, 2022, https://www.biennaleofsydney.art/biennale/22nd-biennale-of-sydney-2020/; Katya García-Antón, ed., *Sovereign Words: Indigenous Art, Curation and Criticism* (Oslo: Valiz/Office for Contemporary Art Norway, 2019).

22   Michelle Raheja, "Visual Prophecies: Imprint and It Starts with a Whisper," in *Visualities: Perspectives on Contemporary American Indian Film and Art*, ed. Denise K. Cummings (East Lansing, Michigan: Michigan State University Press, 2011).

23   *Aboriginal Territories in Cyberspace*, https://abtec.org; *Space Between Us*, www.thespacebetweenus.ca.it Press, 2011).

working against mineral extraction during the DAPL/Standing Rock protests).

FdC I like the notion of art as a shapeshifter, because it is shifting and we want it to keep shifting, i.e., looking for meeting points and a language that can begin to speak across these definitions, forms of listening, non-verbal ways of co-creating across species, shapeshifting together.

CM "Art" itself refers to something else, just a skill, so it can certainly continue to shift.

WM Exactly, Carla. Skill, like *poiesis*, means making; what skill we have to make what, and why.[24]
And again, the question is: What do we want? And what means do we have at hand to achieve the goals we propose to ourselves?

CM Connecting, listening, and feeling, in multiple directions, might be part of what "we" (as you say) want.

FdC Art is a meeting point, and art practice is the wanting to find that meeting point; the seeking and dwelling in that meeting point is artmaking.

WM Listening for sure, and multiple directions; but again, what do we want to do? What are our goals?

DM I have been working from a position learned from Indigenous Elders, employing a "methodology of visiting."

WM If you are an Indigenous person, you know what you want: to get rid of settlers being all over you and recover the land, which is life, spirituality, energy.

24   Mignolo and Vazquez, "Decolonial AestheSis."

We non-Indigenous, what do we want? And what can art do once we know what we want?

DM As Eve Tuck and K. Wayne Yang argue, "Decolonization is not a metaphor."[25]

WM Of course not, it never was a metaphor. Think about the Cold War; do you think Lumumba and Biko and Cabral were poets writing metaphors?

CM Can one generalise though, Walter, as to non-Indigenous needs, and intra-relations? However, recognising we are visitors—all of us non-Indigenous, migrants. Recognising the precarious state that we as visitors are in, might be a path.

WM I go with that. I dwell in the border; migrant consciousness.

DM Often times, a meeting place is *agamiing*, which means "at the lake shore." This is an important vantage point to see the point of colonial meeting, and subsequent violence.

CM A meeting place, a shore, a place where bodies touch, meet, and transform too; a space that invokes movement, horizontality as much as there are still layers, shifting borders. But also, as you mention Dylan, a place that is a reminder of settler-colonial violence, past and present. Or, as Jennifer recalls, of a continued push to conform to some idea of a normative bodily experience. A meeting place where the question of capacities to hear emerges, what remains unknowable and inaccessible to some, and the responsibility embedded in response. A reminder of being visitors, migrants, perhaps also unmooring

25 Eve Tuck and K. Wayne Yang,
    "Decolonization is Not a Metaphor."

notions of what being rooted means. I am sorry we have to end the conversation for the time being, but perhaps this is also just a beginning, a first meeting place. Thank you all.

Global Art

GLOBAL ART: STEPPING NIMBLY WITH STRATEGIC SOUTHERNNESS
Ruth Simbao

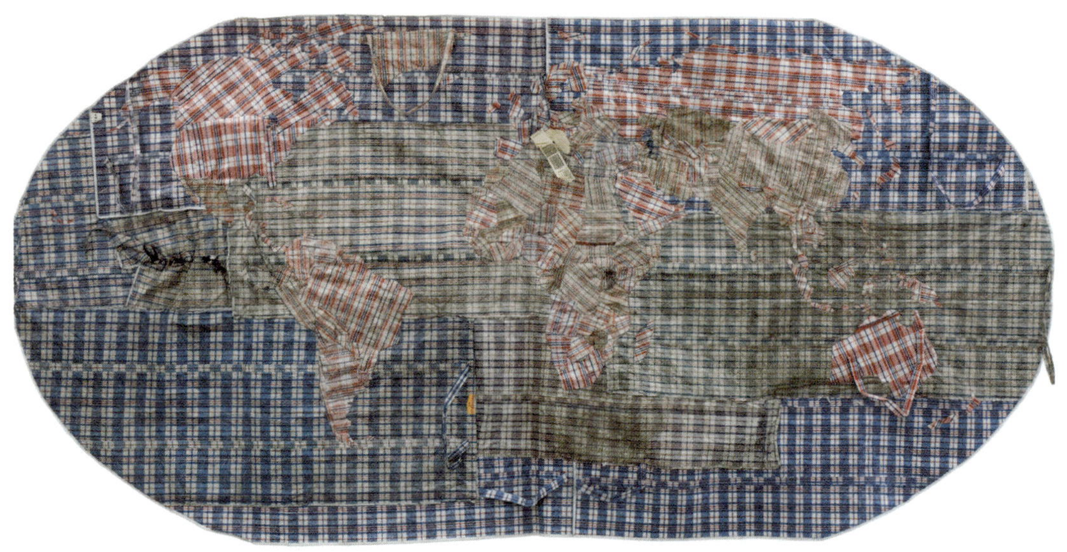

Dan Halter, *Rifugiato Mappa Del Mondo (Refugee Map of The World)*, 2011, constructed out of new and used plastic-weave bags, 83 x 380 centimetres. Map of the world loosely based on infographics showing areas according to immigration and emigration statistics. Areas and routes with increased emigration are more worn than the destination countries. Image courtesy Dan Halter and WHATIFTHEWORLD.

Speaking from South Africa, I don't think there is such a thing as "global art," at least not in the sense of a coherent, agreed-upon phenomenon. Nonetheless, as a scholar, I am intrigued by the discourse that this label has generated in recent years, especially as I attempt to understand what underlies the impetus to talk about art that is deemed global.[1] Within this discourse, there is a general consensus—at least on a theoretical level—that the terms "global art," "global north," and "global south" are inevitably unstable and, to certain degrees, delinked from physical geographies (as Verónica says in the introduction to this book). In my own work, I view the souths as a loose conceptual framework that links to "situational geographies of exclusion and geographies of resistance based on shared histories of colonialism and ongoing processes of decolonization."[2] As a concept, souths (and "norths," for that matter) are simultaneously "contingent, constitutive and process-based."[3] Beyond theory, however, southern experiences are often deeply embedded (as Zoe Butt emphasises in chapter 3), and it is not, I submit, yet viable to drop the language of "souths" and "norths," especially while most art-related and other privileges remain in the norths.[4] What is viable, and indeed *necessary*, is an interrogation of the often incongruous relationship between privilege and constructions of value, and an unsettling of the norths' self-assumed ownership of the framing of global art.[5]

1   See, for example, James Elkins, *Is Art History Global?* (New York: Routledge, 2006); Peter Weibel and Andrea Buddensieg, eds., *Contemporary Art and the Museum: A Global Perspective* (Berlin: Hatje Cantz, 2007); Hans Belting, "From World Art to Global Art: View on a New Panorama," in *The Global Contemporary and the Rise of New Art Worlds*, ed. Hans Belting, Andrea Buddensieg, and Peter Weibel (Cambridge, Massachusetts: MIT Press and the Centre for Art and Media Karlsruhe, 2013); and Peter Weibel, ed., *Global Activism: Art and Conflict in the 21st Century* (Cambridge, Massachusetts: MIT Press, 2015).

2   Ruth Simbao, "Situating Africa: An Alter-Geopolitics of Knowledge, or Chapungu Rises," *African Arts* 50, no. 2 (2017): 1–9.

3   Simbao, "Situating Africa," 1.

4   Ruth Simbao, "What 'Global Art' and Current (Re)turns Fail to See: A Modest Counter-narrative of 'Not-Another-biennial'," *Image & Text* 25 (2015).

5   "'Global art' is a term developed by Hans Belting and Peter Weibel in 2006 for the research programme 'Global art and the Museum' at the Center for Art and Media Karlsruhe, Germany. This was followed by the exhibition 'The Global Contemporary: Art Worlds after 1989' (2012), curated by Andrea Buddensieg and Peter Weibel, as well as the 2013 publication, *The Global Contemporary and the Rise of New Art Worlds*, edited by Belting, Buddensieg and Weibel." Simbao, "'Global Art' and Current (Re)turns," 262.

Considering the northern-dominated generation of "global art" as an art historical term, a number of questions come to the fore. Do the norths simply assume ownership of global change, blindly failing to address the *aftermath* (or *continuance*, depending on one's perspective) of imperial and colonial dominance? Does anxiety about potential irrelevance or loss of power lead the norths to embrace "the global" as a form of cultural revitalisation? If curators, writers, and artists in the norths genuinely seek to collaborate globally, and with the souths, how can this be done to purposefully unsettle accepted frameworks and generate multidirectional epistemologies of reciprocity?

While the global souths are not a physically stable place, living in South Africa and working in other parts of Africa, I am convinced of the need for what I call "strategic southernness."[6] Strategies are seldom permanent, as they aim to address or challenge that which needs to change at a particular time, and agility—the ability to think perceptively, to see what others fail to see, and to step nimbly—is key. As such, the strategies we might employ today or the commonalities we might draw on will be, indeed *should* be, different to our strategies or commonalities of the future, hence the need for ways of thinking, ways of dialoguing, and ways of being that *never* settle.

What I would like to think through in this dialogue with others is what strategies can be employed in our engagement with what is labelled global art. While we might have differing perceptions and/or experiences of global art, are there commonalities within and across

---

6   In my work as a research chair in geopolitics and the arts of Africa, I emphasise the need to work alongside and collaborate with scholars based on the African continent in order to challenge the current situation of northern "consumption" and dominance in terms of the production of internationally recognised knowledge about African art. Rather than talking about "African art" we refer to the "arts of Africa," as a way of acknowledging the complexities and multiplicities of art across the continent. While our art and our socio-political and cultural contexts in which we create knowledge are far from uniform, there is value in strategically working together in order to create the solidarity and momentum needed to raise the voice of Africa-based scholars on international platforms. Our collaborative work has included intra-African publishing workshops, residencies for writers and artists, and co-authorship.

current and future encounters with "southernness" that can lead to fundamental shifts in the problematic logic of addition or accumulation that seems to underpin northern formulations of global art?

In my essay, "What 'Global Art' and Current (Re)turns Fail to See: A Modest Counter-narrative of 'Not-another-biennial'" (2015), I argue that Hans Belting's framing of global art in the book *The Global Contemporary and the Rise of New Art Worlds* celebrates the rise of so-called new art worlds with a logic of addition, implying that "they" have joined "our" core; "they" have risen to "our" standards and "our" understanding of good art.[7]

A logic of addition merely celebrates what has been added to the already-settled core without significant destabilisation of the core itself—the way things are done, the way art is viewed, the way art is valued, and the very defining framework of what art is. On the other hand, a logic of unsettling and of radical unlearning destabilises the normative core, and actively seeks what people fail to see. It takes as its premise the fact that certain ways of doing things need to be undone, many ways of valuing art need to be unlearned, and even the notion of what art is needs to be rethought. While a logic of addition often boils down to tokenistic inclusion under the guise of global art (or a slightly softened notion of a "global contemporary"), if there is, indeed, a desire for art to have some kind of *reach* across the globe, it should not comprise one paternalistic reach that starts from one given point, but it should be a series of "sideways reaches" that are initiated from multiple modalities across the globe.[8]

In thinking through potential strategies that people who self-identify with southernness might employ, I propose exploring different economies of *scale*, *weight*, *direction*, *value*, *orientation*, and *success* in the formation

---

7 Belting, "From World Art to Global Art."

8 My concept of "reaching sideways" refers to the importance of creating knowledge with people in non-individualistic ways, and looks to the works of southern authors rather than gazing upwards to the dominant theories of the north. See Ruth Simbao et al., "Reaching Sideways, Writing *Our* Ways: The Orientation of the Arts of Africa Discourse," *African Arts* 50, no. 2 (2017).

of counter-narratives about art and about the still quite singular art world.[9] As an author, I think that writing is a powerful tool that can be employed to engage with the discourse of global art as it has recently been presented to the world.[10] Activist strategies of writing can create "otherwise modes" that either choose to deliberately ignore the discourse, thus to some degree rendering it irrelevant; to directly challenge and "unwrite" the construct of global art; or to create variations and intersections that both destabilise the core and focus on existing knowledges that fall beyond the narrow framework of global art. Of course, these approaches might overlap and/or alternate at times.

As writers and curators, it is important for us to question who tells the story of global art and in whose books we read these stories. Who writes about a need to rewrite art history, and then who actually rewrites it?[11] Who publishes it, and who positions it in the market? In terms of economies of scale, weight, direction, value, orientation, and success, what do we choose to write about, and why? How often do we choose to write about failure, not as a competitive attack on others but as a way of challenging epistemic normativity and of learning from our own mistakes—a form of unmaking, unlearning, and unbecoming?

Further, do we assume that what we do not see is simply not there,[12] or do we recognise what exists beyond our blinkers—beyond dominant art platforms and beyond the timeframe of dominant narratives of what some call

---

9   Importantly, "southernness" is a concept, experience, and strategy that one chooses as a form of self-identification and is not something that can be imposed onto another person.

10   See Sarah Dornhof et al., eds., *Situating Global Art: Topologies, Temporalities, Trajectories* (Bielefeld: Transcript, 2018).

11   In "What 'Global Art' and Current (Re)turns Fail to See," I argue that authors steeped in the Euro-American domination of the visual arts do not actually have the right to announce the demise of the/their privileged art world and privileged art histories, thereby implying that they are "willing and perhaps key agents of this apparent change." Simbao, "'Global Art' and Current (Re)turns," 263.

12   I ask this question in response to the implication in the book, *The Global Contemporary and the Rise of New Art Worlds*, that either these art worlds beyond the dominant art world did not exist before they were recognised by the norths, or their existence didn't count before they were supposedly discovered by the norths.

the "global turn"?[13] While we are familiar with claims of multidirectional flows that supposedly break down the centres and peripheries of the art world, do we simply celebrate the addition of these global flows to what is viewed by the norths as the core, or do we interrogate these flows with honesty? Is it possible to claim that the global art world is effectively decentred when, as Dan Halter's series *Rifugiato Mappa Del Mondo* (*Refugee Map of The World*, 2011) reveals, our flows in this world are far from just? Whose feet tread more heavily than others? Why is ease of global mobility often viewed as being "light" when it is this supposedly light globe-hopping that creates burdens for many others? In contrast to an elitist "lightness" based on privileged mobility, whose feet are nimble—perceptively, flexibly, strategically, and, most importantly, *justly* so?

13   In "What 'Global Art' and Current (Re)turns Fail to See," I argue that what is framed by the norths as a "global turn" is, in some ways, a *return* (even if somewhat disguised) to the core of northern dominance. With its logic of addition, it amounts to little more than what Gerardo Mosquera refers to as "quantitative internationalization" and a "flat cosmopolitanism" (as cited in Simbao, "'Global Art' and Current (Re)turns," 264).

Dialogue
Ruth Simbao with Carla Macchiavello, Jean-Sylvain Tshilumba Mukendi, and Verónica Tello

RUTH SIMBAO (RS) Warm greetings to you all. I will begin by offering you a short statement and posing questions to specific people. I will then open up the conversation more freely.

As I proposed in my introductory text, "Stepping Nimbly with Strategic Southernness," I question whether global art exists beyond a mere tokenism that creates ideas of the global in self-gratifying ways. Although we tend not to think of it in this way, there are, perhaps, as many globals (or at least perceptions of globals) as there are locals, which I capture in my term "cosmolocalism."[14] A few years ago, I asked the author Tariq Ali how he would describe the local, and his response was, "The local is here and now, and wherever I am."[15] Perhaps the global is no different, as our situatedness, regardless of how multiple or fragmented this might be, is always a lens through which we read, understand, and project the global and, by extension, various conceptualisations of global art.[16]

All of us collaborating here today have, at some point, expressed our recognition that there are multiple and often fragmented *southernnesses* rather than a clearly defined commonality formulated as "the south," and yet we willingly press forward in our dialogues with each other, seeking some form of resonance. We recognise, it seems, a need for what I call

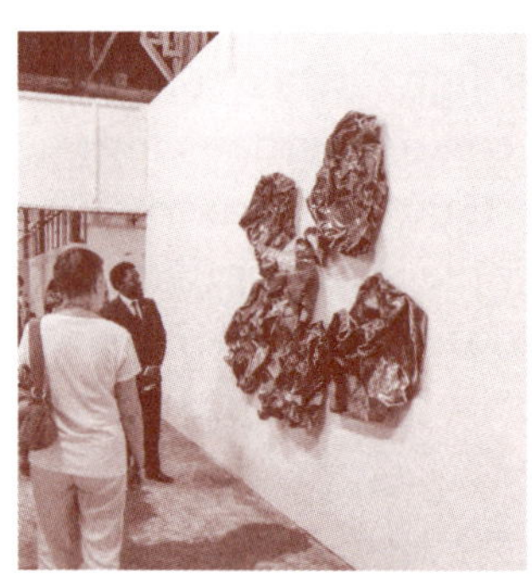

Young Congo Exhibition 2017 at the Kin ArtStudio in Kinshasa—Visitors in front of Fransix Tenda's *Libanda (La Lutte)*, 2017. Copyright Ephraïm Baku. Image courtesy Jean-Sylvain Tshilumba Mukendi.

14   See Ruth Simbao, "Cosmolocal Orientations: Trickster Spatialization and the Politics of Cultural Bargaining in Zambia," *Critical Interventions: Journal of African Art History and Visual Culture* 12, no. 3 (2018), https://doi.org/10.1080/19301944.2018.1532379.

15   Personal conversation with Tariq Ali, Makhanda (then known as Grahamstown), South Africa, April 2011.

16   Ruth Simbao unpacks situational ways of being (and being in place) in the 2016 article, "Infecting the City: Site-Situational Performance and Ambulatory Hermeneutics," *Third Text* 30, no. 102 (2016), https://doi.org/10.1080/09528822.2016.1266776.

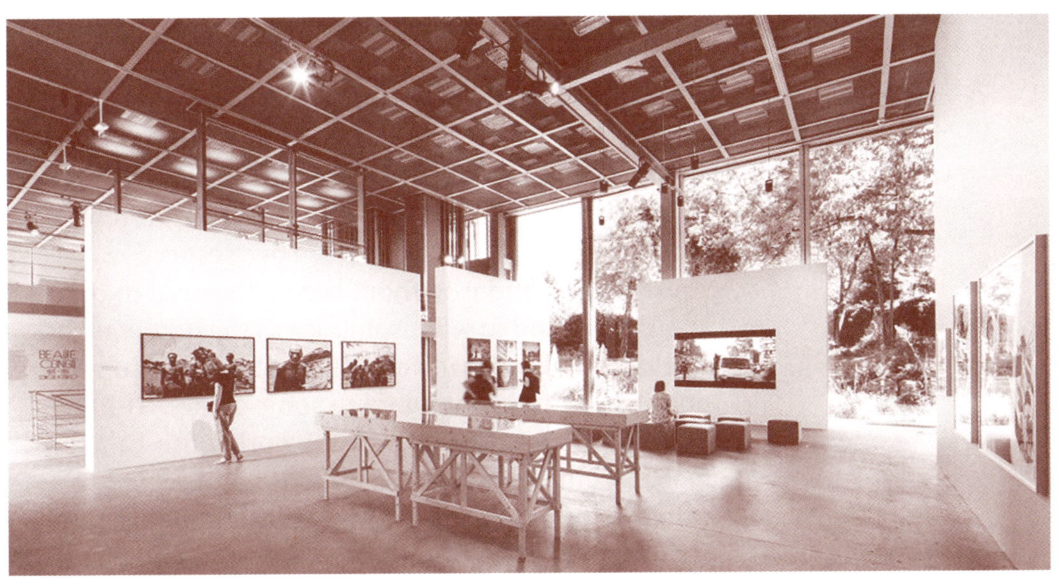

View of the exhibition *Beauté Congo 1926–2015 Congo Kitoko*. Fondation Cartier pour l'art contemporain, Paris, 2015. Photograph: Luc Boegly. Image courtesy Jean-Sylvain Tshilumba Mukendi.

"strategic southernness," a conscious form of self-identifying in a particular way at a particular moment in order to *do* something and *change* something—an activist urge, perhaps.

I think for most of us there are at least two strands to our doing: 1) We simply *do* southernness—that is, we simply practice within our respective southern situations without seeing the need to constantly respond to what some see as the dominant art world, and as such we delegitimate its self-assumed dominance; and 2) we work to some degree with and at times within this broader world of so-called global art in our day-to-day practice, and yet we do things in other ways. That is, we create slippages and lacunae in which we do things differently (whether the differences be large or small); we nudge, we push (sometimes subtly, other times explicitly) as we unmake the systems within which we operate; we unsettle the people driving these systems, and we continue to unlearn ourselves.

What I'd like to do in this dialogue is explore the small, modest strategies that we generate daily as we operate within our respective places in the world. By "places" I refer not to static, closed ideas of place but rather to the recognition of place as dynamic happenings always in relationship. In what ways do we or might we develop, explore and revel in alternative economies of scale, weight, direction, value, orientation, or success? If the simplistic stories of global art and the global south fail, then how do we embrace this failure in a way that enables us to meaningfully reorient these stories and lead them, or perhaps coax them, down different paths?

Verónica, I begin by posing a fairly broad question to you as the project initiator. When you conceived of *Future Souths*, how did you imagine it differing to the typical discourse of global art? If certain discourses of global art tend to emphasise and give credence to a limited number of voices, to value only what they see and *want* to see, to move predominantly in certain directions despite talk of multidirectional flows, to ignore what they deem as inconsequential, to orientate the discourse around themselves, and to drum up success stories to uphold their myths, then how can we enact southern doing in the art world in a way that not only tells different stories but *enables* them too?

VERÓNICA TELLO (VT) That's a great question, Ruth. I'm not sure if I conceived it as being necessarily or intentionally distinct from global art discourse. While I agree with your criticism of global art discourse, I also need to acknowledge that I have benefited from it. Because this discourse—and its claims of having an interest in the souths—has come from the norths (Weibel, Beltin, Elkins), it has with great effect and in a short amount of time entered the academy and legitimised areas of study that were historically not just marginal but also unfundable and unteachable.[17] I wonder in fact if the funding I received for *Future Souths* was somehow indirectly influenced by global art's legitimacy in the academy.[18] Further, my job prospects increased with the institutionalisation of global art: I feel like at some point around 2015 universities in the norths, especially in the US and the United Kingdom, decided they needed to appoint lecturers or assistant professors of global art in an attempt to diversify their curriculum and faculty.[19] Interestingly, advertisements for global art positions often targeted academics from

17   Mignolo and Vazquez, "Decolonial AestheSis."

18   Verónica Tello further comments: For example, at the very moment I was searching for academic positions, there was an interest in diversity recruitment and diversifying curriculum, which had not been as prevalent prior to 2010, and became much more emphasised around 2015–2018. Now, writing this footnote in 2022, it is less common to see advertisements recruiting for global art history positions; whether that's a critique of the limitations of the term "global art," as discussed here, or that different terms are being mobilised in recruitment, is a matter I leave for the reader to discern.

19   For example, in 2018, Tello initiated a new course, entitled "Global Contemporary Art."

the souths, rather than the authors of global art discourse (Weibel, Belting, Elkins). The usual suspects were not what the universities were looking for when recruiting for global art jobs. I'd say that the northern proponents of global art have perhaps inadvertently manoeuvred themselves out of academic jobs, although maybe that's just wishful thinking.

Still, a key motivation for me in initiating *Future Souths* has been to unlearn the norms and standards of art history as propagated by the usual suspects and methods, e.g., writing about art with "critical distance" *à la* Kant, Hegel, Winckelmann, etc. Instead, I want to have intimacy with my subject matter and to speak from an embodied, partial position. As Walter was discussing in the "Souths" dialogue, embodied thinking and writing are vital for delinking from Western/ northern epistemologies. I want to engage with histories, art, and people that I am connected to, and to engage in ways that don't fit into how I was trained to do art history.[20]

When I began *Future Souths* I was still in the early stages of my career, and I got tired of doing art history in the usual ways, for example, writing about a celebrated or undervalued artist and then locating a place for this figure in art history or the canon, even if that meant troubling the canon; or identifying a new impulse, turn, trend, or paradigm of contemporary art practice and articulating it through theoretical frameworks and case studies. By doing either of these two things, which to my mind are the *modus operandi*

20   Verónica Tello further comments: I studied art history at a sandstone university in Melbourne/Naarm and was never encouraged to practice the discipline in any way other than how Kant, Hegel, Winckelmann, and their followers do it. For a further analysis of how to undo normative art history see Verónica Tello, "How to Appear? Writing Art History in Australia after 1973," in *Performance, Resistance and Refugees,* ed. Samid Suliman, Caroline Wake and Suzanne Little (London: Routledge, 2023), 138–154.

of my discipline, I/we keep expanding or at best troubling the canon, a canon that is persistently tied to Western genealogies and epistemologies, rather than unlearning how we do art history. I guess that's connected to how you characterise global art, Ruth, and its logic of addition; in spite of efforts to diversify contemporary art discourse, global art doesn't change the foundations or norms of the discipline, and thus reproduces its Western epistemologies (and its values, directions, etc.). With *Future Souths*, I wanted to keep a space open for failure, or to be more precise, to fail at doing art history.

If I can also offer a Marx-inflected answer to your question, Ruth: I perceive the idea of global art discourse as being interconnected with the international division of labour (after Spivak).[21] That is, who has the means of production, who is accumulating capital (social or otherwise) to narrate the story and produce the aesthetics of global art—this is what I'm interested in.

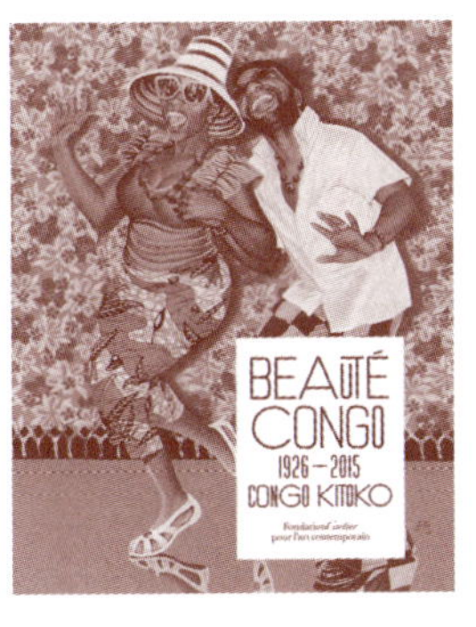

Beauté Congo—1926–2015— Congo Kitoko (Paris: Publication Foundation Cartier pour l'art contemporain, 2015).

RS   Thanks. Let's come back to this later. Jean-Sylvain, in your current work you explore the importance of the small, modest story of a group of Congolese artists taking the reins of their own presentation to the broader art world, and you contrast this to the problematic (yet more well-known) story of European curators who developed the "Beauté Congo" exhibition at the Cartier foundation in Paris.[22] We have, here, two very different stories.

The latter is plugged into the more visible global art scene (a scene that is largely constructed from the

21   Gayatri Chakravorty Spivak, "Can the Subaltern Speak?," in *Marxism and the Interpretation of Culture*, ed. Cary Nelson and Lawrence Grossberg (Basingstoke: Macmillan, 1988).

22   Jean-Sylvain Tshilumba Mukendi, "The Kinshasa-based Kin ArtStudio in the Democratic Republic of Congo: Visual Arts Spaces and the Potential to Challenge Global Art's Representative and Legitimizing Mechanisms" (Master's thesis, Rhodes University, 2019).

north) and thus seems to carry more weight. It is this weight that generates a certain blindness to other stories resulting, as such, in a certain failure. How can southern strategies generate different orientations in global art?

JEAN-SYLVAIN TSHILUMBA MUKENDI (JTM) I understand southern strategies, and more particularly the term "strategies," as efforts to locate the gaps that exist in global art discourses that tend to overlook local expressions and understandings of art creation with its global dynamics as they are happening on a local scale. In my research, that's where criticality lies, in the ability to locate those gaps and deconstruct the "main," "global" narrative.

Then, I wonder if our southernnesses are still willing to refer to such a realm as "global art." I like your proposition of orientations, or of reorientations. I believe that our efforts to refer to the global must start with an understanding of global flows (technological, migratory, economic, etc.) as they are expressed locally. And to follow up on Verónica, the reorientation also has to address ownership of discourse (or who holds the means of production).

RS Let's bring Carla in and we will come back to some of these points. Carla, I am interested in your work on networks of solidarity,[23] and would like to know more about this in relation to southern doing or strategic southernness. How, in particular, could networks of solidarity play out in the contemporary global art scene,

23 Carla Macchiavello, "A Case of Collective Resistance: Museo de la Solidaridad Salvador Allende." In *A los artistas del mundo/To the Artists of the World. Museo de la Solidaridad Salvador Allende. México/Chile* (México: Editorial RM, MUAC [Museo Universitario de Arte Contemporáneo], 2016), 70–94;

Carla Macchiavello, "Weaving Forms of Resistance: The Museo de la Solidaridad and the Museo Internacional de la Resistencia Salvador Allende," *Arts* 9, no. 1 (2020), www.mdpi.com/2076-0752/9/1/12/htm.

in which the language of global networks is shallow at best, and often quite condescending? How does contemporary solidarity relate to, or differ from, what used to be called "Third World solidarity"?[24]

CARLA MACCHIAVELLO (CM) The term you propose, "strategic southernness," reminds me of Gayatri Spivak and bell hooks' notion of "strategic essentialism" in the eighties and nineties (as a way of naming oneself to assert one's subjectivity politically and publicly).[25] I think the notion of southernness is useful now as it helps to build networks, even start dialogues—like this one. Yet, in order to avoid adopting a simplifying view of an enemy (which even solidarity networks had in the sixties and seventies, mirroring the politics of that which it rejected, thus mirroring "strong resistance"), we need to draw other types of lines, other meridians.

RS Yes, I was struck by your comments in your text for *Future Souths* on "Species(isms)," where you discuss caring about the enemy, and even "becoming" the enemy. Can you say a bit more about this?

CM In that text, I am referring to the "dear enemy theory," drawn from scientific discourse.[26] It refers to how beavers, for instance, fear less their competing (yet well-known) neighbours than new incoming strangers.

24 Ruth Simbao expands further on the notion of "Third World solidarity" and the ways that this intersects with and veers away from contemporary networks and alliances in "超越萬隆的側向接觸:当代视觉艺术中的无畏团结与偶然的「中非」剧本" ("Reaching Sideways Beyond Bandung: Audacious Solidarities and Contingent "China–Africa" Scripts in Contemporary Visual Art"), 人間思想 (*Renjian Thought Review*) 10 (2019).

25 Nasrullah Mambrol, "Strategic Essentialism," *Literary Theory and Criticism* 9 (April, 2016), accessed March 9, 2018, https://literariness.org/2016/04/09/strategic-essentialism/; bell hooks, "Essentialism and Experience," *American Literary History* 3, no. 1 (1991).

26 See Rickels, *The Devil Notebooks*.

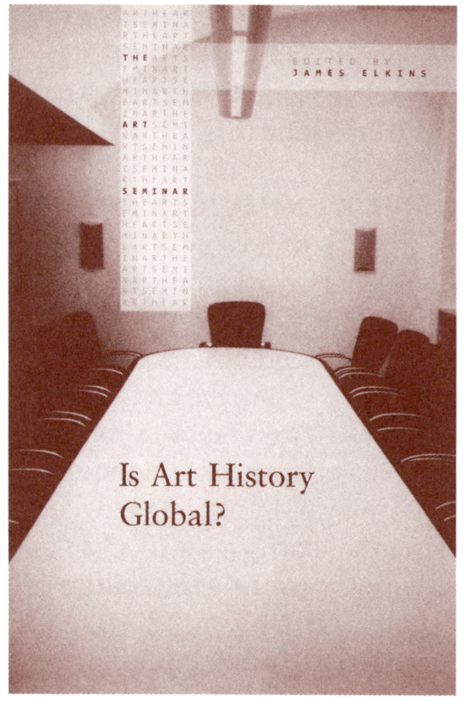

1

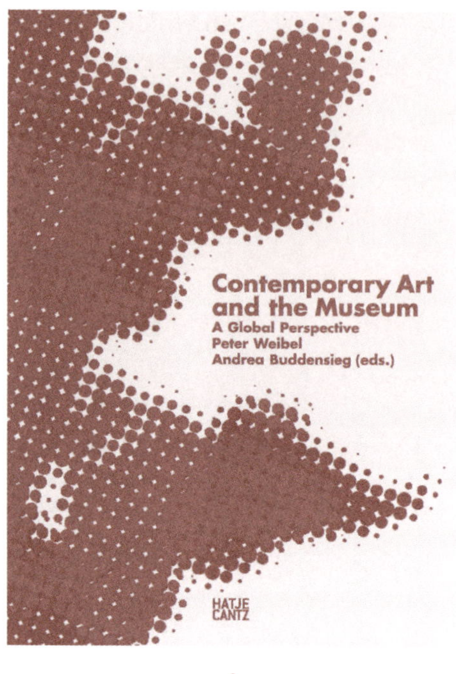

2

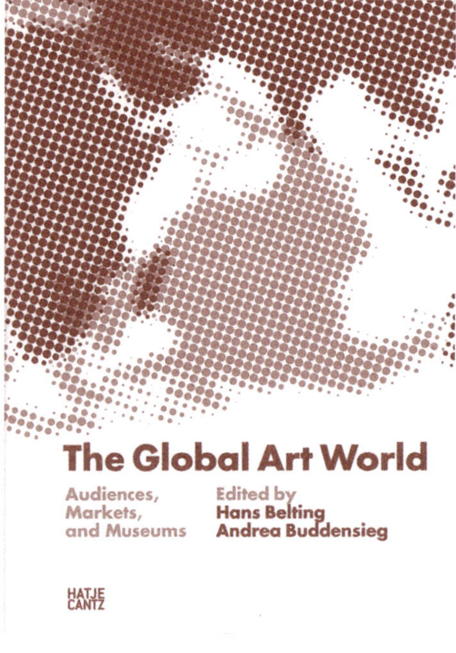

3

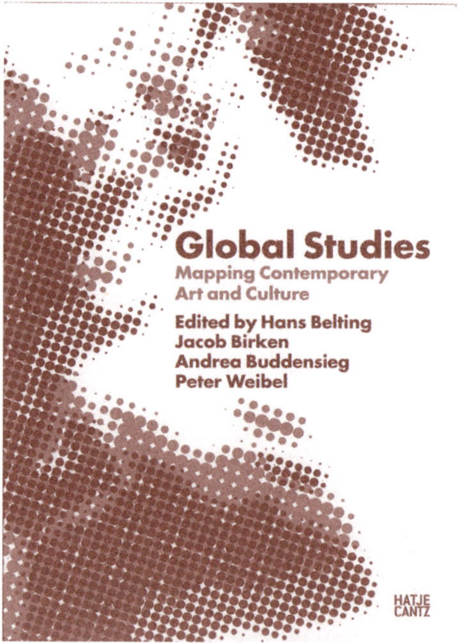

4

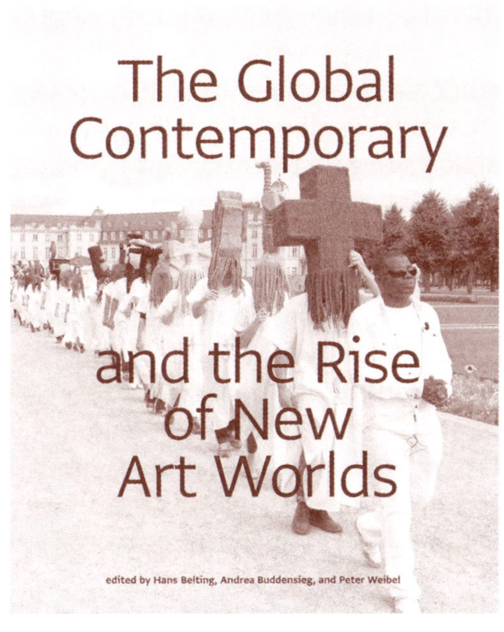

5

6

1   James Elkins, ed., *Is Art History Global?* (New York: Routledge, 2006).

2   Peter Weibel and Andrea Buddensieg, eds., *Contemporary Art and the Museum: A Global Perspective* (Berlin: Hatje Cantz, 2007).

3   Andrea Buddensieg and Hans Belting, eds., *The Global Art World: Audiences, Markets, and Museums* (Berlin: Hatje Cantz, 2009).

4   Hans Belting, Jacob Birken, Andrea Buddensieg, and Peter Weibel, eds., *Global Studies: Mapping Contemporary Art and Culture* (Berlin: Hatje Cantz, 2011).

5   Hans Belting, Andrea Buddensieg, and Peter Weibel, eds., *The Global Contemporary and the Rise of New Art Worlds* (Cambridge, Massachusetts and Karlsruhe: MIT Press, and the Centre for Art and Media Karlsruhe, 2013).

6   Sarah Dornhof et al., eds., *Situating Global Art: Topologies, Temporalities, Trajectories* (Bielefeld: Transcript, 2018).

RS   And the notion of having an enemy connotes winning or losing. On this note, perhaps we can try to draw some threads together via ideas of *failure*. Tshilu (Jean-Sylvain) talks about analysing global flows locally, and the failures of local flows to gain traction; and Verónica, you discuss failure in relation to art historiography, locating ways of moving beyond normative ways of doing art history—and I'd like to push this a bit further. How might we keep spaces open for failure in practical terms? How do we *name* failure? I think it is important to name failure (including our own) in considered ways, and to let the naming sit on our tongues and in our ears. How do we let failure *be*? And then, how do we do something with it? Or is the desire to rush also a tendency to get rid of failure?

VT   I think we are not used to thinking of art as weak (or as an enemy), or if we do think of art as weak it's to point out how this is a heroic gesture in the face of hegemony (the uselessness of art in the face of economic growth, for example) or something like that. In terms of art history, failure could entail acknowledging that the discipline might, in part, be an enemy—and we might need to fail as art historians in order to advance strategic southernness.

RS   Yes, we are not used to thinking of ourselves and our own ideas as potentially weak.

CM   I have been struggling with internal colonialism, acts of appropriation and speaking for others in much of my recent work, and feel that I often fail. Queer/trans activists and Indigenous thinkers and artists in Chile have made me aware of some of my own art historical habits, which I can only translate as this: Who am I leaving behind? Who did I not name and whose names do I not know? Who am I treating as an object of study?

JTM   Indeed, we think that the global undermines agency, and certainly, global art and its internal mechanisms tend to do this. But obviously we are not passive consumers of the global, or passive participants in global art culture as individuals or collectives, as we are practicing now in this dialogue.

VT   Jean-Sylvain, to my mind, when you describe the local/global, it's as if they have a parasitic relationship. Going back to the idea of strategic southernness, how do you see the dialectic of the global/local positing a critique of the hierarchical social relations of coloniality and capital? There seems to be a dependency in the local/global, as you articulate it, which is reflective of geo-economic configurations that go beyond the art world.

JTM   The local cannot be independent from the global… It's the way we look at that reciprocal relationship that needs to change so that it's not parasitic.

CM   The relationship can stop being parasitic if, for example, we refuse to depoliticise the art we produce and study; I refuse to tame it. I cannot generalise, but I often see this happening in academia, museum work, and art history in the norths and souths. In part, I see this happening through regular acts of making safe, whitewashing, reducing problems to something manageable, easily explainable and palatable, not too political or dirty. Even if political, the attitude seems to be: reduce focus on the context, focus only on formal achievements, make connections to relatable/ already known/accepted theories/categories. A lack of commitment to staying with the strange, the uncomfortable.

VT   I think failure is also about sitting with the inevitable alienation that will follow—what you describe, Carla, is a kind of failed or weak method, to not insert oneself or one's discourse into ways of doing things that will be recognised or easily subsumed into well-articulated genealogies/canons. But this is precisely why it's important to build strategic southernness and configure new ways of thinking and new alliances.

RS   And what are the values, Verónica, of sitting with inevitable alienation?

VT   Valuing, or at least not rejecting or repressing, the discomfort and anxiety that comes from being on the margins, which can potentially be generative. There is value, too, in building networks, friendships, with others who also feel this discomfort, although this discomfort will be felt and experienced unevenly and differently within any network.

RS   It strikes me that we, within the souths, sometimes fail to speak enough with each other, to explore our resonances, and to feed our like-mindedness. There are so many more dialogues to have and so many things that need to take place as we enable epistemologies of reciprocity.

VT   Part of the challenge is to develop infrastructures for such reciprocity and epistemologies (which again speaks to who has the means of production, which is a question that definitely guided the initiation of *Future Souths*, as briefly discussed in the introduction).

JTM   Ruth, to answer your question about why it is important to build southern strategies, alliances, and new ways of thinking, beyond creating a network of southern experiences based on the principle of refusal, I think it is important to relate to contexts that can echo the same struggles on the diverse ways the local/global dialectic plays out.

RS   Yes, there are a lot more conversations to be had, and it is important to acknowledge that our points of resonance don't necessarily translate into automatic understanding across contexts, even within the souths. We have to work hard to educate ourselves about each other in various southern contexts, and we can't assume that the experiences of discomfort that we've inevitably felt in broader art world contexts are all the same. For those of us (in the souths or the norths) who care about walking towards more just practices in the arts, we need to learn how to sit with discomfort and sit with failure. In this way, stepping nimbly is not a way of running away from challenging work, but it's the flexibility and perceptibility to deliberately step within and, at some point, *through* the sticky mess of human engagement in uneven worlds.

Contemporaneities

CONTEMPORANEITIES: *AANIKOOBIJIGANAG* (ANCESTORS/DESCENDANTS) AND DECOLONISED TIME

Dylan A. T. Miner

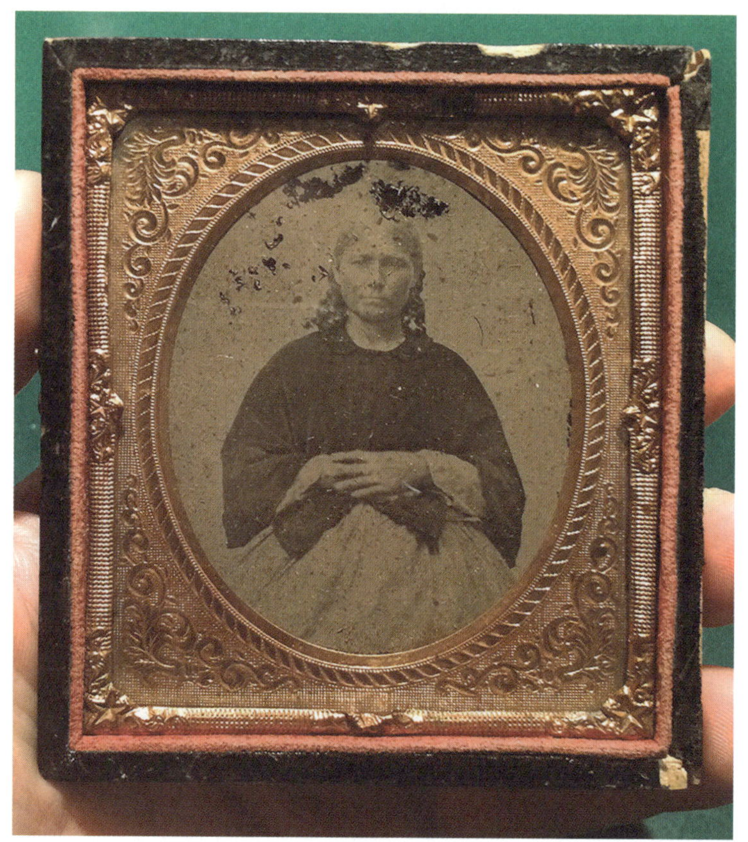

Photograph of Archange Brissette (née L'Hirondelle), Dylan Miner's *gichi-gichi-aaniikoobijigan*.
Image courtesy Dylan Miner

Temporality, much like math and science, is commonly viewed from a singular and univocal perspective. That is, the present moment—the contemporary—exists because of the past and, to some extent, in spite of the future. As radical scholars and artists, those of us participating in *Future Souths* consistently challenge this Eurocentric perspective, even if dominant institutions continue to maintain capitalist and settler-colonial epistemologies and their social institutions.

"Contemporaneity"—or its plural form, "contemporaneities"—is a term increasingly employed to describe the presence of the contemporary in culture, most prevalent in contemporary art discourse. In *Antinomies of Art and Culture: Modernity, Postmodernity, Contemporaneity* (2008), art historian Terry Smith walks us through the intimate relations and distinctions between modernity, postmodernity, and contemporaneity.[1] Smith, alongside figures such as Giorgio Agamben, Peter Osborne, and Boris Groys, has spent significant time engaging the terms "contemporary" and "contemporaneity."[2] In 2009, Smith hosted a workshop at the renowned Sterling and Francine Clark Art Institute focusing on "Contemporaneity in the History of Art."[3] In his reflection on this workshop, Smith asked whether "'contemporary' [is] the name of an art historical period that has succeeded modernism, or does 'contemporaneity' mean that periodisation is past (an anachronism from modernity) both in the general culture and in art?"[4] Or to put it in a slightly different

1   Terry Smith, "Introduction: The Contemporaneity Question." In *Antinomies of Art and Culture: Modernity, Postmodernity, Contemporaneity*, ed. Terry Smith, Okwui Enwezor, and Nancy Condee (Durham, North Carolina: Duke University Press, 2008).

2   Giorgio Agamben, "On Contemporaneity," European Graduate School, June 19, 2008, YouTube video, 7:28, www.youtube.com/watch?v=GsS9VPS_gms; Peter Osborne, *Anywhere or Not at All: Philosophy of Contemporary Art* (London: Verso, 2013); Terry Smith, *What Is Contemporary Art?* (Chicago: University of Chicago Press, Chicago, 2009; Boris Groys, "Comrades of Time," *e-flux journal* 11 (December 2009), www.e-flux.com/journal/comrades-of-time/.

3   Terry Smith, "Contemporaneity in the History of Art: A Clark Workshop 2009, Summaries of Papers and Notes on Discussions," *Contemporaneity: Historical Presence in Visual Culture* 1 (2011), https://doi.org/10.5195/contemp.2011.32.

4   Smith, "Contemporaneity in the History of Art."

way, as art historian Wu Hung states, "Is 'contemporary' an art historical period that has succeeded modernism? Is contemporary art a kind of modernism that has outlived its time?"[5]

Regardless of these internal art historical debates, and even if contemporaneity is potentially already seen as being outmoded, it nonetheless remains an important conceptual and linguistic marker that can be used to acknowledge the coterminous realities of multiple ontologies and epistemologies and the peoples who formed/form/will form them.[6] Does contemporaneity allow for all present-day ontologies and epistemologies to coexist, or is it a particular and linear time-based modality?

At its best, a term like "contemporaneities" allows us to recognise the competing and contestable chronotopes that exist at the same time in the now. But has our increased reliance on digital and global technologies exacerbated the already shrinking capacity to live, think, and be in non-capitalist time? Can Indigenous ontologies exist outside the contours of Aníbal Quijano's coloniality of power?[7] Can Indigeneities be outside the matrices of colonial economic and social relations and their reliance on the nation-state? Are Indigeneities and contemporaneities compatible, or does contemporaneity demolish all temporal and geo-graphic systems in its continued digital standardisation?

While we can pluralise the term "contemporaneity" (which is a noun in English), it nonetheless becomes a thing that is indistinguishable from the settler-colonial and capitalist logics at its core. From an Indigenist perspective, the decolonial is not *an* option. Decolonisation is the *only* option.

---

5   Wu Hung, "From 'Modern' to 'Contemporary': A Case in Post-Cultural Revolutionary Art," *Contemporaneity: Historical Presence in Visual Culture* 1 (2011), http://contemporaneity.pitt.edu/ojs/index.php/contemporaneity/article/view/36/6.

6   As Smith argues in his book of 2009, *What is Contemporary Art?*, to live in contemporaneity is to live with "multiple yet incommensurable temporalities…and [correlative] conceptions of historical development [which] move in multifarious directions." It is defined by multiple ways of being in time, at the same time as others, as a means to rupture any singular concept of time. Smith, *What Is Contemporary Art?*, 197–198.

7   Quijano, "Coloniality of Power, Eurocentrism, and Latin America."

Decoloniality and its study is the objectification—possibly what Aimé Césaire would call "thingification"—of Indigenous and colonised movements towards decolonisation.[8] While decoloniality is a thing, decolonisation is an active process. Just as Indigenous languages commonly focus on verbs, we too must recognise *time* as a living process and not as a thingified and objectified period (the Indigenous is not *past*).

While each term—and the presumed periodisations that are linked to them—must be seen in dialectic relation with the others, they are nonetheless still seen as successive and chronological: modernity >> postmodernity >> contemporaneity. As the failures and fissures are located in one period, it gives way to the next. Contemporaneity replaces postcoloniality which replaces postmodernity which replaces modernity which replaces (insert text here *ad infinitum*).

From my vantage point living on Mikinak-minis (Turtle Island, or Indigenous North America), the dominance and colonial control of British, French, Spanish, American, Canadian, and Mexican ontologies is clear. Quijano's coloniality of power is palpable, yet it is not inescapable. Indigenous knowledge and communities assert survivance in spite of colonial institutions and infrastructures.

When I think about the contemporary and contemporaneities—which from an Indigenous perspective are indistinguishable from the past and the future—I cannot help but think about the Anishinaabemowin word *aanikoobijigan* (*aanikoobijiganag* in its plural form), which simultaneously names an ancestor and a descendant. That is to say, when I speak of my *aanikoobijiganag*, I am naming my ancestors and descendants three generations out from me. *Aanikoobijiganag* signifies both my great-grandparents and my great-grandchildren. They are inextricable and indistinguishable but linked together through me.

The stem of *aanikoobijigan* is also shared with the word *aanikoobidoon*, which means "to string it together"

8   Aimé Césaire, *Discourse on Colonialism,* trans. Joan Pinkham (New York: Monthly Review Press, 2001).

or "extend it by tying." I wonder how *aanikoobijiganag* (ancestors/descendants) and *aanikoobidoon* (extending by tying) can better help us understand or undermine contemporaneity and its potential relationship with decoloniality and thingification.

Dialogue
Dylan A. T. Miner with Jennifer Biddle, Walter D. Mignolo,
Jean-Sylvain Tshilumba Mukendi, Ruth Simbao, and Verónica Tello

DYLAN A. T. MINER (DM) I am writing this while drinking coffee (*mshkikiwaaboo* or medicine water in Anishinaabemowin) at my kitchen table in Nkwejong, the place where the waters meet. Some know this as Lansing, Michigan, the US. It is the traditional homeland of the Anishinaabeg and other peoples. My university sits on 1819 Treaty of Saginaw lands.[9]

Taanishi Kiyawow Nimiyou ayawn. Dishinikshon Dylan Miner. *Michigumme nki nitwikin. Ndatochkan Universit de l'Etat de Michigan. Deu lii zanfan dayaawaawak. Ni moushoom taypwawsh Michif, taypwawsh Otepemisiwak. Gee paytohtahnahn Bootaagani-minis miinawaa Waasaaksing miinawaa Shebeshekong miinawaa Penetanguishene. Meena ka wawpamitin. Marsii.*

Aanii boozhoo niijii-bimaadiziig. Bangii eta go ninitaa-nishnabemowin. Dylan Miner *nindizhinikaaz zhaaganaashiimong. Niin nindoodem Wiisaakodewinini. Bootaagani-minis miinawaa Waasaaksing miinawaa Shebeshekong miinawaa Penetanguishene onjibaa Mishomis. Michigan niin nindoonjibaa. Nkewjong nindaa. Spartananishinaabeg nindanokii. Miigwech bizindawiyeg.*

I have been taught to introduce myself in ancestral languages—I use Michif and Anishinaabemowin—as well as to acknowledge land. So, even though meeting and dialoguing digitally, I think this practice is crucial to continue.

I will begin with a brief introduction, a paraphrase from my above text, "Contemporaneities," and then allow my collaborators to enter into dialogue.

9   Dylan is referring to Michigan State University. For further information see Beth Bonsall, "Recognizing the land MSU occupies," MSU Today, 2020, accessed February 28, 2022, https://msutoday.msu.edu/news/2020/taking-steps-to-use-the-msu-land-acknowledgement-more-broadly.

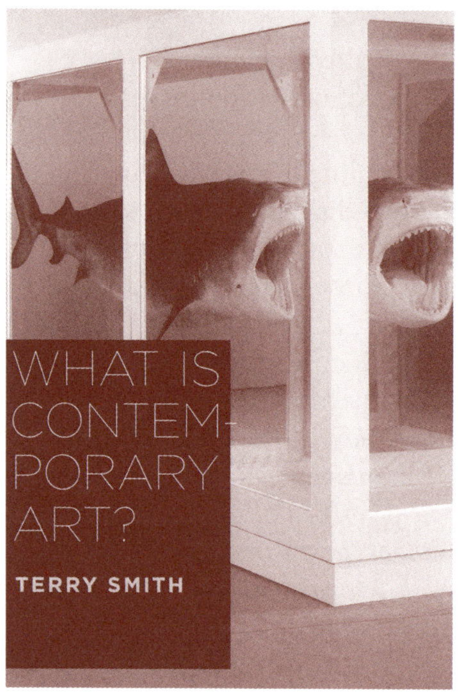

1

THE CONTEMPORARY CONDITION

The Contemporary Condition: Introductory Thoughts on Contemporaneity & Contemporary Art

Geoff Cox & Jacob Lund

Sternberg Press

2

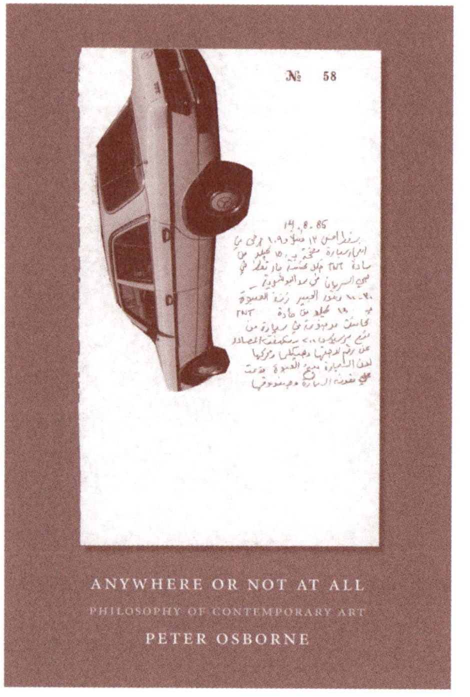

3

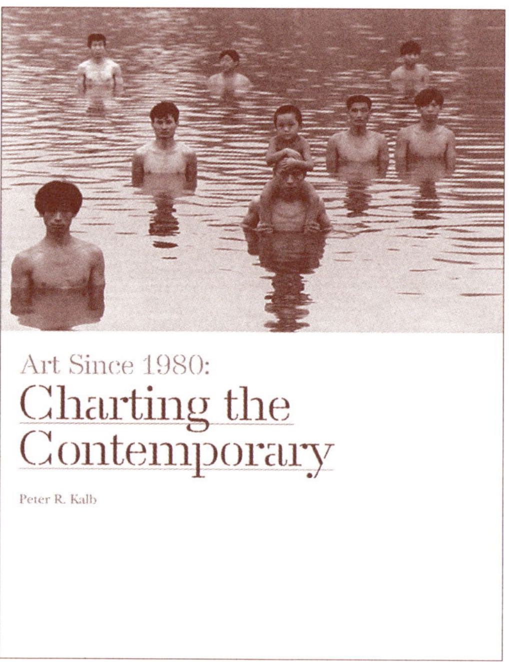

4

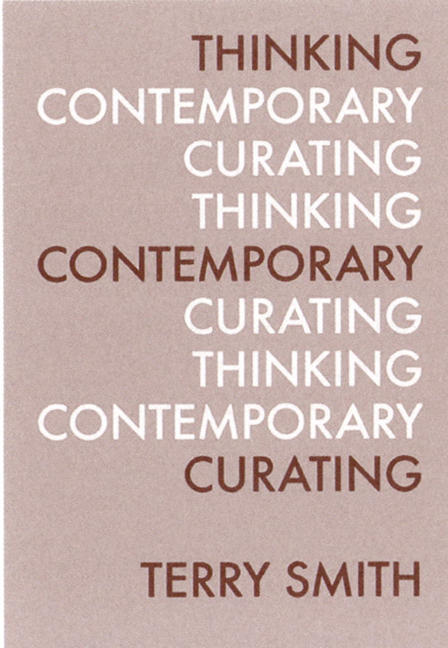

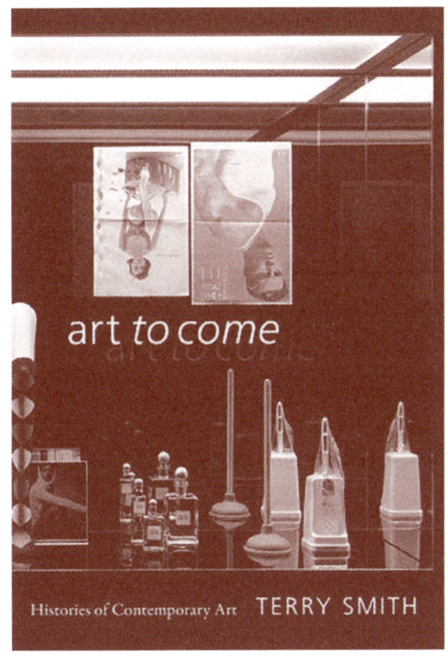

5

6

1   Terry Smith, *What Is Contemporary Art?*
     (Chicago: University of Chicago Press, 2009).

2   Terry Smith, *Thinking Contemporary
     Curating* (New York: Independent Curators
     International (ICI), 2012).

3   Peter Osborne, *Anywhere or Not at All:
     Philosophy of Contemporary Art* (London:
     Verso, 2013).

4   Peter R. Kalb, *Art Since 1980: Charting the
     Contemporary* (London: Laurence King
     Publishing, 2013).

5   Geoff Cox and Jacob Lund, *The Contemporary
     Condition: Introductory Thoughts on
     Contemporaneity and Contemporary Art*
     (Berlin and Aarhus: Sternberg Press, Aarhus
     University, and ARoS Art Museum, 2016).

6   Terry Smith, *Art to Come: Histories
     of Contemporary Art* (Durham: Duke
     University Press, 2019).

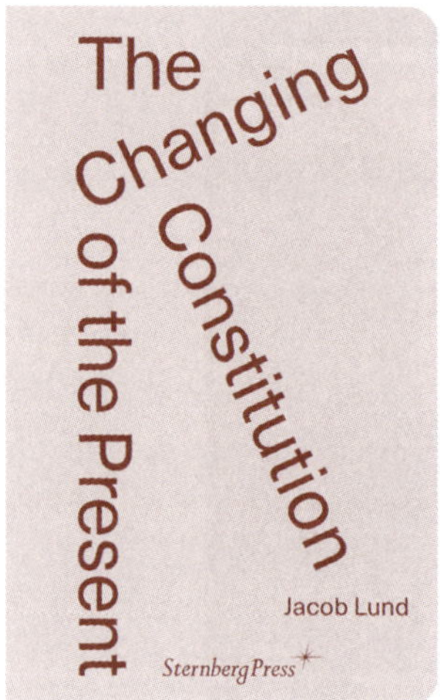

Jacob Lund, *The Changing Constitution of the Present: Essays on the Work of Art in Times of Contemporaneity* (London: Sternberg Press, 2022).

Contemporaneity has become an important conceptual and linguistic marker that can be used to acknowledge the coterminous realities of multiple ontologies and epistemologies, and the peoples who formed/form/will form them. Does contemporaneity allow for all present-day ontologies and epistemologies to coexist, or is it a particular (Western) and linear time-based modality? Are Indigeneities and contemporaneities compatible, or does contemporaneity demolish all temporal and geographic systems in its continued desire for (global) standardisation?

Would anyone like to commence?

WALTER D. MIGNOLO (WM) I will begin to address your questions by invoking Johannes Fabian's concept of the "denial of coevalness" (developed in *Time and the Other: How Anthropology Makes its Object*).[10] Through this concept, Fabian reveals not only the way in which Western epistemology, in the form of anthropology, denied the coexistence/co-presence of subjects, casting the anthropologists as present and the "other" as out of time/in the past, he also reveals how the Renaissance—and its scientific/mathematical/maritime "discoveries"—colonised and appropriated time and space. Through the epistemologies it advanced, and the correlative empires it built, it erased conceptions of time/space that were incongruous with modernist teleology. For example, it erased the Nahuatl concept of *tlacahutli* (part of the language of Aztlán, ancestral home of the Aztecs), which connotes more than time and space; it is time *and* space *and* movement.[11] Western epistemology took away movement,

10   Johannes Fabian, *Time and the Other: How Anthropology Makes its Object* (New York: Columbia University Press, 1983).

11   Mignolo is drawing on the work of Daniel Astorga Poblete on the Nahuatl concept of *tlacahutli*: Daniel Astorga Poblete, "La fluidez del género en el tlacauhtli: El Mapa de Cholula de 1581," *Estudios de cultura náhuatl* 56 (Julio–Diciembre de 2018), http://www.historicas.unam.mx/publicaciones/revistas/nahuatl/pdf/ecn56/ecn056.html

establishing colonial differences: it cast the West as always forward-casting, and the rest as not.

After Aníbal Quijano, I would say that there is coexistence today but with power differentials: 1) if Indigenous epistemologies and ontologies were not coexisting, it would not be possible to have a politics of re-emergence and re-existence as we have today in Indigenous organisations; and 2) they coexist through border epistemology, which is what Leanne Betasamosake Simpson does so greatly—her book *Dancing on our Turtle's Back* (2011) is an exemplar of coexisting border epistemology.[12]

RUTH SIMBAO (RS) Yes, but what about quality of coexistence?

WM What do you mean by quality?

RS   I was thinking about an exhibition in the US shortly after the "end" of Apartheid called *Coexistence* (2003).[13] It attempted to showcase a supposedly new South Africa, and for many it raised critical questions about whether or not coexistence was wanted or needed.[14] Coexistence seemed facile and easily invoked rhetorically, in spite of deep underlying injustices. This is why I am raising questions about the quality of coexistence, and its potential complacency—are we merely seeking to coexist? To refer back to Dylan's

12   Leanne Betasamosake Simpson, *Dancing on our Turtle's Back: Stories of Nishnaabeg Re-Creation, Resurgence, and a New Emergence* (Winnipeg: Arbiter Ring, 2011).

13   Pamela Allara, Marilyn Martin, and Zola Mtshiza, *Coexistence: Contemporary Cultural Production in South Africa*, Rose Art Museum, Brandeis University, Waltham, Massachusetts, January 22–June 29, 2003, and South African National Gallery, Iziko Museums of Cape Town, Cape Town, South Africa, September 24, 2003–March 2004.

14   See, for example, Mark Auslander, "Coexistence: Contemporary Cultural Production in South Africa," *American Anthropologist* 105, no. 3 (2003); and Ruth Kerkham, "Coexistence: Contemporary Cultural Production in South Africa [Review]," *Nka: Journal of Contemporary African Art* 18 (2003).

question, "Does contemporaneity allow for all present-day ontologies and epistemologies to coexist"? I would say that the answer is no, if one seeks some form of justice and reciprocity in this coexistence.

WM   Ah, for me, coexistence is inherently embodying conflict and power differentials at all levels and in all spheres. If we want to coexist in harmony and plenitude, that is another thing; and that is what, in my view, we do want. How we can contribute to that is what we are talking about here today.

RS   I think that in a South African context, the rhetoric of coexistence was just too easy after Apartheid. If we can extend this dialogue on coexistence: for me, it is interesting to connect it with Indigenous critiques of the recent Truth and Reconciliation Commission in Canada.[15] From an Indigenous perspective, there could never be reconciliation, because there was never conciliation.

JENNIFER BIDDLE (JB) *Wiyarrpa Ngaju-jurna Nampijinpa.* I'm saluting and returning the respectful disruption to English dominance that Dylan began this dialogue with, spoken and alphabetic (now in editing this written version), by introductory protocol I have been tutored to use from long-term, First Nations Warlpiri collaborators, to introduce myself formally first before I speak (with hope that my rudimentary evocation of Warlpiri here does not do unintended violence in my mouth as a non-Warlpiri, settler-colonial student of Warlpiri). Warlpiri is the name of a language, a people, and a Country (that itself speaks Warlpiri, as Wanta Steve Patrick Jampijinpa models) in what is called in English the Central Desert of

15   To learn more about the Truth and Reconciliation Commission of Canada, see https://www.rcaanc-cirnac.gc.ca/eng/145012 4405592/1529106060525.

the Northern Territory of Australia.[16] This is not the Country, however, where I come from, nor is it the Country from which I am speaking today; double, triple, forked-tongued, and split-lipped as I am positioned here, again, on Country that is not my own, mouthing terms not my own. Thus I respectfully acknowledge where I join this conversation from (and from where I have edited this dialogue): the Gadigal and Bidjigal land of the Eora Nation, otherwise known as central Sydney.

Ruth, Dylan: Métis scholar, artist, and activist David Garneau distinguishes between the terms "reconciliation" and "conciliation" precisely on these grounds: that there can be no reconciliation or coexistence possible in a context in which Indigenous people, language, and Country remain in an iniquitous structural impasse of having to reconcile to what remain dominant colonial terms, structures, and values.[17]

DM *Maarsii/Miigwetch*, Jennifer. Exactly! Is coexistence just another word that those in positions of power both value and use in order to try to get colonised peoples to agree to their own colonisation?

VERÓNICA TELLO (VT) Yes, the idea of coexistence is easily valued/desired/commodified—and I think that's what Dylan was touching on with his questioning of whether the concept of contemporaneities is a catalyst for critical multiplicities or just another formation of coloniality.

16 Wanta Steve Jampijinpa Patrick, "*Pulya-ranyi*: Winds of Change," *Cultural Studies Review* 21, no. 1 (2015). See also Jennifer Biddle and Wanta Steve Jampijinpa Patrick, "Not Just Ceremony, Not Just Dance, Not Just Idea: Milpirri as Hyper-Realism, a Key Word Discussion," *Visual Anthropology Review* 34, no. 1 (2018).

17 David Garneau, "Imaginary Spaces of Conciliation and Reconciliation," *West Coast Line* 46, no. 2 (2012).

WM   I know, the rhetoric of coexistence is a state rhetoric that tries to hide the conflict and power differential. Contemporaneity is part of the rhetoric of modernity to maintain power differentials and time management, of course.

JB   Yes, my problem with the concept of "contemporaneity" is in much the same terms, given its deep Western/colonial underpinnings, and I wonder if it is the best term to utilise. I am thinking of ways to move beyond decolonising and towards something more like Yamatji art historian and curator Stephen Gilchrist's notion of "Indigenising,"[18] a gesture not dissimilar to the one you are making Dylan, it seems to me, in invoking the idea of *aanikoobijiganag*.

JEAN-SYLVAIN TSHILUMBA MUKENDI (JTM) If we move away from a Western/colonial understanding of contemporaneity does that alter the power differential that Walter referred to before? Can that readjust the prism we apply to our coexistence? And how?

DM   If my ancestors are my descendants and vice versa, invoking the idea of *aanikoobijiganag* I raised above, does this productively expand and critique the concept of the contemporary or who my contemporaries are? I am also interested in *aanikoobijiganag* (ancestors/descendants) because it does not create a distinction between histories and futurities; they are the same.

VT   Dylan and Jean-Sylvain: Yes, absolutely, and I also love the embodied relationship to time that is inherent to *aanikoobijiganag*. The concept of contemporaneity, as I read it, does also support a similar potentiality—of

18   Stephen Gilchrist, "Indigenising Curatorial Practice," in Quentin Sprague, ed, *The World is Not a Foreign Land*, ed. Quentin Sprague (Melbourne: Ian Potter Museum of Art, University of Melbourne, 2014).

being with others in time (including ancestors, grand-parents, etc., as discussed in chapter 1, "Futures")—and by doing so, it does redefine what is at stake in the present, and in experiences of co-presence.[19]

RS   Verónica, I like this linking of contemporaneities and potentialities, and with being with others in time.

VT   As I read it, contemporaneity is more than just what comes after modernity—it's a way to rethink time and coexistence, including working through concepts and methods of collaboration, and what we make of being in time together (which includes the labour of dialoguing here today).[20]

However, contemporaneity, as a concept and/or navigational tool through which to articulate the potentialities of the now, has to date emerged out of the global norths and fairly Eurocentric discourses (Groys, Osborne, Agamben).[21] This raises important questions around the politics of epistemology, central to the discourses and politics of decoloniality. To put

19   Verónica Tello, "Counter-Memory and and–and."

20   Tello, "Counter-Memory and and–and," and Verónica Tello, "What is Contemporary about Institutional Critique?," *Third Text* 34, no. 6 (2020), https://doi.org/10.1080/09528822.2020.1841409.

21   Verónica Tello further comments: I would add that I don't place Smith in the same genre as Groys, Agamben, and Osborne, for the reason that Smith's discourse on contemporaneity emerges out of his grappling with his settler-colonial position in Australia and First Nations ontologies and temporalities, a genealogy of thought that can be traced back to his 1974 essay "The Provincialism Problem," and which he pursues in his 2001 pamphlet, published by Sydney-based Artspace, *What is Contemporary Art? Contemporary Art, Contemporaneity and Art to Come*; and his 2002 book *Transformations in Australian Art* (2002). To my mind, Smith's engagement with contemporaneity is embodied, and pursues a critique of universal readings of time and history via postcolonial consciousness and a critical settler-colonial studies methodology. I don't find such approaches apparent in Osborne's readings of contemporaneity, which proceed via genealogies of continental philosophy without any self-critique on the limitations and colonial violence of such an approach. Terry Smith, "The Provincialism Problem," *Artforum* 13, no. 1 (September, 1974); Terry Smith, *What is Contemporary Art? Contemporary Art, Contemporaneity and Art to Come* (pamphlet), Artspace Critical Issues Series (Sydney: Artspace, 2001); Terry Smith, *Transformations in Australian Art, Volume 1 and 2: The 19th Century—Landscape, Colony and Nation* (Sydney: Craftsman House, 2002).

it more simply: Whose knowledge, histories and temporalities matter? Who is shaping how we read and use the concept of contemporaneity? These questions cannot be raised without also considering geopolitics, coloniality, and land grabs. The question of contemporaneity is not just about which and whose epistemologies and time(s) matter; it's also about space, place, and land—the colonisation of land, knowledge, and bodies. Or, as Walter and Dylan put it before, it's about the colonising of time and space through the project of modernity.

RS   Even to separate the word "time" from space/place (land) is problematic. Too often space/place is "thingified" in Western thought. Europeans viewed the continent of Africa as a thing. Frozen in time. A thing to be taken.

VT   Thingification is a vital tool of coloniality, for controlling space/time.

DM   Yes, Robin D. G. Kelly writes:

> The Africans, the Indians, the Asians cannot possess civilisation or a culture equal to that of the imperialists, or the latter have no purpose, no justification for the exploitation and domination of the rest of the world. The colonial encounter, in other words, requires a reinvention of the colonised, the deliberate destruction of her past, what Césaire calls "thingification."[22]

WM   Exactly. There are no ontological Indians, and no ontological Blacks. They are an epistemic construction

22   Robin D. G. Kelley, "A Poetics of Anticolonialism," *Monthly Review* (November 1, 1999), https://monthlyreview. org/1999/11/01/a-poetics-of-anticolonialism/.

of epistemology. To do that you have to control knowledge and live in a civilisation that privileges objects (or things) over (human, non-human) relations. With this in mind, I propose two interrelated levels of analysis:

1   The analytic of coloniality (Fabian's "denial of coevalness," and 1500, or the colonisation of the Américas).
2   The prospective and potentialities of decoloniality.

The first refers to how the colonial matrix of power was built, managed, transformed, and controlled; and what we, such as in this dialogue, are doing to delink from it. The second refers to listening to the land, or engaging in processes of decolonising knowing, sensing, believing. I don't mean for Indigenous peoples; they already have all of it. I mean for non-Indigenous peoples.

vT   Perhaps we could engage with these two levels via the politics of space/time, or land and time, vis-a-vis contemporaneity (to critique thingification, including the thingification of land). What happens when the land stops becoming a thing and instead becomes a catalyst for experiencing time/history? How does it shift conceptions of the contemporary?

DM   What about if we think not of land as much as moving through land? We can do this by engaging more explicitly with the Nahuatl idea of *tlacahutli* that Walter raised before.

RS   Space *and* time *and* movement.

DM   Yes. By thinking of moving, or more specifically *migrating,* through land I think it's possible to undermine the dialectic of time/space central to Western epistemologies and catalyse non-linear, decolonial temporalities.

VT   Yes, migratory flows are attuned to circular, non-linear time, and they trouble any division between place/time, space/time. There is no either/or, or an absolute "here and now," for a migratory subject.

DM   In my book, *Creating Aztlán: Chicano Art, Indigenous Sovereignty, and Lowriding Across Turtle Island* (2014), I grappled with how migration can shift conceptions of time through an analysis of "lowriding."[23] Lowriding is a mode of migration but not in a literal sense. It is closer to the form of migration that birds experience.

RS   Can you further explain your use of lowriding?

DM   It is an Indigenous practice used throughout Xicanx communities in the US, transforming cars and bikes to move slowly through the land. I have taken that to connect to other ways of being that are non- and anti-capitalist and decolonial. Namely, I adopt lowriding as a metaphor and method for engaging with the land that is Indigenist. Moving slowly is deeply congruous with Indigenous ways of being and knowing the land—establishing deep roots is necessary, even if incompatible with the speed and precarity of global capital. Lowriding resists settler-colonial, capitalist relations to the land, which always seek to occupy and extract value from it. It enables one to traverse different spaces, dwelling and engaging with the multiple social structures that exist/coexist on the land, and the histories, temporalities, and concepts of the future that shape subjectivities. Through a lowriding practice, I engage with Indigenous not settler-colonialist readings of the land—lowriding is an Indigenous ontology and epistemology, and it is Aztlán, not the US, that I connect and think with.

JB   Lowriding keeps in movement, and keeps in Indigenous terms and hands as I understand it,

23   Miner, *Creating Aztlán*.

relations with Country of a certain energetics or ontology of movement as you put it, Dylan, not a thingification relationality.

DM   When lowriding, we must continue moving—the bike needs movement or it falls.

At this point, I think it's worth returning to a question I was trying to intimate in the introductory essay, "Contemporaneities: *Aanikoobijiganag* (Ancestors/Descendants) and Decolonised Time." Are Indigenous knowledges always contained by the settler state?[24] By Western temporalities?

WM   I go back to Fabian's "denial of coevalness." Denial of contemporaneity is a powerful tool of Western knowledge.

DM   Walter, why turn to Fabian? Why not cite the Land? Why not cite the plant beings?

WM   I am mentioning Fabian because he pointed out the trick of Western epistemic power. So, if we are talking about contemporaneity, I start from how contemporaneity has been constructed. If I can use a metaphor: There is nothing outside "The Matrix." Since 1500 and through time now we are all in The Matrix, just like the movie.

DM   This question is for everyone: Is privileging 1500 (or 1492 or 1519) simply a reification of colonial authority because it assumes a certain form of linear time?

WM   It is when the coexistence of many civilisations or cultures and cosmologies began to be absorbed and linearised.

24   For another discussion on a related topic, see Dylan Miner, "*Makataimeshekiakiak,* Settler Colonialism, and the Specter of Indigenous Liberation," in *Re-Collecting Black Hawk: Landscape, Memory, and Power in the American Midwest*, ed. Nicholas A. Brown and Sarah E. Kanouse (Pittsburgh: University of Pittsburgh Press, 2015).

VT   1500 is like 1989 or 9/11: it is a way to narrate the world that privileges Western epistemologies/hegemony. These temporal points of reference need to be approached through a deconstructive lens, then perhaps they can become a useful way to understand the matrix.

DM   How can we think through temporalities, or from temporalities, as Walter argues, that are not linear/teleological? How can we write about "history"?

JTM   We can construct epistemologies that embrace the multiple (time–space–movement) relations that make up one's sense of the contemporary.

WM   In my view, and learning from Indigenous epistemologies, we are all in the present, always changing—though not in a linear sense. The past is in front of us because we can see it; the future is behind us because we cannot. So, the temporality of the present is what counts—where we are (place), the moment we are in, and the things we do in our coexistence with the movement of Earth.
      Dylan, to speak more directly to question of history/historiography: We the Quijano followers talk about heterogeneous historical structural relations that take you in different directions and temporalities, relations, or nodes.

VT   Yes, but I've just been thinking that there is a tendency to stick with the monumental years like 1500, even if critical (decolonial) historiography is trying to deconstruct how we know what we know of the world.

WM   But you have to construct it as a heterogeneous historical structural node. That is one way of doing it.

VT   I guess if we have a history in motion, such as lowriding or something similar, it wouldn't privilege particular moments.

WM And it depends on where you start: from Guaman
    Poma, or from Las Casas and Sepulveda?

VT· Yes, but a networked/mobile history could also not
    have a starting point.
            Or you could start from somewhere in order to
    create a web rather than a line, thus the starting point
    would eventually be erased and/or irrelevant.

WM That is fine, but I am talking about the Western
    construction of the colonial matrix of power when
    I talk about 1500.

DM From an Indigenous perspective, the start is time
    immemorial. There is no beginning, nor end.

WM Tell me how would you tell a story without a
    starting point?

VT It's hard to answer that as someone who writes in
    essay form—it's perhaps easier for non-academic
    writing.

WM What are the gains if you manage to tell a story
    that has no beginning?

RS Many gains. In any case, telling a story—and writing
    history—often relies on other stories already told.
    They are always continuations.

DM Maybe relations and constellations make
    sense here, because unlike narratives, they are
    continuous.

WM But how do you construct relations and constellations?
    And why do you need relations and constellations?
    What is the gain for you by doing that?

RS Do we construct them?

VT   I imagine relations and constellations already exist and don't need to be constructed as much as located or animated.

JB   Yes, they exist, but as I understand it, they need to be activated, iterated, made animate by those who know and are authorised—responsive and responsible—for these histories, relations, and constellations. This is an active "remembering forward" or "remembering the future," as First Nations Warlpiri concepts and practices of temporality have been translated.

WM   That is fine, but where do these relations/constellations take you? And why do you want to do history in that way? Why do you want to do what you want to do?

RS   It doesn't matter where it takes me. Writing/reading history connects me with previous, and future, generations. It is relational. I am thinking about historical interconnectivity. I am because you are.

VT   That sounds akin to *aanikoobijiganag* (ancestors/descendants), and *aanikoobidoon* (extending by tying). Walter, I don't think of historiography—and the temporalities and socialities invoked and grappled with in the process—as a process that will eventually allow me to arrive at a certain (pre-determined or located) end point, or a singular end point, which I'm sure you don't either.

WM   Not getting to a place, but a direction: What do we want? You have to start from somewhere, and where you start will take you on a ride. Beginnings are politically constructed, and they are there to regulate and liberate.

DM   Lowriding has no start or end points, it is constant (slow) movement.

wm   The future doesn't exist—we are creating it in the
     present, and so the question is: What do we want?

rs   Interrelatedness (not a specific direction).

vt   Yes, but perhaps even though interrelatedness
     is key, it is the "we" that we are struggling
     with here. The various futurities and power
     differentials within that "we" need to be
     maintained and interrogated. Perhaps this is why
     we are struggling with this question of a start/end
     point, and what "we" want.

dm   Yes, and as Tuck and Yang argue, "decolonization is
     not a metaphor."[25] That definitely is one thing.

jb   Yes. And critically important. The question of
     futurities and what is at stake for Indigenous
     life worlds, peoples, Country, practices—under
     occupation, colonised—is not the same as it is for
     non-Indigenous.

dm   Let me pause, as we get toward the end of the dialogue,
     to raise a final question, as a way to both finish the
     conversation and leave it open. What kind of futurities
     can Indigenous and non-Indigenous contemporary
     struggles collaborate on, without erasing the inherent
     differences in how they conceive time and history?
     Can contemporaneities, with their connotation of
     coexistence, accommodate Indigeneities?
         Using linear notions of time, we have reached
     the end of this dialogue, unfortunately. Thank you all
     for your kind and generous offerings. If we were in the
     sugar bush, we would continue until the snow melted.
     But unfortunately colonial-capitalist temporalities are
     still encapsulating us.
         Maarsii/Chii miigwetch, for collectively thinking
     (and writing) together. *Baamaapii miinawaa.*

25   Tuck and Yang, "Decolonization is Not
     a Metaphor," 1-40.

Agamben, Giorgio. "On Contemporaneity." European Graduate School. June 19, 2008. YouTube video, 7:28. www.youtube.com/watch?v=GsS9VPS_gms.

Allen, Susan L., and Amy B Weisgram Engstrom. "Inclusivity in Contemporary Art: Assessing the Walker's Scaffold Controversy." *Sua Sponte* 44 (2018): 172–192.

Altinbas, Deniz. "South–South Cooperation: A Counter-Hegemonic Movement?" In *The Rise of the Global South: Philosophical, Geopolitical and Economic Trends of the 21st Century*, edited by Justin Dargin, 29–65. Singapore: World Scientific Publishing, 2013.

Ancic, Ivana. "Belgrade, the 1961 Non-aligned Conference." Global South Studies. Accessed February 28, 2022, https://globalsouthstudies.as.virginia.edu/key-moments/belgrade-1961-non-aligned-conference

Anzaldúa, Gloria. *Borderlands/La Frontera: The New Mestiza*. San Francisco: Aunt Lute Books, 1987.

Astorga Poblete, Daniel. "La fluidez del género en el tlacauhtli: El Mapa de Cholula de 1581." *Estudios de Cultura Náhuatl* 56 (2018): 137–159. www.historicas.unam.mx/publicaciones/revistas/nahuatl/pdf/ecn56/ecn056.html.

Auslander, Mark. "Coexistence: Contemporary Cultural Production in South Africa." *American Anthropologist* 105, no. 3 (2003): 621–623.

Barrett, Frances. "Meatus: A Curatorial Passage." PhD diss., Monash University, 2021.

Belting, Hans. "From World Art to Global Art: View on a New Panorama." In *The Global Contemporary and the Rise of New Art Worlds*, edited by Belting, Hans, Andrea Buddensieg, and Peter Weibel, 178–185. Cambridge, Massachusetts: MIT Press, and the Centre for Art and Media Karlsruhe, 2013.

Bey, Marquis. *Them Goon Rules: Fugitive Essays on Radical Black Feminism*. Phoenix: University of Arizona Press, 2019.

Biddle, Jennifer, and Wanta Steve Jampijinpa Patrick. "Not Just Ceremony, Not Just Dance, Not Just Idea: Milpirri as Hyper-Realism, a Key Word Discussion." *Visual Anthropology Review* 34, no. 1 (2018): 27–35.

Biddle, Jennifer Loureide. *Remote Avant-Garde: Aboriginal Art under Occupation*. Durham, North Carolina: Duke University Press, 2016.

Butler, Rex, ed. *What is Appropriation? An Anthology of writings on Australian Art in the 1980s & 1990s*, 2nd ed. Brisbane: IMA Publishing, 2004.

Butt, Zoe. "Spirit of Friendship: Artist Groups in Vietnam Since 1975." *Southeast of Now: Directions in Contemporary and Modern Art in Asia* 2, no. 1 (2018): 145–79.

Bystrom, K. and Joseph R. Slaughter, eds. *The Global South Atlantic*. New York: Fordham University Press: 2017.

Camnitzer, Luis. *Conceptualism in Latin American Art: Didactics of Liberation*. Austin: University of Texas Press, 2007.

Campt, Tina. *Image Matters: Archive, Photography, and the African Diaspora in Europe*. Durham, North Carolina: Duke University Press, 2012.

Carr, Barry. "Marxism and Anarchism in the Formation of the Mexican Communist Party, 1910–19." *Hispanic American Historical Review* 63, no. 2 (1983): 277–305.

Carroll, Khadija von Zinnenburg. *The Contested Crown: Repatriation Politics between Europe and Mexico*. Chicago: University of Chicago Press, 2022.

Casimir, Jean. *The Haitians: A Decolonial History*. Chapel Hill, North Carolina: University of North Carolina Press, 2020.

Césaire, Aimé. *Discourse on Colonialism*, translated by Joan Pinkham. New York: Monthly Review Press, 2001.

Chakrabarty, Dipesh. *Provincialising Europe: Postcolonial Thought and Historical Difference—New Edition*. New Jersey: Princeton University Press, 2007.

Comaroff, Jean, and John Comaroff. *Theory from the South: Or, How Euro-America is Evolving Toward Africa*. New York: Routledge, 2012.

Connell, Raewyn. *Southern Theory: Social Science and the Global Dynamics of Knowledge*. London: Polity Press, 2007.

Dados, Nour, and Raewyn Connell, "The Global South." *Contexts* 11, no. 1 (2012): 12–13.

Dargin, Justin, ed. *The Rise of the Global South: Philosophical, Geopolitical and Economic Trends of the 21st Century*. Singapore: World Scientific Publishing, 2013.

Darwin, Charles. *The Voyage of the Beagle*. London: Penguin, 1989.

Demos, T. J. *Against the Anthropocene: Visual Culture and Environment Today*. Berlin: Sternberg Press, 2017.

———, "Learning from documenta 14: Athens, Post-Democracy, and Decolonisation." *Third Text Online*. Accessed March 1, 2020, http://thirdtext.org/demos-documenta.

Dornhof, Sarah, Nanne Buurman, Birgit Hopfener, and Barbara Lutz, eds. *Situating Global Art: Topologies, Temporalities, Trajectories*. Bielefeld: Transcript, 2018.

Elkins, James. *Is Art History Global?* New York: Routledge, 2006.

Fabian, Johannes. *Time and the Other: How Anthropology Makes its Object*. New York: Columbia University Press, 1983.

Foster, Hal. "An Archival Impulse." *October* 110 (Autumn 2004): 3–22.

Francis, David, Imraan Valodia and Edward Webster. *Inequality Studies from the Global South*. London: Routledge, 2020.

Frank, Chandra. "Fugitive Desires." Paper presented at 198 Contemporary Arts & Learning, London, March 3–4, 2017.

www.chandrafrank.com/new-events/2017/2/26/opening-fugitive-desires-at-198

———, "Sister Outsider and Audre Lorde in the Netherlands: On Transnational Queer Feminisms and Archival Methodological Practices." *Feminist Review* 121 (2019): 9–23.

Franklin, Jonathan. "Pinochet"s Widow under Investigation on Suspicion of Swindling Million." *The Guardian*, August 19, 2016. www.theguardian.com/world/2016/aug/19/pinochet-widow-lucia-hiriart-cema-chile.

Fukuyama, Francis. "The End of History?" *National Interest*, no. 16 (Summer 1989): 3–18.

Fuller, Timothy, David Satter, David Stove, and Frederick L. Will. "More Responses to Fukuyama." *The National Interest* 17 (1989): 93–100. www.jstor.org/stable/42896764.

García-Antón, Katya, ed. *Sovereign Words: Indigenous Art, Curation and Criticism*. Oslo: Valiz/Office for Contemporary Art Norway, 2019.

Gardner, Anthony, ed. *Mapping South: Journeys in South–South Cultural Relations*. Melbourne: The South Project Inc, 2013.

Gardner, Anthony and Charles Green. *Biennials, Triennials, and documenta: The Exhibitions that Created Contemporary Art*. Wiley-Blackwell, 2016.

Garneau, David. "Imaginary Spaces of Conciliation and Reconciliation." *West Coast Line* 46, no. 2 (2012): 28–38.

Garraty, J.A, M.C. Carnes and American Council of Learned Societies. *American National Biography*. New York: Oxford University Press, 1999.

Gilchrist, Stephen. "Indigenising Curatorial Practice." In *The World is Not a Foreign Land*, edited by Quentin Sprague, 55–59. Melbourne: Ian Potter Museum of Art, University of Melbourne, 2014.

Glissant, Édouard. *Poetics of Relation*, translated by Betsy Wing. Ann Arbor, Michigan: University of Michigan Press.

Global Ultra Luxury Faction (G.U.L.F.). "On Direct Action: An Address to Cultural Workers." *eflux journal* 65 (May/August 2015). http://supercommunity-pdf.e-flux.com/pdf/supercommunity/article_1213.pdf.

González, Jennifer A., C. Ondine Chavoya, Chon Noriega, and Terezita Romo, eds. *Chicano and Chicana Art: A Critical Anthology*. Durham, North Carolina: Duke University Press, 2019.

González Jiménez, Alejandra. "Entanglements: Volkswagen de México and Global Capitalism." PhD diss., University of Toronto, 2017.

Groys, Boris. "Comrades of Time." *e-flux journal* 11 (December 2009). www.e-flux.com/journal/comrades-of-time/.

Haraway, Donna. 1988. "Situated Knowledges: The Science Question in Feminism and the Privilege of Partial Perspective." *Feminist Studies* 14, no. 3 (1988): 575–599.

———. *Staying with the Trouble: Making Kin in the Chthulucene*. Durham, North Carolina: Duke University Press, 2016.

Hartman, Saidiya. *Wayward Lives, Beautiful Experiments: Intimate Histories of Social Upheaval*. London: Serpents Tail, 2019.

Harvey, David. "Neoliberalism as Creative Destruction." *The Annals of the American Academy of Political and Social Science* 610 (March 2007): 22–44.

Hlavajova, Maria, and Simon Sheikh. "Formering the West." In *Former West: Art and the Contemporary after 1989*, edited by Maria Hlavajova and Simon Sheikh, 19–28. Cambridge, Massachusetts: MIT Press, Cambridge.

hooks, bell. "Essentialism and Experience." *American Literary History* 3, no. 1 (1991): 172–183.

Hung, Wu. "From 'Modern' to 'Contemporary': A Case in Post-cultural Revolutionary Art." *Contemporaneity: Historical Presence in Visual Culture* 1 (2011). http://contemporaneity.pitt.edu/ojs/index.php/contemporaneity/article/view/36/6.

Jones, Amelia. "Ethnic Envy and Other Aggressions in the Contemporary 'Global' Art Complex." *Journal of Contemporary African Art*, no. 48 (May, 2021).

Joy, Charlotte. *Heritage Justice*. Cambridge: Cambridge University Press, 2020.

Kant, Immanuel. *Critique of Pure Reason*. London: Penguin, 2008.

Kelley, Robin D. G. "A Poetics of Anticolonialism." *Monthly Review* (1 November 1999). https://monthlyreview.org/1999/11/01/a-poetics-of-anticolonialism/.

Kerkham, Ruth. "Coexistence: Contemporary Cultural Production in South Africa [Review]." *Nka: Journal of Contemporary African Art* 18 (2003): 92–93.

Klein, Naomi. *The Shock Doctrine: The Rise of Disaster Capitalism*. Toronto: Knopf Canada, 2007.

Lambert-Beatty, Carrie. "Make-Believe: Parafiction and Plausibility." *October* 129 (Summer 2009): 51–84.

Lawrence, Jack. *The Revenge of History: Why the Past Endures, a Critique of Francis Fukuyama*. Luzkow Lewiston, New York: Edwin Mellen Press, 2003.

Lezcano, Mario Parada. "End of the Road for Chile's Neoliberal Healthcare System?" *Peoples Dispatch*. Accessed January 7, 2022, https://peoplesdispatch.org/2022/01/07/end-of-the-road-for-chiles-neoliberal-healthcare-system/.

Lippard, Lucy R. *Undermining: A Wild Ride Through Land Use, Politics, and Art in the Changing West*. New York: The New Press, 2014.

Lorde, Audre. *The Master's Tools Will Never Dismantle the Master's House*. London: Penguin, 2018.

———. *Zami: A New Spelling of My Name— A Biomythography*. New York: Crossing Press, 1982.

Lopez, Alfred J. "The (Post) Global South." *Global South* 1, no. 1 (Winter, 2007): 1–11.

Love, Heather. *Feeling Backward: Loss and the Politics of Queer History*. Cambridge, Massachusetts: Harvard University Press, 2007.

Lugones, Maria. "Heterosexualism and the Colonial/Modern Gender System." *Hypatia* 22, no. 1 (2007): 186–219.

———. "The Coloniality of Gender." *Worlds & Knowledges Otherwise* 2, no. 2 (Spring 2008): 1–9.

Macchiavello, Carla. "A Case of Collective Resistance: Museo de la Solidaridad Salvador Allende." In *A los artistas del mundo/To the Artists of the World. Museo de la Solidaridad Salvador Allende. México/Chile*, 70–94. México: Editorial RM, MUAC (Museo Universitario de Arte Contemporáneo), 2016.

———. "Vanguardia de exportación: La originalidad de la 'Escena de Avanzada' y otros mitos chilenos." In *Ensayos sobre artes visuales: Prácticas y discursos de los años '70 y '80 en Chile*, 85–112. Santiago: LOM Ediciones—Centro de Documentación de Artes Visuales, 2011.

———. "Weaving Forms of Resistance: The Museo de la Solidaridad and the Museo Internacional de la Resistencia Salvador Allende." *Arts* 9, no. 1 (2020). www.mdpi.com/2076-0752/9/1/12/htm.

Maffie, James. "Aztec Philosophy." *Internet Encyclopedia of Philosophy*. Accessed March 1, 2022, https://iep.utm.edu/aztec/.

Majewska, Ewa. "Everyday Struggles and the Politics of Failure." Paper presented at Weak Resistance, Institute for Cultural Inquiry, Berlin, May 27, 2015, www.ici-berlin.org/events/weak-resistance/.

———. "Peripheries, Housewives, and Artists in Revolt: Notes from the 'Former East.'" In *Former West: Art and The Contemporary After 1989*, edited by Maria Hlavajova and Simon Sheikh, 601–604. Cambridge, Massachusetts: MIT Press, 2016.

———. "Weak Resistance." *Krisis Journal for Contemporary Philosophy*, no. 2 (2018).

Mambrol, Nasrullah. "Strategic Essentialism." *Literary Theory and Criticism* (April 9, 2016). https://literariness.org/2016/04/09/strategic-essentialism/.

Mignolo, Walter D. *The Darker Side of the Renaissance: Literacy, Territoriality, and Colonization*. Ann Arbor, Michigan: University of Michigan Press, 2003.

———. *The Darker Side of Western Modernity: Global Futures, Decolonial Options*. Durham, North Carolina: Duke University Press, 2011.

———. "The Enduring Enchantment (Or the Epistemic Privilege of Modernity and Where to Go from Here)." *South Atlantic Quarterly* 101, no. 4 (Fall 2002): 927–954.

———. "Epistemic Disobedience, Independent Thought and Decolonial Freedom." *Theory, Culture & Society* 26, no. 7–8 (2009): 159–181.

———. "The Global South and World Dis/Order." *Journal of Anthropological Research* 67, no. 2 (2011): 165–188.

Mignolo, Walter D., and Rolando Vázquez. "Decolonial AestheSis: Colonial Wounds/Decolonial Healings." *Social Text Online*, July 15, 2013. Accessed February 20, 2021. https://socialtextjournal.org/periscope_article/decolonial-aesthesis-colonial-woundsdecolonial-healings.

Mignolo, Walter D., and Catherine E. Walsh. *On Decoloniality: Concepts, Analytics, Praxis*. Durham, North Carolina: Duke University Press, 2018.

Mignolo, Walter D., Marc Woons and Sebastian Weier. "Interview with Walter D. Mignolo." In *Critical Epistemologies of Global Politics*, edited by Marc Woons and Sebastian Weier, 219–235. Bristol: E-International Relations Publishing, 2017.

Miner, Dylan A. T. *Creating Aztlán: Chicano Art, Indigenous Sovereignty, and Lowriding Across Turtle Island*. Tucson: University of Arizona Press, 2014.

———. *"Gaagegoo Dabakaanan miiniwaa Debenjigejig* (No Borders, Indigenous Sovereignty)." *Decolonisation* (blog). October 1, 2015, https://decolonization. wordpress.com/2015/10/01/gaagegoo-dabakaanan-miiniwaa-debenjigejig-no-borders-indigenous-sovereignty/h

———. *"Makataimeshekiakiak*, Settler Colonialism, and the Specter of Indigenous Liberation." In *Re-Collecting Black Hawk: Landscape, Memory, and Power in the American Midwest*, edited by Nicholas A. Brown and Sarah E. Kanouse, 219–235. Pittsburgh: University of Pittsburgh Press, 2015.

———. *"Mawadisidiwag Miinawaa Wiidanokiindiwag //* They Visit and Work Together." In *Makers, Crafters, Educators: Working for Cultural Change*, edited by Elizabeth Garber, Lisa Hochtritt and Manisha Sharma, 132–133. London: Routledge, 2018.

Mitropoulos, Angela. *Contract and Contagion: From Biopolitics to Oikonomia*. Wivenhoe, New York: Minor Compositions, 2012.

Moraga, Cherríe. *Native Country of the Heart: A Memoir*. New York: Farrar, Straus, and Giroux, 2019.

Moraga, Cherríe, and Gloria Anzaldúa, eds. *This Bridge Called My Back: Writings by Radical Women of Color*. New York: State University New York Press, 1981.

Moreton-Robinson, Aileen. "I Still Call Australia Home: Indigenous Belonging and Place in a White Postcolonizing Society." In *Uprootings/Regroundings: Questions of Home and Migration*, edited by Sara Ahmed, Claudia Castada, Anne-Marie Fortier and Mimi Sheller, 23–40. London: Routledge, 2003.

Mosquera, Gerardo. "El arte latinoamericano deja de serlo." *ARCO Latino* (1996): 7–10.

Mueller, John. "Did History End? Assessing the Fukuyama Thesis." *Political Science Quarterly* 129, no. 1 (2014): 35–54.

Murray, Kevin, ed. "The South South Way." *Artlink Australia* 27, no.2 (June, 2007).

Nguyen, James. "Translating Diaspora in the Settler-Colony," *Antithesis* 31 (2021): 58–65.

Noys, Benjamin. "Ends in Sight: Marx/Fukuyama/Hobsbawm/Anderson." *Historical Materialism: Research in Critical Marxist Theory* 17, no. 4 (2009): 157–163.

O'Reilly, Rachel. "Dematerializations of the Land/Water Object," *e-flux journal* 90 (April 2018). http://worker01.e-flux.com/pdf/article_191918.pdf.

Orellana, Antonia. "1972–2016: Las historias tras las dos visitas de Angela Davis a Chile." *El Disconcieto*. August 20, 2016, www.eldesconcierto.cl/nacional/2016/07/20/1972-2016-las-historias-tras-las-dos-visitas-de-angela-davis-a-chile.html.

Osborne, Peter. *Anywhere or Not at All: Philosophy of Contemporary Art*. London: Verso, 2013.

Papastergiadis, Nikos. The End of the Global South and the Cultures of the South. *Thesis Eleven* 142, no. 1(2017): 69–90.

Patrick, Wanta Steve Jampijinpa. *"Pulya-ranyi*: Winds of Change." *Cultural Studies Review* 21, no. 1 (2015): 121–131.

Pérez, Laura E. *Eros Ideologies: Writings on Art, Spirituality, and the Decolonial*. Durham, North Carolina and London: Duke University Press, 2019.

Piedalue, Amy, and Susmita Rishi. "Unsettling the South through Postcolonial Feminist Theory." *Feminist Studies* 43, no. 3 (2017): 548–570.

Quijano, Aníbal. "Coloniality of Power, Eurocentrism, and Latin America." Nepantla: Views from South 1, no. 3 (2000): 533–580.

Raheja, Michelle. "Visual Prophecies: Imprint and It Starts with a Whisper." In *Visualities: Perspectives on Contemporary American Indian Film and Art*, edited by Denise K. Cummings, 3–40. East Lansing, Michigan: Michigan State University Press, 2011.

Ramírez, Mari Carmen. "Tactics for Thriving on Adversity: Conceptualism in Latin America, 1960–1980." In *Global Conceptualisms: Points of Origin, 1950s–1980s*, edited by Luis Camnitzer, Jane Farver, and Rachel Weiss (Queens, New York: Queens Museum of Art, 1999), 53-71.

Rich, Adrienne. *Blood, Bread, and Poetry: Selected Prose 1979–1985*. New York: W. W. Norton & Company, 1994.

Richard, Nelly. "Latin American Cultures: Mimicry or Difference?" In *The Fifth Biennale of Sydney: Private Symbol, Social Metaphor*, edited by Leon Paroissien (Sydney: Biennale of Sydney, 1984), n.p.

———. "Margins and Institutions: Art in Chile after 1973." *Art & Text* 21, translated by Juan Dávila and Paul Foss (1986).

———. *Masculine/Feminine: Practices of Difference(s)*. Durham, North Carolina: Duke University Press: 2004.

———. *Masculino/Femenino: Practicas De La Diferencia Y Cultura Democratica*. Santiago: Fondo de Desarrollo de la cultura y las Artes, 1993.

Rickard, Jolene. "Sovereignty: A Line in the Sand." *Aperture* 139 (1995): 51–61.

Rickels, Laurence A. *The Devil Notebooks*. Minneapolis, MN: University of Minnesota Press, Minneapolis, 2008.

Rikou, Elpida, and Eleana Yalouri. "Learning from documenta: A Research Project Between Art and Anthropology." *On Curating* 33 (2017): 132–138. www.on-curating.org/issue-33-reader/learning-from-documenta-a-research-project-between-art-and-anthropology.html#.YeoIBS8RpTY.

Rosell, F., and T. Bjørkøyli. "A Test of the Dear Enemy Phenomenon in the Eurasian Beaver." *Animal Behaviour* 63 (2002): 1073–1078.

Rotarou, Elena S., and Dikaios Sakellariou. "Inequalities in Access to Health Care for People with Disabilities in Chile: The Limits of Universal Health Coverage." *Critical Public Health* 27, no. 5 (2017): 604–616. https://doi.org/10.1080/095815 96.2016.1275524

Sakellariou, Dikaios, and Elena S. Rotarou. "The Effects of Neoliberal Policies on Access to Healthcare for People with Disabilities." *International Journal for Equity in Health* 16 (2017): 199. https://doi.org/10.1186/s12939-017-0699-3.

Santos, Boaventura de Sousa. *Epistemologies of the South: Justice Against Epistemicide*. London: Routledge, 2014.

Simbao, Ruth. "Cosmolocal Orientations: Trickster Spatialization and the Politics of Cultural Bargaining in Zambia." *Critical Interventions: Journal of African Art History and Visual Culture* 12, no. 3 (2018): 251–274. https://doi.org/10.1080/193019 44.2018.1532379.

———. "Infecting the City: Site-Situational Performance and Ambulatory Hermeneutics." *Third Text* 30, no. 102 (2016): 1–26. https://doi.org/10.1080/095 28822.2016.1266776.

———. "超越萬隆的側向接觸：当代视觉艺术中的无畏团结与偶然的「中非」剧本" ("Reaching Sideways Beyond Bandung: Audacious Solidarities and Contingent 'China–Africa' Scripts in Contemporary Visual Art"). 人間思想 (*Renjian Thought Review*) 10 (2019): 14–51.

———. "Situating Africa: An Alter-Geopolitics of Knowledge, or Chapungu Rises." *African Arts* 50, no. 2 (2017): 1–9.

———. "What 'Global Art' and Current (Re)turns Fail to See: A Modest Counter-narrative of "Not-another-biennial."" *Image & Text* 25 (2015): 261–286.

Simbao, Ruth, William B. Miko, Eyitayo Tolulope Ijisakin, Romuald Tchibozo, Masimba Hwati, Kristin NG-Yang, Patrick Mudekereza, Aidah Nalubowa, Genevieve Hyacinthe, Lee-Roy Jason, Eman Abdou, Rehema Chachage, Amanda Tumusiime, Suzana Sousa and Fadzai Muchemwa. "Reaching Sideways, Writing *Our* Ways: The Orientation of the Arts of Africa Discourse." *African Arts* 50, no. 2 (2017): 10–29.

Simpson, Leanne Betasamosake. *Dancing on our Turtle's Back: Stories of Nishnaabeg Re-Creation, Resurgence, and a New Emergence.* Winnipeg: Arbiter Ring, 2011.

———. "Indigenous Resurgence and Co-resistance." *Critical Ethnic Studies* 2, no. 2 (2016): 19–34.

———. "Land as Pedagogy: Nishnaabeg Intelligence and Rebellious Transfor-mation." *Decolonization: Indigeneity, Education & Society* 3, no. 3 (2014): 1–25.

Slater, David. *Geopolitics and the Post-Colonial: Rethinking North-South Relations.* Hoboken, New Jersey: Wiley Publishing, 2008.

Smith, Terry. "Contemporaneity in the History of Art: A Clark Workshop 2009, Summaries of Papers and Notes on Discussions." *Contemporaneity: Historical Presence in Visual Culture* 1 (2011): 3–34. https://doi.org/10.5195/contemp.2011.32.

———. "Introduction: The Contemporaneity Question." In *Antinomies of Art and Culture: Modernity, Postmodernity, Contemporaneity*, edited by Terry Smith, Okwui Enwezor and Nancy Condee, 1–22. Durham, North Carolina: Duke University Press, 2008.

———. "The Provincialism Problem," *Artforum* 13, no. 1 (September, 1974): 54–59.

———. *Transformations in Australian Art, Volume 1 and 2: The 19th Century—Landscape, Colony and Nation.* Sydney: Craftsman House, 2002.

———. *What Is Contemporary Art?* Chicago: University of Chicago Press, 2009.

———. *What is Contemporary Art? Contemporary Art, Contemporaneity and Art to Come* (pamphlet). Artspace Critical Issues Series. Sydney: Artspace, 2001.

Spieker, Sven. *The Big Archive: Art from Bureaucracy.* Cambridge, Massachusetts: MIT Press, 2008.

Spivak, Gayatri Chakravorty. "Can the Subaltern Speak?" In *Marxism and the Interpretation of Culture*, edited by Cary Nelson and Lawrence Grossberg, 271–313. Basingstoke: Macmillan, 1988.

Swaby, Nydia A., and Chandra Frank. "Archival Experiments, Notes and (Dis)orientations." *Feminist Review* 124 (2020): 4–16.

Tawale, Salote, Ruth McDougall, June Miskell, and Amy Barrett-Lenard. *I Don't See Colour.* Perth: Perth Institute of Contemporary Arts, 2021.

Tello, Verónica. "Counter-Memory and and-and: Aesthetics and Temporalities for Living Together." *Memory Studies* 15, no. 2 (2022): 390–401. https://doi.org/10.1177%2F1750698019876002.

———. "How to Appear? Writing Art History in Australia after 1973." In *Performance, Resistance and Refugees*, edited by Samid Suliman, Caroline Wake and Suzanne Little, 138–154. London: Routledge, 2022.

———. "What is Contemporary about Institutional Critique?" *Third Text* 34, no. 6 (2020): 635–649. https://doi.org/10.1080/09528822.2020.1841409.

———. *Counter-Memorial Aesthetics: Refugee Histories and Contemporary Art.* London and New York: Bloomsbury, 2013.

———. "The Aesthetics of Counter-Memory: Contemporary art and Australian Refugee Histories After Tampa." PhD diss., University of Melbourne, 2013.

Tello, Verónica, and Sebastián Valenzuela-Valdivia. "A Partial History of South–

South Art Criticism: Juan Dávila"s Collaborations with *Art & Text* and Chilean Art Workers during the Pinochet Dictatorship, 1981–1990." *Third Text* 35, no. 6 (2021): 709–731. https://doi.org/10.1080/09528822.2021.2019954.

Thorne, Sam. *School: A Recent History of Self-Organized Art Education*. Berlin: Sternberg Press, 2016.

Tinker, George. *American Indian Liberation: A Theology of Sovereignty*. Maryknoll, New York: Orbis Books, 2008.

Traba, Marta. "La Cultura de la Resistencia." In *Mirar en América, selección y prólogo de Ana Pizarro*. Caracas: Biblioteca Ayacucho, 2005.

Tshilumba Mukendi, Jean-Sylvain. "The Kinshasa-based Kin ArtStudio in the Democratic Republic of Congo: Visual Arts Spaces and the Potential to Challenge Global Art's Representative and Legitimizing Mechanisms." Master's thesis, Rhodes University, 2019.

Tuck, Eve, and K. Wayne Yang. "Decolonization is Not a Metaphor." *Decolonization: Indigeneity, Education & Society* 1, no. 1 (2012): 1–4.

Twu, Marianne. "Slavery and Segregation." Duke Human Rights Center. https://humanrights.fhi.duke.edu/who-we-are/history-of-human-rights-at-duke/slavery-and-segregation/.

Unger, Jean-Pierre, Pierre De Paepe, Giorgio Solimano Cantuarias, and Oscar Arteaga Herrera. "Chile's Neoliberal Health Reform: An Assessment and a Critique." *PLoS Medicine* 5, no. 4 (2008), 0542–0547.

Vega, Paula Clemente. "The 2017 Venice Biennale and the Colonial Other." *Third Text Online*, November 1, 2018, http://thirdtext.org/vega-2017-venice-biennale.

Vicuña, Cecilia. *PALABRARmas*. Santiago: RIL Editores, 2005.

Vishmidt, Marina. *Speculation as a Mode of Production*. London: Brill, 2018.

Weibel, Peter, ed. *Global Activism: Art and Conflict in the 21st Century*. Cambridge, Massachusetts: MIT Press, 2015.

Weibel, Peter, and Andrea Buddensieg, eds. *Contemporary Art and the Museum: A Global Perspective*. Berlin: Hatje Cantz, 2007

Weiss, Srdjan Jovanović, and Katherine Carl. *Lost Highway Expedition Photobook*. Ljubljana: Centrala Foundation for Future Cities, School of Missing Studies and Škuc Gallery, 2007.

Rachel Weiss, *Making Art Global (Part I): The Third Havana Biennial 1989*. London: Afterall, 2011.

Wekker, Gloria. *White Innocence: Paradoxes of Colonialism and Race*. Durham, North Carolina: Duke University Press, 2016.

Whittle, Alberta. "Biting the Hand that Feeds You: A Strategy of Wayward Curating." *Critical Arts* 33, no. 6 (2019): 110–123.

VERÓNICA TELLO is a Chilean-Australian art historian, writer, editor, teacher, and curator. Her research predominantly focuses on transnational art histories—and their archives—in and out of Australia, Chile, the Pacific, and Latin America. Tello is lead researcher on the Australian Research Council project *Parallel Structures* (2021–2024), which experiments with the structures of museums in collaboration with emerging diasporic and Indigenous writers and curators. In 2016, she published her first book, *Counter-Memorial Aesthetics: Refugee Histories and the Politics of Contemporary Art* (Bloomsbury). She is currently finalising a manuscript on the exhibition history of *Art in Chile: An Audio-Visual Documentation* (1986, co-curated by Juan Dávila and Nelly Richard), and the accompanying catalogue/book *Margins and Institutions: Art in Chile Since 1973*. Her writings have appeared in *Third Text, Memory Studies, Afterall*, and *Artforum*. She is a Sydney editor of *Memo Review* and editor-in-chief of the *Australian and New Zealand Journal of Art*. Tello is a senior lecturer in contemporary art history and theory at UNSW Art & Design.

JENNIFER BIDDLE is founding director of the Visual Anthropology and Visual Culture program, a research program specialising in practice-led Indigenous and Asia-Pacific research at UNSW, where she is also a professor in the School of Art & Design. She is Gough Whitlam and Malcom Fraser Chair in Australian Studies at Harvard University (2022–2023). An anthropologist with a background in linguistics, she has worked with northern Warlpiri in Lajamanu for over two decades and, more recently, in partnership with (select) Central and Western Desert community art organisations. Her most recent monograph, *Remote Avant-Garde: Aboriginal Art under Occupation*, was published by Duke University Press and models the importance of new and emergent desert Aboriginal aesthetics as an art of survival.

ZOE BUTT is a curator and writer. Her curatorial practice centres on building critically thinking and historically conscious artistic communities, fostering dialogue among cultures of the globalising souths. Butt was artistic director of the Factory Contemporary Arts Centre, Ho Chi Minh City (2017–2021); executive director and curator, Sàn Art, Ho Chi Minh City (2009–2016); director, International Programs, Long March Project, Beijing (2007–2009); and assistant curator, Contemporary Asian Art, Queensland Art Gallery, Brisbane (2001–2007). This latter post particularly focused on the development of its Asia-Pacific Triennial of Contemporary Art. Her work has been published by Hatje Cantz, *ArtReview*, Independent Curators International, *ArtAsiaPacific*, Printed Project, Lalit Kala Akademi, JRP-Ringier, Routledge, and Sternberg Press, among others. Notable endeavours include *Sharjah Biennial 14: Leaving the Echo Chamber—Journey Beyond the Arrow* (2019), *Pollination* (2018–),

Conscious Realities (2013–2016), *Embedded South(s)* (2016), and *San Art Laboratory* (2012–2015). Butt is a CCL/MoMA International Curatorial Fellow; a member of the Asia Society's "Asia 21" initiative; and a member of the Asian Art Council, Solomon R. Guggenheim Museum. She lives and works in Chiang Mai (Thailand) and Ho Chi Minh City (Vietnam).

FERNANDO DO CAMPO is an artist currently based in Sydney. Since 2015 he has produced the *HSSH (House Sparrow Society for Humans)*. Recent projects have used a practice of birdwatching, curating, painting, fiction, and post-humanist writing to examine the documented and undocumented histories of introduced species in the global south. Solo exhibitions include *The Kookaburra Self-Relocation Project (WHOSLAUGHINGJACKASS)*, MONA FOMA 2020, and *To companion a companion* (2021–2022), co-presented by Contemporary Art Tasmania, Hobart; UNSW Galleries, Sydney; and Perth Institute of Contemporary Art, Perth and. He is a lecturer at UNSW Art & Design.

KATHERINE CARL is co-founder (with Srdjan Jovanović Weiss) of the School of Missing Studies, Balkans (2005–). Her PhD, entitled "Aoristic Avant-Garde: Experimental Art in 1960s and 1970s Yugoslavia," was awarded by the State University of New York, Stony Brook in 2009. Carl is currently deputy director of the Center for the Humanities and Curator of the James Gallery, CUNY Graduate Center. Curatorial projects include *NSK State Art: New York the Impossible Return* (with Tevž Logar), the *Lenin Museum* (Yevgeniy Fiks), and *A World Redrawn: Eisenstein and Brecht in Hollywood* (all at James Gallery, CUNY). Previous roles include curator of contemporary exhibitions at the Drawing Center (2004–2007); Dia Art Foundation (1999–2003); manager of the international artists exchange program ArtsLink (1996–1997); and program specialist at the National Endowment for the Arts (1991–1995). Carl has taught art history, theory, and criticism and curatorial methods in the PhD Program in Art History at the Graduate Center (CUNY, 2014), Tyler School of Art (2010), Parsons (2009), Moore College of Art (2009), and New York University (2002–3). Carl's co-edited books are *Evasions of Power* (2011) and *Lost Highway Expedition Photobook* (2007), as part of her participation in the School of Missing Studies. Her writing has been included in *Speculation Now* (Vera List Center and Duke University Press, 2015) and *Toward Participation as a Critical Spatial Practice* (Sternberg Press, 2016).

EDGAR ALEJANDRO HERNÁNDEZ is an editor, researcher, curator, and art critic. He is co-author of the books *Limitless: Contemporary Art in Mexico City 2000–2010* and *Déjà vu: Celda Contemporánea*

2004/2007, and editor of *Abuso mutuo: Ensayos e intervenciones sobre arte postmexicano 1992–2013* by Cuauhtémoc Medina, and *El arte de mostrar el arte mexicano* by Olivier Debroise. He has curated *Miasma* (2017) and *Museo Guggenheim Aguascalientes* (2015, 2016, and 2018) with Rolando López, and *Aquatania: Parte I* (2016 and 2017), with Cristóbal Gracia. He has taught at the Universities of Guadalajara, Ciudad Juárez, Autonomous of Aguascalientes, de las Américas Puebla, Autonomous of Nuevo León, and the National Autonomous University of Mexico. He has written about contemporary art in the newspapers *El Universal, Reforma*, and *Excélsior*, and the magazines *Gatopardo, Letras Libres, Chilango, Revista de la Universidad de México, Utopía, Código, Vice, Ramona, Artishock, Terremoto, Harper's Bazaar*, and *Forbes*. Hernández is director of Promotora Cultural Cubo Blanco.

CHANDRA FRANK is a feminist researcher and independent curator. She works on the intersections of archives, waterways, gender, sexuality, and race. Her curatorial practice explores the politics of care, experimental forms of narration, and the colonial grammar embedded within display and exhibition arrangements. Frank earned a PhD in media, communications, and cultural studies from Goldsmiths, University of London. She has published in peer-reviewed journals and exhibition catalogues, including *Feminist Review*, the Small Axe VLOSA catalogue, *The Place is Here* publication, *FOAM Magazine, Stedelijk Studies*, and the collection *Tongues*. She recently co-edited a special issue on "Archives" for *Feminist Review*. Chandra has written for, among others, *Africa is a Country, Discover Society*, and *Warscapes*. In 2016, she was a curatorial fellow at the Institute of the Creative Arts (University of Cape Town). Her curated exhibitions include *Re(as)sisting Narratives* (Amsterdam/Cape Town), *Fugitive Desires* (London), and *Proclamation 73* (Durban), co-curated with Zara Julius. Frank curated the 2016 "Archives Matter" Conference at the Centre for Feminist Research at Goldsmiths. Exhibitions include *Ecologies of Elsewhere* at the CAC in Cincinnati (spring 2023). Frank is assistant professor of communication, film, and media studies and women's, gender, and sexuality studies at the University of Cincinnati.

SRDJAN JOVANOVIĆ WEISS was born in Yugoslavia and mainly lived and worked in New York. He started as an avid swimmer and mathematician and developed into a researcher and architect working on special projects in spatial and visual cultures. He founded the NAO.NYC (Normal Architecture Office) for design based in New York and co-founded the School of Missing Studies (with Katherin Carl) for the experimental studies of cities marked by or currently undergoing abrupt transition. He was ex-head of research at Herzog & de Meuron Architects; served as a visiting professor at Columbia, Cornell, Penn, and Harvard Universities; and was a research fellow at Forensic Architecture. Selected books include *Socialist Architecture: The Reappearing Act* (The Green Box Berlin, 2017); *Socialist Architecture: The Vanishing Act* (JRP Ringier, 2012, with Armin Linke); *Almost Architecture* (Merz & Solitude Akademie, 2006); *Evasions of Power: On the Architecture of Adjustment* (ed., Slought, 2008); and *Lost Highway Expedition* (ed., School of Missing Studies, 2007). Weiss' last book project, *Better than Weather: On the Human Desire for Artificial Comfort,* was developed via his art residency at *Potsdam Institute for Climate Impacts Research by DAAD Berlin,* and published by The Green Box, Berlin.

ROLANDO LÓPEZ is an artist with a bachelor of graphic design and a master's in social sciences from the Autonomous University of Aguascalientes. In 2014 he initiated the ongoing project *Museo Guggenheim Aguascalientes,* through which he has played the roles of artist, historian, anthropologist, coordinator, curator, researcher, inventor, and museum designer. This project has been exhibited in Mexico City (2015), Querétaro, Mx. (2016), San Antonio, E.U.A. (2017), and at the XLVI International Cervantino Festival (2018, Guanajuato, Mx.). He is a graduate of the SOMA educational project (Mexico D.F. 2013.) Awards include the 2020 Cisneros Fontanals Art Foundation (CIFO/Miami, Florida, US) scholarship and commission and the 2017 KADIST (Artist Circle Award/Summer) for emerging artists. He has carried out the artistic production residencies in the EESI École Européenne Supérieure de l'Image/Angouleme, France (2014) and in Artpace/San Antonio, Texas, US (2017).

CARLA MACCHIAVELLO is an art historian and educator, born in Santiago, Chile, and based in New York. Her research centres on Latin American contemporary art, networks of solidarity and resistance, migrant identities in video art, artistic pedagogies, and art practices aimed at social and environmental change. Her work has been published in international journals, catalogues, and edited books. She co-edits the periodical *Más allá del fin/Beyond the End* for Ensayos, a trans-disciplinary research practice engaging in matters related to the political ecology of Tierra del Fuego. She is part of the creative team of *Turba Tol Hol Hol Tol* for the Chilean pavilion at the Venice Art Biennale of 2022, co-editing its rumours, script, and catalogue. Carla joined City University New York (CUNY) in 2015, after working as an assistant professor in art history at Universidad de los Andes, Bogota, Colombia (2010–2014). She received a PhD from Stony Brook University in 2010 and studied aesthetics at the Pontificia Universidad Católica de Chile in Santiago. She is currently an associate professor in art history at Borough of Manhattan Community College/CUNY.

WALTER D. MIGNOLO is William H. Wannamaker Professor and director of the Center for Global Studies and the Humanities at Duke University. Over the past thirty years, Mignolo's research and teaching has been devoted to understanding and unravelling the historical foundation of the modern/colonial world system and imaginary since 1500. In his research, the modern/colonial world system and imaginary is tantamount to the historical foundation of Western Civilisation and its expansion around the globe. His research stands on four basic premises: 1) that there was no world-system before 1500 and the integration of America in the Western Christian (European) imaginary; 2) that the world-system generated the idea of "newness" (the New World) and modernity; 3) that there is no modernity without coloniality, and coloniality is constitutive rather than derivative of modernity; and 4) that the modern/colonial imaginary was mounted and maintained on the invention of the Human and of Humanity, which provided the point of reference for the invention of racism and sexism together with the invention of nature. Mignolo was awarded the Katherine Singer Kovaks prize (MLA) for *The Darker Side of the Renaissance: Literacy, Territoriality, and Colonization* (1996) and the Frantz Fanon Prize by the Caribbean Philosophical Association for *The Idea of Latin America* (2006). His work has been translated into German, Italian, French, Swedish, Rumanian, Spanish, Portuguese, Mandarin, and Korean. *On Decoloniality: Concepts, Analysis, Praxis*, co-authored with Catherine Walsh, was published in 2018 (with an Italian translation in progress), and in 2021 Mignolo published *The Politics of Decolonial Investigations*. Because of the political dimension of his work, in the past fifteen years Mignolo's energy has been increasingly devoted to the public sphere working with artists, curators, and journalists; writing op-eds; giving frequent interviews in English and Spanish; and co-organising and co-teaching summer schools in Middelburg, Bremen, and at UNC-Duke. He is also frequently delivering workshops for faculty and graduate students in South and Central America, Asia, and Europe.

DYLAN A.T. MINER, PhD is an artist, activist, scholar, and transformational leader. He is dean and professor in the Residential College in the Arts and Humanities (RCAH) at Michigan State University. He is a founding member of the artist collective Justseeds. As an artist, he has hung nearly thirty solo art exhibitions, as well as participated in more than 115 group exhibitions. He has created graphics for numerous community organisations, social justice campaigns, and environmental organisations. Miner has published extensively, including chapters published in books by Duke University Press, Yale University Press, and Oxford University Press, among many others. His book *Creating Aztlán: Chicano Art, Indigenous*

Sovereignty, and Lowriding Across Turtle Island (2014) was published by the University of Arizona Press. Born and raised in Michigan, Miner is a registered citizen of the Métis Nation of Ontario.

ANGELA MITROPOULOS is a theorist and academic based in Sydney, Australia. Her writings track shifting boundaries and movements in the history of philosophy, science, aesthetics, politics, and economics. Mitropoulos is the author of *Contract and Contagion: From Biopolitics to Oikonomia* (2012, Minor Compositions) and *Pandemonium: Proliferating Borders of Capital and the Pandemic Swerve* (2020, Pluto Press). Other publications include "Encoding the Law of the Household and the Standardisation of Uncertainty" (in *Mapping Precariousness, Labour Insecurity and Uncertain Livelihoods*, Ashgate, 2017) and "Archipelago of Risk: Uncertainty, Borders, and Migration Detention Systems" (in *New Formations*, 84–85). Mitropoulos has also been interviewed on her theoretical and activist work for a number of publications, which appear under the titles "Cross-Border Operations" (in the US magazine *New Inquiry*, November 18, 2015), "Border, Theory, Contract" (in the Canadian journal, *Public* 28, no. 55 (2017)), and "On Borders, Race, Fascism, Labour, Precarity" (in the UK magazine, *Base* 3, no. 1 (2016)).

JAMES NGUYEN is an artist and researcher, born in Vietnam and currently based in Naarm/Melbourne. Nguyen's interdisciplinary practice moves between live and online performance, video, drawing, and installation. He is interested in personal history and migrant absurdities, often working with his family and friends to examine the politics of art, self-representation, displacement, and diaspora. Nguyen has been the recipient of several prizes and awards, including the Australian Centre for Contemporary Art and the Copyright Agency's Cultural Fund's 2023 Commission, the Clitheroe Foundation Scholarship, the Nillumbik Art Prize for Contemporary Art, and the Anne & Gordon Samstag International Visual Arts Scholarship. His work has been included in group exhibitions across Australia, including *The National* in 2019. Recent solo exhibitions include *Re:Tuning* (with Victoria Pham and collaborators), Sydney Opera House, 2022; *Re.Sounding* (with Victoria Pham and collaborators), Samstag Museum, Adelaide, 2021; *Homesickness* (with Nguyen Thi Kim Nhung), a commission by the Australian War Memorial, Canberra, 2018; and *BuffaloDeer* (with Nguyen Ngoc Cu), Westspace, Melbourne, 2016. Nguyen completed a PhD at UNSW Art & Design.

RACHEL O'REILLY is an artist, writer/poet, curator, and PhD researcher at Goldsmiths' Centre for Research Architecture. She teaches the theory seminar "At the Limits of the Writerly" on planetarity, political economy, and poetics at the Dutch Art Institute. She was previously a curator at the Australian Cinematheque at the Gallery of Modern Art | Australian Cinematheque, Brisbane, and researcher at the Jan van Eyck Academy. Her artistic work and research have been presented internationally, most recently at Van Abbemuseum, Eindhoven; E-flux, New York; and UNSW Galleries, Sydney. Recent curatorial collaborations include *Ex-Embassy* with Sonja Hornung and *Planetary Records: Performing Justice between Art and Law* with Natasha Ginwala. She co-wrote *On Neutrality* with Jelena Vesic and Vlidi Jeric for the Non-Aligned Modernisms series (MCA, Belgrade), publishes with Danny Butt on artistic autonomy in settler-colonial space, and currently co-edits *Feminist Takes on Black Wave Film* with Antonia Majaca and Jelena Vesic for Sternberg Press.

RUTH SIMBAO is a professor in the Fine Art Department at Rhodes University, South Africa, and teaches art history and visual culture. Her research interests include contemporary art with a particular focus on Africa, the geopolitics of art and society, geopolitics in relation to biennialisation, "strategic southernness" and the global souths, theories of "place," contra-flow diasporas, cosmopolitanism and cosmolocalism, redefinitions of "the local," the power of small spaces and modest gestures, artists' responses to xenophobia, China–Africa relations and the arts, contemporary cultural festivals and globalisation, performance theory and live art, the performance of heritage in Zambia, and site-situational art. In recent years Simbao founded the following research initiatives, projects and networks: Visual and Performing Arts of Africa (ViPAA) (2011 to present), Residencies for Artists and Writers (RAW) (2014 to present), and Art & Culture: Writers in Africa (ACWA) (2015). She has published in various journals including *African Arts, Art South Africa, NKA: Journal of Contemporary African Art, JACANA: Journal of African Culture and New Approaches, Third Text, Kronos: Southern African Histories, Parachute, Mix, Lola, De Arte, Image & Text, Social Dynamics* and the *International Journal of African Historical Studies*. Ruth Simbao is a co-editor of the book, *Visualising China in Southern Africa: Biography, Circulation, Transgression* (Wits University Press 2022), and is currently working on two books—*Audacious Art Histories: Situating the Arts of Africa* and *The Art of Pushing Back: Zambia's Long March with China.*

SALOTE TAWALE was born in Suva, Fiji Islands and grew up in the south-eastern suburbs of Melbourne, Australia. Cultural identity is a central focus in her research; the inherent conflict of being from a mixed heritage (Fiji and Australia) that simultaneously includes and excludes Tawale from colonial Australia is a significant consideration in her arts practice. Intrinsically performative, employing photography, video, drawing, sculpture, installation, and live actions, Tawale re-forms and performs her identity and experience of translocated Indigeneity, which is removed from land and separated from traditional practices, and consequently repositioned within immigrant, settler-colonial histories in Australia. Her expanded form of self-portraiture focuses on the self in relation to both art and contemporary politics and is heavily influenced by feminist video art practices of the 1970s. Her work has appeared at the Asia-Pacific Triennial of Contemporary Art, the Australian Centre for Contemporary Art, and the Biennale of Sydney. Tawale is currently a lecturer of screen arts at Sydney College of the Arts, University of Sydney.

JEAN-SYLVAIN TSHILUMBA MUKENDI is a member the *Arts of Africa and the Global South* research initiative (NRF/Mellon) at Rhodes University, South Africa. His research interests currently focus on independent art spaces in Africa, the relevance of the "global" in contemporary visual art, and African artists' status and position within the art world. They also include contemporary photography, sociocultural discourses embedded within visual representations of the continent, issues of cultural production in African metropolises, diasporic identities, creative responses to Western cultural hegemony, cross-continental cultural exchanges, and the social effects of sub-Saharan rapid urban transformation. Tshilumba completed a masters of arts in arts and sciences at Maastricht University (the Netherlands) in 2012. The same year, he took part in the Graduate Liberal Studies Symposium at the University of Southern California Dornsife College of Letters, Arts and Sciences. In 2014, he worked as an assistant within the research department of the Prince Claus Fund (Amsterdam). In 2016 and 2017, he was awarded an Andrew W. Mellon postgraduate bursary as part of the NRF SARChI Chair research initiative. In 2013 and 2016, he engaged for several months with the Kin ArtStudio, a Kinshasa-based art studio and platform for contemporary visual art created by the artist Vitshois Mwilambwe Bondo. Tshilumba has been an assistant editor of the *Prince Claus Fund 2013 Africa Call Review*. In 2016, he contributed to the publication *Créer en postcolonie: Voix et dissidences belgo-congolaises 2010–2015*, edited by Bozar Books and Africalia Belgium. He has published in *Art Africa*. Recent curatorial and artistic projects include *Les Mitrailleurs*, a photo-project realised with Maxence Dedry in Kinshasa, DRC.

Future Souths: Dialogues on Art, Place, and History, published in 2023 by Discipline in collaboration with Third Text Publications, an affiliate of *Third Text* journal.

Essays by Verónica Tello, Dylan A. T. Miner, Zoe Butt, Edgar Alejandro Hernández, Rolando López, Carla Macchiavello, Walter D. Mignolo, Rachel O'Reilly, and Ruth Simbao, and dialogues with the aforementioned and Jennifer Biddle, Katherine Carl, Fernando do Campo, Chandra Frank, Srdjan Jovanović Weiss, Angela Mitropoulos, James Nguyen, Salote Tawale, and Jean-Sylvain Tshilumba Mukendi; and copyediting by Nicholas Croggon, Helen Hughes, and Jennifer Sijnja.

Designed by Zenobia Ahmed and Alexandra Margetic.
Typeset in Borges (PampaType).

ISBN: 978-0-9945388-6-4
Printed in Estonia

Essays and dialogues published in this volume have been subject to a double anonymous peer-review process.

Discipline is primarily based on Kulin Nation land, principally on the lands of the Wurundjeri. The publishers acknowledge the Wurundjeri as the original owners of this land, and pay their utmost respect to their Elders, past and present.
> www.discipline.net.au

Third Text Publications is an affiliate of *Third Text: Critical Perspectives on Contemporary Art and Culture* (Print ISSN 0952-8822, Online ISSN 1475-5297). *Third Text* is published bimonthly in January, March, May, July, September, and November for a total of 6 issues per year by Routledge, an imprint of Taylor & Francis Group, 4 Park Square, Milton Park, Abingdon, Oxon, OX14 4RN, UK.
Editor in Chief: Richard Dyer. rdyer@thirdtext.org.
> www.thirdtext.org

Future Souths has been generously supported through funds from Create NSW and UNSW Art & Design.